THE
GUINNESS
BOOK
OF
ESPI⊕NAGE

MARK LLOYD

THE
GUINNESS
BOOK
OF
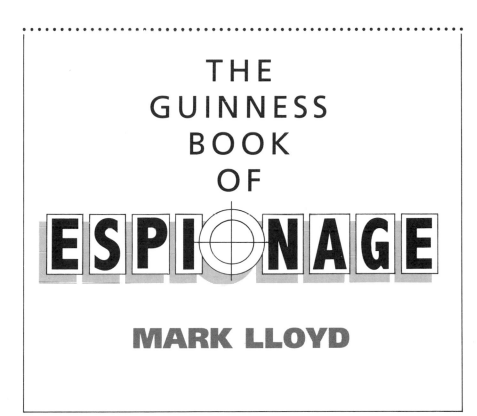

MARK LLOYD

DA CAPO PRESS • NEW YORK

Editor: Beatrice Frei
Design: John Rivers
Picture editing and research: Image Select International
Photography: Mike Good
Artwork: Guy Taylor

First published in the United States of America in 1994 by Da Capo Press, Inc.
233 Spring Street, New York, NY 10013

First published in the United Kingdom in 1994 by Guinness Publishing Ltd.
This Publication Copyright © Guinness Publishing Ltd., 1994
33 London Road, Enfield, Middlesex.

Typeset in Frutiger by Ace Filmsetting Ltd, Frome, Somerset
Printed and bound in Great Britain by The Bath Press, Bath

Library of Congress Cataloging-in-Publication Data

Lloyd, Mark. 1948-
    The Guinness book of espionage/Mark Lloyd.
        p.   cm.
    Includes bibliographical references and index.
    ISBN 0-306-80584-7
    1. Espionage--History.   2. Intelligence service--History.
    3. Secret service--History.   I. Title.
    JF1525.16L56   1994   94-8562
    327.12'09--dc20   CIP

CONTENTS

INTRODUCTION

Espionage is one of the oldest, most fascinating and most enduring of all human pursuits. Sun Tzu – a Chinese ruler of the Confucian era still much read in military circles – wrote of the necessity for spies more than 2400 years ago. During the 5th century AD the Emperor Justinian sent monks to China, ostensibly as commercial envoys but in reality as thieves to steal the secret of the silk worm industry. While being entertained by their unsuspecting hosts they collected moth eggs, concealing them in the hollowed out ends of their walking sticks.

In more recent times espionage has been conducted by kings, governments and generals alike in the pursuit of often crucial intelligence that could not otherwise have been gained by more 'honourable' means. It would be dangerously naive to suggest that espionage has somehow abated with the thawing of East–West relations. In the early months of 1994 alone Russia accused Britain of running an agent network from its embassy in Moscow (an accusation which the Foreign Office hardly bothered to deny) while the United States unearthed a former KGB spy network which continued to operate well after the disintegration of the former Soviet Union.

Within the last decade the security services of many countries have become more open, and on the face of it more accountable. The United States has introduced the Freedom of Information Act, Russia has opened the doors of the (now largely redundant) Lubyanka to selected television crews, and Britain has at last admitted the existence of MI5 and MI6! Yet budgets remain a closely guarded secret, as do the scope and numbers of operators abroad.

The introduction of modern technology with all its vulnerabilities has brought the threat of commercial espionage to the board rooms of all but the smallest of companies. Firms of security 'experts' have mushroomed to meet this threat, but nobody seriously believes that it will ever be truly defeated.

To counter espionage you must first understand it. To do this you must be aware of its history, its motives and the motivations of those who risk life and liberty in its pursuit. It is hoped that the following pages will give the reader an insight into this most complex and fascinating of subjects.

O N E

FACTS & FABLES IN THE EARLY HISTORY OF ESPIONAGE

EARLY EXAMPLES OF ESPIONAGE

EGYPTIAN BEGINNINGS

Nearly 4000 years ago, a master scribe in the Egyptian Nile town of Menet Khufu sketched out a series of hieroglyphs telling the story of the life of his lord, the nobleman Khnumhotep II, and in so doing opened the recorded history of cryptography. He did not use a formal system of secret writing, but instead employed some unusual hieroglyphic symbols here and there in place of the more conventional ones. The intention was not to make the text hard to read but to impart a dignity and authority to it. In so doing, it incorporated a deliberate transformation of the writing, the first essential element of cryptography.

As the Egyptian civilisation prospered, the writings on the tombs of the venerated became more contrived. Many became tinctured for the first time with the second essential of cryptography—secrecy. In a few cases the secrecy was intended to increase the mystery and magical powers of certain religious texts. But more often it resulted from the desire of the inscriber to induce the traveller to read his master's inscription, thereby conferring upon the deceased the blessings therein. The addition of secrecy to the transformation mentioned above produced the world's first true cryptography.

ORIENTAL ADVANCES

Classical China was the only early civilisation to employ ideographic writing, yet never seemed to develop any real cryptography. It did, however, introduce primitive codes. The 11th-century treatise 'Wu-ching stung-yao' ('Essentials for Military Classics') listed 40 plain-text items, ranging from requests for bows and arrows to the report of a victory, to which were assigned the first 40 ideograms of a poem. When a commander wished to request, for example, more arrows he simply wrote the corresponding ideogram in a specified place on an ordinary dispatch and stamped his seal on it.

India introduced and developed a series of secret communications. The 'Artha-sastra', the classic work on statecraft attributed to Kautilya, not only described India as riddled with spies but recommended the use of secret writing. Even Vatsyayana's masterpiece of eroticism, the 'Kama Sutra', lists secret writing as one of the 64 arts, or yogas, that women should know and practise.

The last great civilisation of antiquity, the Mesopotamian, paralleled and then surpassed Egypt in the evolution of cryptography. During the last period of cuneiform writing, a few decades before the advent of Christianity, scribes preparing the colophons in Uruk (in modern-day Iraq) converted their names into numbers in an attempt to amuse, or frustrate, the passing reader.

EARLY MILITARY CRYPTOGRAPHY

The Spartans introduced the 'skytale', the first system of military cryptography, in the 5th century BC. A strip of papyrus, leather or parchment was tightly wrapped around a staff of wood of a given diameter. The secret message was then written on the parchment down the length of the staff, unwound and sent for delivery. The message made no sense until wrapped around a staff of identical diameter, after which the message became immediately legible.

A century later, the Greek writer Polybius, devised a system of signalling destined to last two and a half millennia to the days of the SOE. Letters were arranged into a square numbered vertically and horizontally. Using Arabic numerals and the Roman alphabet by way of example the square looked as follows:

	1	2	3	4	5
1	F	A	S	O	IJ
2	U	T	G	Y	R
3	C	L	B	N	X
4	P	D	Q	V	H
5	K	W	Z	E	M

Each letter was then changed into two numbers; B became 33, O 14 and W 52. The word 'bow' therefore read '33 14 52'. The message was then transmitted vast distances by torches; three torches in each hand becoming B, one in the right hand and four in the left O and five in the right hand and two in the left W.

During the 1st century BC, Julius Caesar sent many of his plain-text dispatches in a simple cipher still universally known as the Caesar alphabet. Letters were replaced by letters standing three places down the alphabet:

plain:	a	b	c	d	e	f	g	h	i	j	k	l	m
cipher:	d	e	f	g	h	i	j	k	l	m	n	o	p

plain:	n	o	p	q	r	s	t	u	v	w	x	y	z
cipher:	q	r	s	t	u	v	w	x	y	z	a	b	c

Thus (translating from *De Bello Gallicos*): 'The foremost man among the Helvetii, in rank and wealth, was Orgetorix' became 'Wkh iruhprvw pdq dprqj wkh Khoyhwwl, lq udqn dqn zhdowk, zdv Rujhwrula'. Clearly this code would have proved of little worth against a sophisticated adversary. Yet, in a world in which literacy was rare, it was perfectly effective. As will be seen in Chapter Two, the Caesar alphabet survived to World War II, when a variant was used by the SOE as a secondary cipher to add to the complexity of already coded messages.

WESTERN CONSOLIDATION

Modern Western cryptography emerged directly from the flowering of modern diplomacy. Ambassadors' reports were prone to interception and therefore were usually encoded. As the

EARLY CIPHERING DEVICES

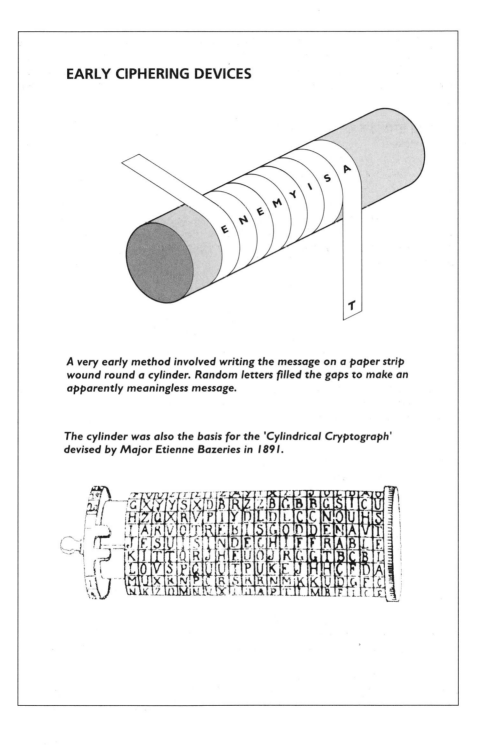

A very early method involved writing the message on a paper strip wound round a cylinder. Random letters filled the gaps to make an apparently meaningless message.

The cylinder was also the basis for the 'Cylindrical Cryptograph' devised by Major Etienne Bazeries in 1891.

Excellent examples of a primitive substitution cipher device (above) and a primitive code table (right), employed by Giovanni Battista Posta c.1430. Guy Taylor

art of code-breaking improved, so it became necessary for states to employ full-time cipher secretaries occupied in making up new keys, coding and decoding messages and breaking the codes of rivals.

Arguably the most successful Renaissance cryptanalyst was Giovanni Soro, taken into the employ of the Venetian Council of Ten in 1506. Venice was then ruled by a combination of espionage, subterfuge and diplomacy in which the ability to know the innermost thoughts of the neighbouring principalities was crucial. By 1510, Soro had forced other courts to sharpen their ciphers to such a degree that even the Papal Curia was sending him codes which their own analysts in Rome could not break.

Eighty years later the ability of Thomas Phelippes, a cryptographer in the employ of the English secret service, to break the codes of the French and Spanish Courts brought about the downfall of Mary Queen of Scots. In 1586, a former page of Mary's, Anthony Babington, began to organise a plot to have courtiers assassinate Queen Elizabeth I, incite a general Catholic uprising in England, and crown Mary. Babington gained the support of Philip II of Spain, who promised to send an expedition to help, once Elizabeth was dead. Such a plot required at least the tacit approval of Mary, and to obtain this, Babington had to communicate with her.

This was no easy task as Mary was then being held incommunicado. But a former seminarian named Gilbert Gifford, recruited by Babington as a messenger, discovered ways of smuggling Mary's letters to her in a beer mug. The system worked so well that the French ambassador eventually entrusted Gifford with two full years' backlog of correspondence.

Mary took great care to ensure her personal security. She insisted that important letters be written in her presence and read to her before they were enciphered. The actual encipherment was usually undertaken by her secretary, Gilbert Curll, less often by his subordinate, Jacques Nau. However, unknown to Mary or Babington, Gifford was in fact a double agent in the pay of the English spymaster Walsingham. All correspondence was intercepted, copied and passed on to the unsuspecting Scottish queen.

Phelippes was able to decipher the relatively primitive codes with ease and was soon able to furnish Walsingham with a full report of the plot on Elizabeth's life. Early in July 1586, Babington specified the details of his plan to Mary in a letter, referring to the Spanish invasion, her own deliverance and the death of Elizabeth. Mary pondered her reply for a week and eventually concurred. She had her reply ciphered by Curll and dispatched to Babington on 17 July. Its contents, which were soon divulged to Walsingham, were to cost her her life. Babington and his co-conspirators were arrested and horribly put to death. The Star Chamber convicted Mary of treason and a reluctant Elizabeth signed her death warrant. On 7 February 1587, Mary was executed at Fotheringhay Castle, Northants, England.

MAJOR ESPIONAGE FIRSTS

SUN TZU (c. 510 BC)

Sun Tzu is generally credited with instigating the first fully operational espionage network. His book *Ping Fa* ('The Principles of War'), published in c. 510 BC, is the earliest known textbook on the art of general warfare and as such remains required reading in many military academies. Its lessons were applied by Mao Tse-tung during the Long March and by the Japanese prior to Pearl Harbor.

Sun Tzu was born in Ch'i state, on the mouth of the Yellow River, but spent most of his life in the service of Ho Lu, the king of the neighbouring state of Wu. Under Sun Tzu's generalship, Ho Lu's troops occupied the city of Ying, the capital of the Ch'u state to the west, and ranged far to the north, defeating the armies of the feudal princedoms of Ch'i and Chin.

Sun Tzu believed that to wage war economically while defending the state against others, it was necessary to employ a permanent espionage service spying on neighbours and enemies alike. Sun Tzu introduced a rigid hierarchy of spies to include local spies, internal spies, converted spies and 'condemned spies'. He argued that espionage should be regarded as honourable, with agents granted access to their political and military leaders at all times.

Captured agents should be treated with benevolence, 'tempted with bribes, led away and comfortably housed'. He realised that if such men could be turned they would be in a position to report on their previous masters' strengths and weaknesses. In particular their knowledge of which officials might most easily be bribed would prove of inestimable use to local and inward spies sent to exploit them.

Condemned spies were less fortunate. Unknown to them they were fed completely false information by Sun Tzu's agents, sent into enemy territory and if necessary compromised. When they were captured and tortured, the information which they were able to divulge was wholly incorrect, leading the enemy to miscalculate his response. When the enemy learned of his mistake the spy was put to death, but by then it was often too late, easing Ho Lu to yet another victory.

Alexander the Great was one of the first great generals to realise the full potential of intelligence as a weapon of war.

Erich Lessing/AKG, Berlin

ALEXANDER THE GREAT (356–323 BC)

Under the tutelage of Aristotle, Alexander the Great, King of Macedonia, became the first ruler to utilise intelligence as a weapon of government. Using a system of identical staves and scrolls, he devised a simple but highly effective system of covert ciphers. The scroll containing the hidden message was secreted in an overtly straightforward report, but was wound spirally around the staff in such a way that the secret message could be deciphered from the characters which appeared in a straight line along the staff.

Alexander, who trusted few people, introduced a primitive form of 'Cabinet Noir' (internal monitoring) when he instigated postal censorship into the army. Disruptive elements were sacked, enabling him to maintain morale, even under the most difficult of conditions.

SIR FRANCIS WALSINGHAM (1530–90)

Sir Francis Walsingham is credited with creating the first viable secret service in England. A forthright Protestant, he studied law as a young man, but was forced to flee to the Continent when the Roman Catholic Mary Tudor ascended the throne in 1553. On Elizabeth's accession five years later he felt it safe to return. The experience which he had gained in foreign parts brought him to the notice of Secretary of State Lord Burghley, who engaged him for espionage work in Europe. Using the private agent network which he had built up inside the French Court, Walsingham was successfully able to report on a series of Jesuit-inspired intrigues against the Queen.

Walsingham was recalled in 1569 to assume the appointment of chief of the secret service. Within a year, however, he was returned to France, promoted to English Ambassador and given direct control over all agents working in that country. When Burghley was elevated to Lord High Treasurer in 1573, Walsingham was recalled once again, this time to succeed his mentor as Secretary of State.

Walsingham found the Queen a grateful, if parsimonious, employer who demanded concrete results for as small a financial outlay as possible. He was forced to subsidise the English secret service to such a degree that he virtually bankrupted himself, yet he continued to provide Elizabeth with so complete an umbrella of protection that none of the numerous plots to assassinate her came near to fruition.

Walsingham regarded all English envoys abroad with suspicion until their loyalty was absolutely proven. When Sir Edward Stafford was made Ambassador in Paris in 1583 he was quick to accept Spanish money in return for his services as a spy. Aware of the existence of a problem but unable to prove it, Walsingham sent a trusted agent called Rogers to keep an eye on Stafford in Paris. Rogers' reports were damning yet Stafford was allowed to remain at liberty. Walsingham believed that if Stafford had the trust of the Spanish they would believe anything he told them and began to ensure that the ambassador became the recipient of some highly plausible, though equally inaccurate, disinformation. It is highly unlikely that Stafford ever realised that he was being used as a double agent. He was never brought to trial and returned to England with his reputation intact.

Sir Francis Walsingham was the greatest spymaster of his time. Yet his services to Queen Elizabeth went almost unrewarded and he died in near poverty in 1590. Popperfoto

By 1587 Walsingham had become convinced, partly from intelligence supplied by Stafford, that Spain was amassing a vast armada of ships for an invasion of England. In the spring he drew up a 'Plot for Intelligence out of Spain' in which he set out in immaculate detail his plans: to intercept correspondence between the French Ambassador and Spain; to have agents at Nantes, Rouen, Le Havre and Dieppe; to set up an intelligence network in Cracow to monitor the Vatican attitudes towards Spain; to arrange intelligence-gathering facilities in Brussels, Leyden, Denmark and the Spanish Court and to arrange for coast watchers to travel from port to port in Spain assessing the overall readiness of the fleet.

Walsingham relied for much of his information on intelligence gleaned by Antony Standon, a thoroughly unconventional and wholly reckless agent whom he sent to Spain. In 1586, Standon obtained copies of the reports from the Grand Admiral of the Armada, the Marquis of Santa Cruz, giving precise details of the number of ships available, their sea state, crews and armed forces. From these reports Walsingham was able to deduce that the fleet could not sail until 1587. Pressure was put on King Philip's bankers in Genoa to delay loans to Spain so that funding for the Armada was effectively controlled by the English secret service. At the same time, acting on disclosures of where various units of the Spanish fleet were stationed, Sir Francis Drake was dispatched to 'singe the King of Spain's beard'.

Conscious of the fact that the Armada could be delayed but not defeated by subterfuge, Standen arranged for a series of watchers to monitor its eventual progress along the French coast. As soon as the fleet was sighted, dispatches were sent to England and Walsingham, allowing Grand Admiral Lord Howard of Effingham to establish the precise size, disposition, strengths and weaknesses of the enemy forces. If history shows Drake as unworried when he first heard news of the Armada off the coast of England it is because, by then, not only did he know when and where to expect it but how to defeat it.

Walsingham is among the few heads of intelligence never to have used the service in the furtherance of his own ends. When he died in 1590, Queen Elizabeth, and England, lost a true friend.

CARDINAL RICHELIEU (1585–1642)

Cardinal Richelieu gave France her first organised system of espionage. The son of a noble family from Poitou, Armand du Plessis was consecrated Bishop of Lucon in 1605. Under the patronage of the Queen Mother, Marie de Medici, he was appointed a Minister of State seven years later, but was driven from office shortly after the assassination of the King's Secretary, Concini, in 1617.

He was appointed Cardinal in 1622 and in 1624 was recalled to State office by King Louis XIII. He was confirmed in the post of chief minister in 1629 and awarded the Dukedom of Richelieu in 1631. From then to his death in 1642, Richelieu virtually ruled France, masterminding the country's intelligence service and creating the omnipotent Cabinet Noir, which was designed to intercept and analyse correspondence between the French Court and the lesser nobility.

A statesman first and a man of the Church second, Richelieu's policy as chief minister was to make France great through the absolute power of its monarchy. By introducing an internal policy of religious tolerance while wresting control of foreign policy from the Hapsburgs, he successfully frustrated the aspirations of Gaston of Orleans and the Duke de Cinq-Mars, both of whom had conspired to take the French throne.

Richelieu employed a widespread system of espionage throughout France to ensure that

A politician first and churchman second, Cardinal Richelieu virtually ruled France from 1631 to his death in 1642. Popperfoto

he was kept fully aware of the thoughts and deeds of both Church and nobility. In this he was ably served by his chief adviser and mentor, the Capuchin father Joseph du Tremblay, the effective director of his secret service. Superficially a mild and gentle man, du Tremblay possessed a mind so subtle and intriguing that it earned him the title 'Son Eminence Grise'— the Grey Cardinal—in recognition of the shadow world of intrigue in which he delved in the service of his master.

At the height of his power Richelieu forged an alliance with the Protestant leader Gustavus Adolphus of Sweden which so weakened the position of the German princes that it enabled France to seize Alsace. He weakened the power of Spain by encouraging risings in Portugal and Catalonia and contrived the downfall and eventual murder of the great soldier Wallenstein.

Richelieu's espionage network was unique in that it owed its sole allegiance to him rather than to the Crown. He paid his agents out of his own purse—which he more than adequately refilled from state funds—and demanded their absolute loyalty in return. In this Cardinal Richelieu of France and Sir Francis Walsingham of England were the complete antithesis.

MAJOR JOHN ANDRE (1751–80)

John Andre, an officer of the 54th Regiment of Foot, is the only spy to be honoured by a memorial tablet at Westminster Abbey. Born the son of a Swiss merchant in London, Andre proved incredibly popular when appointed to the post of Adjutant-General in New York. When the American general Benedict Arnold made surrender overtures to the British in 1780, Andre was delegated to negotiate with him.

Andre was provided with a pass in the name of a fictitious merchant, John Anderson, but regretfully his disguise proved inadequate. When stopped by a suspicious American patrol, Andre made the fatal mistake of admitting that he was a British officer and offering them a bribe. He was arrested as a spy, tried by a military board and sentenced to death. Despite numerous pleas for mitigation from Americans who had known him, Andre was hanged at Tappan on 2 October 1780.

JAMES ROBERTSON

Arthur Wellesley, Duke of Wellington, was a far from conventional soldier. He availed himself freely of the services of agents when other, more conservative, commanders would not, and gained greatly from their information. One of the ablest and most unusual of these agents was James Robertson. A product of the Scottish Benedictine monastery at Regensburg, in allusion to which he was nicknamed 'Brother James', Robertson spoke fluent German.

Robertson's first mission, on behalf of the Foreign Office, was to establish the fate of 15 000 Spanish troops stranded in Denmark. Before Napoleon launched his surprise attack on Spain he had convinced his erstwhile allies that Denmark was under threat from Britain, persuading them to dispatch 15 000 of their best troops to protect it.

Robertson went first to the British Secret Service covert listening post on Heligoland, from where he was smuggled in a small craft up the mouth of the River Weser into Germany. Disguised as 'Adam Rohrauer', he learned that the Spanish forces had been fragmented and marooned on a series of small coastal islands thus rendering them ineffective. Crossing to the island of Funen, Robertson met the Spanish commander, the Marquis de la Romana, to whom he offered safe passage home for him and his men in Royal Navy warships.

After an eventful journey Robertson successfully returned to Heligoland, from where he was able to liaise with the British Admiral Keates. Some 9000 of the 15 000 troops were taken aboard ship a few days later and successfully returned to Spain to play a crucial part in Wellington's Peninsular Campaign.

BRIGADIER GENERAL GRENVILLE M. DODGE

Under the direction of General Ulysses S. Grant, a large Union secret service force operated all over the Confederacy. It was the most effective service of its kind to be employed during the American Civil War (1861–65) and represented the first large-scale use of espionage in modern warfare.

Grant learned the potential of espionage as early as September 1861, when an agent informed him that Confederate forces were preparing to advance on Paducah, Kentucky, a city strategically situated at the junction of the Ohio and Tennessee rivers. Grant quickly moved to secure the town, which was occupied without a fight.

Seven months later, however, Grant learned a salutary lesson when his agents failed to advise him that 40 000 Confederates had gathered to launch a surprise attack on his lines at Shiloh Church, Tennessee. Determined that he would never be caught short of intelligence again, Grant set about building an espionage apparatus of his own, assigning its administration to Brigadier General Grenville M. Dodge. Born in Massachusetts and educated (with a degree in military and civil engineering) in Vermont and New Hampshire, Dodge had spent his early working life in the service of the Mississippi & Missouri Railroad.

When war came he had been mustered into service as Colonel of the 4th Iowa Infantry. While on outpost duty at Rolla, Missouri, he had formed the 1st Tennessee Cavalry, regular troops who performed many of the functions of spies, for service west of the Mississippi. Their scouting activities soon generated a network of civilian informants, who used women to pass through the Confederate lines with intelligence for Dodge's troops.

At Pea Ridge, Dodge had three horses shot from beneath him, was wounded and promoted to Brigadier General. After a month's leave of absence he was transferred to western Tennessee, where his experience with scouts and spies was repeated. In October 1862, Dodge was summoned to Grant's headquarters in Jackson, Tennessee, given command of a division and ordered to set up a comprehensive spy network.

Dodge amassed a force of 117 field agents operating from Memphis to Mobile and from Atlanta to Richmond. Each agent was paid according to the difficulty and danger of his or her assignment, and received expenses of between $5000 and $10000 in Confederate money to defray the costs before embarking on each mission. Subsequently he hit upon the expediency of selling confiscated Confederate cotton to defray his considerable financial outgoings; an activity which, although patently illegal, enjoyed the tacit support of Grant.

Dodge enjoyed his greatest successes in support of Grant's Vicksburg Campaign of 1863. His agents were able to report that rumours that Confederate General Joseph Johnston possessed 60000 troops with which to assail the Union Army in its rear were vastly exaggerated, allowing Grant to concentrate the bulk of his forces on the forthcoming offensive.

Later, a spy named Sanborn accurately informed Dodge of the forces available to the Confederates as they made a stand at Champion's Hill outside Vicksburg. Simultaneously another of Dodge's agents, Jane Featherstone, monitored a Confederate force camped 50 miles to the east, while an illiterate girl named Mary Malone reported on outlying enemy positions in Mississippi and Alabama.

During the War and after, Dodge fiercely protected the identity of his agents. He alone knew their names; even his staff officers knew only the number assigned to each spy. Even when pressed by Major General Stephen A. Hurlbut, the commander of the Union XVI Corps in Memphis, to disclose the names of agents operating within his area, Dodge refused, appealing successfully to Grant for support.

EARLY ESPIONAGE AGENCIES

THE NINJA

The Ninja (the name derives from the word 'ninijitsu'—the 'art of making oneself invisible') served the shoguns of 12th-century Japan. They were drawn from the physical and social cream of samurai youth and were reputed to be able to walk on water, to obtain intelligence while invisible and to appear and disappear at will.

Although clearly many of their capabilities were little more than mythological, they were certainly trained to the highest standards. From infancy they learned to walk tightropes, to hang motionless from the branches of trees and to swim for long distances under water. They became the masters of disguise, camouflage and reconnaissance, from which grew the fable of their invisibility. Whether used as espionage agents or war lords their usefulness to the shoguns was immeasurable, as was reflected by their extremely high status in Japanese society.

CABINET NOIR

The Cabinet Noir (a secret police organisation) was the creation of Cardinal Richelieu. Designed to intercept and analyse correspondence within the French Court and between the lesser nobility, it did much to preserve the sometimes tenuous security of the throne of King Louis XIII.

Richelieu used his secret police machine to whittle away, and finally destroy, the power of the great nobles. The constant attempts, first of Gaston of Orleans and later of the Duke de Cinq-Mars, to usurp the throne were discovered and eventually countered from within the Cabinet Noir.

Richelieu built an intelligence machine of gigantic proportions with tentacles in every part of France and in every country in which France had an interest. Much of the Cabinet Noir's work was paternalistic. The Cardinal was as keen to smother domestic disorder within the nobility, which might lead to a scandal at Court, as he was to suppress acts of patent treason. The Cardinal died in 1642, but the influence of the Cabinet Noir lived on for a further 150 years, until destroyed by the French Revolution.

THE OPRICHNINA

Russia's first political police, the Oprichnina, was founded in 1565 by Ivan the Terrible, the first Grand Duke of Muscovy to be crowned Tsar. The 6000 Oprichniki dressed in black, rode black

Tsar Ivan IV's total mastery of the Boyars would not have been complete had it not been for the reign of terror introduced by the Oprichnina.
AKG/Berlin

horses and carried on their saddles the emblems of a dog's head and a broom, symbolising their mission to sniff out and sweep away treason.

The power of the Oprichniki was as absolute as it was savage. Generations of Boyars, landowning gentry of whom Ivan was particularly suspicious, were listed as traitors and either summararily executed or banished for life to Kazan, their property being confiscated. Whole cities were terrorised; most of the inhabitants of Novgorod were massacred in a five-week orgy of cruelty in 1570.

Having allowed it a seven-year reign of terror, Ivan began to fear the power of his own secret police force, and the whole organisation was disbanded in 1572 with the surviving Oprichniki being dispossessed of their estates.

THE OCHRANA

The Ochrana was born in the reign of Tsar Alexander II, but did not grow to its full might until the final quarter of the 19th century. By 1900, the organisation had over 100 000 agents on its payroll operating from bases in every major city in Russia and in several capitals abroad. Although the Ochrana did gain concrete results it was easily infiltrated by the many revolutionary groups working within Russia and was easily destroyed by the Bolsheviks when they seized power in 1917.

Although it was not directly responsible for the organisation of actual pogroms, the

A portrait of Tsar Nicholas II, painted in 1914 shortly before the outbreak of World War I.
Image Select International, London

Ochrana was particularly anti-Semitic, forcing many Jews into the arms of the Marxists. In 1891, an Ochrana official, Komissarov, received an official reward of 10 000 roubles for aiding the incitement of anti-Jewish riots by allowing the police presses to be used for the publication of inflammatory leaflets.

By the reign of Nicholas II there were almost 5000 revolutionary émigrés preparing for the overthrow of Tsarism. The Ochrana's Foreign Agency (Zagranichnaya Agentura) set up its headquarters in the Russian Embassy in Paris, the main émigré centre, in 1882. Under the leadership of Pyotr Rachkovsky, a one-time Ochrana prisoner given the option of exile in Siberia or a career in the political police, it quickly mushroomed.

Utilising 'external' surveillance operators (plain-clothes detectives, concierges and servants) in support of its 'internal' agents (police spies, turned and double agents) it began to gather a wealth of intelligence, much of which remained unevaluated. Far from objecting to Foreign Agency operations on French soil, the Sûreté welcomed them as a means of extending its own intelligence-gathering.

Smaller Foreign Agency groups were tolerated in London, Berlin and Rome, and were made particularly welcome after a spate of anarchist assassinations had claimed the lives of President Carnot of France (1894), Prime Minister Antonio Canovas del Castillo of Spain (1897), Empress Elizabeth of Austria-Hungary (1898) and King Umberto of Italy (1900).

The Foreign Agency did not limit itself to intelligence gathering. It also pioneered a wide variety of 'active measures', geared to influence foreign governments and public opinion, and 'special actions', involving acts of violence, many of them engineered with the aid of *agents provocateurs*.

The Ochrana made its greatest contribution to Tsarist foreign policy in the field of Signals Intelligence (SIGINT). Cabinets noirs were placed in the post offices in St Petersburg, Moscow, Warsaw, Odessa, Kiev, Kharkov, Riga, Vilna, Tomsk and Tiflis to intercept mail to and from known or suspected dissidents. Coded letters were deciphered and new codes sent to Ivan Zybin, the Ochrana's chief cryptanalyst, for breaking.

Diplomatic messages sent by electric telegraph were routinely intercepted. Under Aleksandr Savinsky, head of the Foreign Ministry's cabinet noir from 1901 to 1910, active measures were taken to purchase, or where possible steal, embassy codes and ciphers, as well as plain-text versions of diplomatic telegrams for comparison with the coded originals.

Russian decryption continued routinely until the outbreak of World War I, although, ironically, the Ochrana was unable to breach a new German code introduced in 1912. A number of cryptanalysts were recruited by the Bolsheviks in 1917–18. The majority, however, were rounded up and summarily executed.

OFFICE OF NAVAL INTELLIGENCE

The United States Bureau of Navigation appointed an 'Officer of Intelligence' in 1882. Tasked with 'collecting and recording such naval information as may be useful to the Department in time of war, as well as in peace' the Office of Naval Intelligence became the first true government intelligence agency to function in Washington.

The ONI's first head, Lieutenant Theodorus Mason, proved his agency's worth in 1898 when over 600 people within the United States were denounced as spies during the Spanish–American War. Most of the denunciations came from within the United States. However, a number were uncovered by a Texan agent of Spanish descent, who was infiltrated into Madrid. Masquerading as Fernandez del Campo, a wealthy American with Spanish sympathies, he discovered the presence of a fleet being prepared for an attack against an American cruiser squadron in the Philippines.

The agent escaped to Tangiers, from whence he cabled the ONI. The United States Navy responded by reinforcing its fleet in the Pacific and ultimately won a major victory. Despite the obvious successes of the ONI, the United States government could not come to terms with the concept of foreign espionage. The office remained small, with no more than eight desk officers and seven attachés, until the entry of the United States into World War I in 1917.

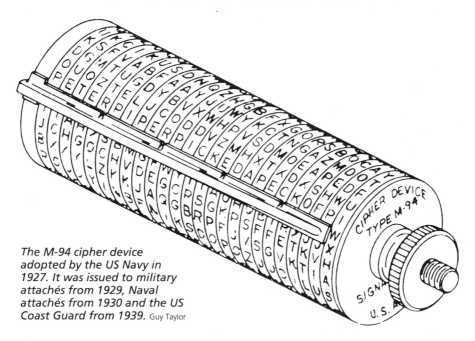

The M-94 cipher device adopted by the US Navy in 1927. It was issued to military attachés from 1929, Naval attachés from 1930 and the US Coast Guard from 1939. Guy Taylor

A PROFILE OF THE AGENT IN HISTORY

CHRISTOPHER MARLOWE (1564–93)

Christopher Marlowe was a considerable poet and playwright. He was also an accomplished spy. While studying at Cambridge University, Marlowe was 'talent spotted' by John Dee, astrologer to Queen Elizabeth I, and recruited by Sir Francis Walsingham, head of the English secret service.

In 1587, the Duc de Guise, the head of the Catholic Church in France, began a long-term attempt to rescue his niece, Mary Queen of Scots, from the clutches of Queen Elizabeth. He planned to offer hospitality to English students with pro-Catholic tendencies at the Jesuit stronghold in Rheims; his ultimate intention was to involve them in plots against the Tudor throne. When Walsingham discovered that Father Robert Parsons, a well-known Jesuit campaigner, had succeeded in planting a Catholic agent in Cambridge he decided to use this route to infiltrate a double agent into the seminary. From him he would obtain detailed information of the conspiracies being plotted there, which he was sure would be intensified after the impending execution of Mary.

The double agent chosen was Christopher Marlowe. Marlowe suddenly left Cambridge in February 1587, and on his return in July was arraigned by the University for being absent without leave, and more seriously for having gone to the Jesuit seminary at Rheims. In the seminary Marlowe had been so loud in his detestation of the Protestant establishment in England that he had been admitted to the schemes then being hatched to create a Catholic resistance movement in England. Unknown to the academic authorities, however, he had dallied just long enough to learn the names of the principal players in the intrigue before returning with the information to Walsingham.

On the secret and direct orders of the Secretary of State all charges against Marlowe were dropped, allowing the student to continue with his studies.

Gradually, for reasons which are still unclear, Marlowe fell from grace. In May 1593, he was arrested at the house of Thomas Walsingham, a cousin of the Secretary of State; although released on bail, he was ordered to answer charges which could have resulted in his being sent to the Tower. Ten days later he was allegedly killed in a drunken brawl in a tavern in Deptford. There are some suggestions that he did not die at all but in fact staged his murder to enable him to escape to the Continent with a new identity.

It is more likely that Marlowe was the victim of an espionage assassination. Frizer, Marlowe's alleged killer, was given a free pardon and no one has yet satisfactorily explained why Robert Poley, a known agent in the pay of Walsingham, was staying in the Deptford tavern at the time.

DANIEL DEFOE (1660–1731)

Daniel Defoe was one of the great authors of the late 17th and early 18th centuries. He was also one of the British monarchy's finest agents. Although best known as the author of *Robinson Crusoe* and *Moll Flanders*, Defoe also worked in 'the honourable, though secret, services' of Queen Anne. Outwardly rebellious, a revolutionary pamphleteer, pilloried and twice imprisoned for seditious libel, his background was hardly suited to the world of royal espionage.

His acute brain, eye for detail and capacity for tireless observation brought Defoe to the attention of Robert Harley, Earl of Oxford, who engineered his release from prison under licence. Defoe proved an excellent servant to Harley and later to Lord Goldsmith, so much so that the latter actually recommended him as his successor when he was forced from office in 1710.

As Defoe progressed deeper into the murky world of espionage he seemingly lost all political conviction, cheerfully betraying those who trusted and befriended him. He became adept at laying bare the sympathies of covert Jacobites, often availing himself of their hospitality the more easily to monitor their private conversations.

As the Jacobite threat grew, George I sent Defoe on a tour of the country. Travelling incognito, sometimes as 'Alexander Goldsmith' and sometimes as 'Claude Guilot', he continued to unearth elements of potential Jacobite resistance while organising a series of pro-Hanoverian agent networks answerable directly to him.

Daniel Defoe, notable author and unlikely secret agent in the service of Queen Anne.
Popperfoto

Despite his obvious successes as a spy Defoe remained a prolific author while in the service of King George, finding time to write *Tour Through England and Wales* as a lucrative sideline to his espionage.

BENJAMIN FRANKLIN (1706–90)

Benjamin Franklin helped to frame the American Declaration of Independence. Superficially he was sober in thought and deed and a diplomat of unquestioned integrity. Privately he was a British double agent with unusually exotic social tastes. As a member of the notorious Hell-Fire Club he met a number of British dignitaries, including the Prime Minister, Lord Bute, and the future Chancellor of the Exchequer, Sir Francis Dashwood, with whom he later corresponded secretly.

While American Ambassador to Paris, Franklin allowed his friend and chief assistant Edward Bancroft to organise a British Secret Service cell within the Embassy. All information gleaned from Washington, together with a great deal of intelligence passed by the French, found its way to London. As matters deteriorated between Britain and her rebellious colony, Franklin passed on information to London relating to the sailing dates and cargoes of ships bound for Washington's army.

Franklin's aim was to have a foot in both camps. He knew that King George would pay a handsome reward to anyone who could return the Colonies to the British fold, yet he had to

Scientist, inventor and politician, Benjamin Franklin attempted to have a foot in both camps, with disastrous results.
Erich Lessing/AKG, Berlin

prepare for the realities of secession. His instincts proved right. At the time of the peace negotiations, John Quincy Adams, destined to be the second President of the United States, expressed considerable doubt as to Franklin's loyalty. He was, however, unable to produce sufficient evidence to pursue the matter.

BELLE BOYD (1844–1901)

The daughter of a Shenandoah Valley farmer and merchant, Belle Boyd was a mere seventeen years old when the American Civil War so fatefully intruded into her life. When Union soldiers occupied her home town of Martinsburg, invaded her house and insulted her mother she took a pistol and shot dead a sergeant. Her youthfulness and sex saved her from serious punishment, and from that day onwards she spied for the Confederacy.

In 1861, Belle became a Confederate courier, running messages and medicine through the Union lines. As the war progressed she travelled far into the enemy lines and beyond, occasionally bringing back intelligence of the greatest timeliness and importance. When she provided General 'Stonewall' Jackson with information which led to the successful surprise attack on Union forces at Fort Royal, Virginia, the general, usually a man of few words, wrote to her personally on behalf of the Army congratulating her on her actions. She never divulged the contents of the letter.

Belle's greatest failings were her extrovert nature and her love of publicity. She talked incessantly about her exploits, real or imagined, preferably to reporters, and allowed herself to become a celebrity in the South. She was arrested six times, imprisoned twice and only saved from the gallows on the personal intercession of Abraham Lincoln. Eventually, late in the war, Union authorities lost patience with her and had her deported to Canada.

Belle Boyd was described by her biographer Joseph Hergesheimer, as 'the most famous woman concerned with official secret activities in the Civil War'. An impartial Press referred to her as 'the Siren of the Shenandoah', 'the Rebel Joan of Arc' and 'the Secesh Cleopatra'. She regarded her fame more circumspectly. 'From the force of circumstances,' she wrote, 'and not through any desire of my own, I became a celebrity.'

After the war, Belle, the reluctant but so successful spy, travelled the world giving lectures on her experiences in the world of espionage. Later she married a Federal naval officer, Sam Wylde Hardinge, who resigned his commission to be with the woman he loved.

ALLAN PINKERTON (1819–85)

Born in Glasgow, Allan Pinkerton showed an early interest in the world of Chartism before emigrating to the United States in 1842. In 1850, he formed Pinkerton's National Detective agency, gaining a considerable reputation within a few years.

By the late 1850s it had become clear that the quarrel between the North and South would almost certainly end in bloodshed. The election of Abraham Lincoln as President in 1860 made open warfare almost inevitable. The South at once began to send agents north to spread anti-Federal propaganda and to seek likely targets for future sabotage.

Aware of the South's activities, the prominent men of the North began to protect their investments. Samuel M. Felton of the Philadelphia, Wilmington & Baltimore Railroad hired Pinkerton and a number of his operatives to protect the railroad from secessionist plotters in Maryland. Pinkerton moved to Baltimore in February 1861 where it was believed that the headquarters of the conspirators had been established. He was accompanied by the highly experienced Timothy Webster and by Henry Davies, a former inhabitant of New Orleans, who had already made the acquaintance of some of the prominent dissidents.

Davies quickly discovered that Marshal Kane, chief of the Baltimore Police, was also a Southern sympathiser who had made it clear that he would do nothing to prevent an attempt on Lincoln's life. Davies so completely won the trust of the conspirators that he was actually allowed to attend the final meeting at which Lincoln's assassin was to be selected. Although he was unable to obtain details of the proposed perpetrator or his intended means of assassination the intelligence gained allowed Pinkerton to ensure that the attempt on the President's life was frustrated.

Pinkerton's handling of the affair had been superb. When war broke out not long afterwards and Lincoln became aware of the pressing need for an espionage service, the grateful President asked Pinkerton to organise it. Although Pinkerton was an excellent detective he had little or no idea of how to acquire and process military intelligence. In the months that followed the embryonic Secret Service lurched from one disaster to another, culminating in the capture and execution of Webster.

Pinkerton accepted his failure as a director of intelligence, but the North could find no one to replace him until the emergence of Lafayette Baker, who subsequently proved himself to be one of the most brilliant spies in history and an accomplished director of intelligence. After the war, Pinkerton returned to domestic detective work, concentrating on the infiltration of the Molly Maguires and the Ku Klux Klan.

Lord Baden-Powell, soldier extraordinary, founder of the scout movement and an active agent. Oil painting by David Jagger

LORD BADEN-POWELL (1857–1941)

Though better known as founder of the Boy Scout movement, Baden-Powell was also an active spy. His penchant for dressing up, love of charades and often embarrassing eccentricity ideally suited him to the world of 19th-century espionage.

Baden-Powell was commissioned into the 13th Hussars on leaving school in 1876. After seven years' service in India his regiment was posted to Natal, South Africa, where the young officer carried out his first intelligence assignment, a covert reconnaissance of the 600-mile frontier of the province. After two years in England Baden-Powell returned to South Africa in 1887, and in the following year acted as intelligence officer for the Flying Column in the Zululand campaign against Dinizulu.

In 1890, he was appointed Military Secretary to his uncle, the Governor of Malta, and in 1891 became intelligence officer for the Mediterranean. Free to act on his own initiative, Baden-Powell now exploited his powers of tracking and observation, coupled with his considerable skills as a thespian, to the benefit of the British Secret Service. When asked to obtain details of the guns in the Herzegovinian fortress of Cattara he disguised himself as an entomologist, taking care to learn how to handle a butterfly net before embarking upon his expedition. A skilled artist, he made sketches of those butterflies he was likely to meet prior to setting out, later secretly incorporating details of the guns and fortifications into their wing patterns.

Subsequently, when ordered to investigate a rumour that a large dry dock was being constructed in Hamburg, he posed as a drunk, saturating his clothes in brandy to enhance the effect. He was swiftly arrested by the German military, but believing him to be too drunk and incapable of finding out any secrets, they released him.

Early in the second Boer War Baden-Powell was given the task of reconnoitring into the Drakensburg Mountains, during which time he succeeded in making friends with a number of Boer farmers. During the subsequent defence of Mafeking, he recruited and trained a number of Zulu scouts, steadfastly refusing to accept the credit for their considerable intelligence-gathering successes. Throughout the campaign, Baden-Powell was convinced that the hand of Germany was guiding the Boer fighters, but was unable to convince the authorities in London.

Despite his outward eccentricities, Lord Baden-Powell was extraordinarily discreet. It is known that he served his country in the field of espionage throughout Europe and southern Africa, in Turkey, Algeria, Tunisia and deep into the Sahara. However, his records are too circumspect to give a full indication of his considerable services to his country.

MATA HARI (1876–1917)

Ironically Mata Hari is one of the best-known spies in history, yet she was one of the worst. Born Margarete Gertrud Zelle, in Leeuwarden in Holland, she displayed an early independence and zest for life. At the age of seventeen she answered a 'lonely hearts' advertisement, through which she met her future husband, John MacLeod, a 38-year-old officer from the Dutch East Indies.

After their marriage the couple returned to Java, where their domestic situation quickly deteriorated. MacLeod was a brute, a drunkard and an adulterer who treated his wife, son (who died in infancy) and daughter shamefully. In 1901, the family returned to Holland. The following year MacLeod deserted his wife, taking his daughter with him. Margarete success-fully fought for custody in the courts, but, when MacLeod failed to pay the maintenance ordered, was forced, in 1905, to leave the little girl with relatives.

Margarete disappeared, to resurface at the Musée Guimet in Paris as Mata Hari, the daughter of a temple dancer who had died giving birth to her and who had been trained by the priests and dedicated to the god Siva. She was an immediate success, performing well enough to gain universal acceptance. She took dozens of lovers from among the rich and social elite of Europe, demanding massive fees in exchange for her services.

When World War I broke out, Mata Hari was in Berlin, where she had recently befriended the Chief of Police, who subsequently enlisted her into the ranks of the German Secret Service. She felt no great loyalty for Germany, having slept with senior diplomats from both sides, and was never fully trusted by her masters.

In August 1914, Italian intelligence advised the French that Mata Hari had renounced the fiction of her Hindu birth to become Berlinoise, and from that moment, wherever she went in Paris, London, Antwerp or Brussels, she was shadowed. Overtly she carried on her life as before, dancing naked on the stage and dispensing her services liberally to those who could afford her. Covertly, however, she began to use neutral diplomats to send low-grade intelligence reports to Germany.

Devoid of enough evidence for a prosecution, the French eventually decided to deport her. To the authorities' surprise Mata Hari at once began to plead her innocence, offering to work for the Allies if required. In order to test her alleged loyalty to the Allies she was sent on a mission to occupied Brussels, to the headquarters of General von Bissing, Governor-General of Belgium. From there she passed, with German help, to neutral Holland, from whence she took ship to Spain.

En route, when her ship docked in England, she was taken to the offices of Sir Basil Thomson, chief of the Special Branch in London; she admitted being a spy, but in the service of France. Knowing her story to be untrue, yet unwilling to arrest her, Thomson beseeched her to give up the dangerous world of espionage before releasing her to continue on her journey.

Once safely in Spain, Mata Hari made contact with the German naval and military attachés. However, she was becoming too expensive for their dwindling resources and was, in any case, now clearly compromised. After a series of cables between Berlin and Madrid, deliberately sent in a code which the Germans knew the French had broken, her masters ordered her to return to France.

On arrival in Paris she collected but did not cash a cheque for 15 000 pesetas. When she was arrested she still had the cheque in her possession. Her trial, held in camera, lasted two

The archetypal image of the international spy, Mata Hari, in her costume as a Hindu princess.
AKG, Berlin

days and was a foregone conclusion. She was sentenced to death on 25 July. Despite numerous pleas for clemency, many of them from her former lovers, she was executed by firing squad on 15 October 1917.

WILLIAM SOMERSET MAUGHAM (1874–1965)

The world famous novelist and playwright W. Somerset Maugham also worked for British intelligence.
Popperfoto

Somerset Maugham, the archetypical Briton, was in fact born in the British Embassy in Paris. He grew up completely bilingual, the very personification of the *entente cordiale*; he was completely at home in both France and Britain. Maugham studied medicine for seven years before deciding to become a professional writer. During World War I he joined the Red Cross in France as a dresser, ambulance driver and interpreter. Later he transferred to the SIS, spending a year as an agent in Geneva.

In 1917, Tsarist Russia exploded in internal strife. Maugham was sent to St Petersburg to support the Provisional Government in its attempt to prevent the Bolsheviks from negotiating an independent peace with Germany. Although he failed in his primary aim (the Bolsheviks acceded to the terms of the Treaty of Brest–Litovsk in February 1918) he submitted considerable intelligence on the German spy network in Russia.

Maugham's outline suggestions for 'a Propaganda and Secret Service organisation in Russia to combat German influence' were well received in London but ultimately were not adopted. When in Russia, Maugham used the cover name 'Somerville'; which he later gave as a code-name to a character in his espionage novel *Ashenden*.

A VERY SPECIAL COURAGE; WORLD WAR II

THE NEED FOR ESPIONAGE—EARLY DAYS AND FUNDAMENTAL MISTAKES

By the summer of 1939 Europe was moving inexorably towards war. France and Britain had mobilised their reserves and Germany had no fewer than 120 divisions poised for action. Yet, when war was finally declared on 3 September, the security services were caught almost wholly unprepared.

Early attempts by the German Intelligence Service, or Abwehr, to penetrate Britain met with almost total failure. Few of the agents planted in Britain as pre-war sleepers were well trained and virtually none were nationals. Most fell victim to internment upon the outbreak of hostilities, while others were incarcerated under Regulation 18 B, an emergency measure of draconian proportions introduced as a counter to anticipated Fifth Column agitation.

THE CELTIC FRINGE

Attempts by Berlin to exploit anti-British sentiments among the Irish met with little success. Although IRA activities on mainland Britain increased after the Munich Agreement of September 1938, few Irishmen proved themselves willing German proxies once hostilities had commenced. Even those, such as Sean Russell, who actively collaborated with the Germans did little to hide their contempt for the political ideals of Naziism.

A few agents were infiltrated into the Irish Republic. However, poorly trained, improperly selected and inadequately equipped they were soon captured. Typical of these hapless amateurs was an Austrian named Ernst Weber-Drohl. A former wrestler and weight-lifter, he had visited Ireland years earlier and had fallen in love with a local woman by whom he had fathered two children before returning to Austria.

Weber-Drohl was put ashore by submarine with instructions to re-establish contact with his former lover notwithstanding the fact that they had not communicated for more than a decade. Not surprisingly she shunned him. Alone and confused he was quickly arrested by the police, fined and released. With his cover gone, his radio confiscated and his funds dwindling he was easily suborned by the XX Committee, a World War II organization formed by British counter-intelligence, to handle turned agents.

The position of Germans in Ireland was made no easier when the IRA began to adopt a policy of securing operational funds by selling foreign agents for cash. When Herman Goertz, an ageing Hamburg lawyer in the service of the Abwehr, was infiltrated into the country, he paid with his life for his masters' failure to warn him of this particular intrigue. Tasked with soliciting support for a peaceful German invasion of the Irish Republic as a prelude to an assault on Britain (code-named Operation Green), Goertz' mission was doomed from the outset by its very amateurism.

As a prelude to catastrophe, Goertz was parachuted not into the Irish Republic as anticipated but across the border into Ulster. His radio set was destroyed on landing, his flashlight failed to function and a small spade provided for burying his equipment was lost. To compound his problems he had been ordered to jump wearing the uniform of a Luftwaffe captain, complete with his own World War I decorations, in the naive belief that this would add credibility to his mission.

Once he discovered that he was in Ulster he declined to use any of his considerable reserves of British and Irish currency for the purchase of food for fear of drawing attention to himself. Instead he headed for the border, swam the Boyne—losing his invisible ink (his sole remaining means of covert communication) in the process—and entered the comparative safety of the Irish Republic.

Having shed his Luftwaffe jacket, though not his medals, which he kept for sentimental reasons, Goertz now headed for Dublin, where he sought refuge in a safe house belonging to a man whose name he had been given in Berlin. Unknown to him the house belonged to a double agent in the service of British intelligence. His money was stolen and, on 22 May 1940, the house was raided by the police. Goertz escaped, after which a large reward was offered for his capture. Destitute, demoralised and highly conspicuous in the by now dishabilled residue of his uniform, he was spotted by the IRA and handed over to the authorities. While in custody the gallant, if wholly inept, Goertz took his life by swallowing a cyanide capsule provided for such contingencies by the Abwehr.

A pre-war attempt by the Abwehr to establish an agency network within the Welsh nationalist movement (though not the Welsh Nationalist Party itself) met with greater, if still limited, success. Although there are suggestions that he was eventually captured and turned by the XX Committee, German reports intimate that one Welshman, Arthur Owens, was considered the most valuable Abwehr agent in Britain.

Arthur Owens

Arthur Owens volunteered his services to the Abwehr in 1937. A regular visitor to Germany in his legitimate capacity as an electrical salesman, a radical nationalist, near destitute and with acute domestic problems, he was a textbook traitor. When war came Owen continued to travel abroad, seemingly ignored by MI5 and MI6 surveillance, taking with him maps, blueprints and diagrams of bases, installations and armaments factories.

When travel to Germany became impractical, Owens made a number of trips to meet his Abwehr handlers in Lisbon, then the espionage clearing-house of the world. Despite his known political convictions, and the fact that all visitors to Portugal were automatically investigated, Owens was seemingly allowed to travel with impunity.

It seems likely that an SIS officer did target Owens, but kept his findings secret for his own, very personal reasons. The unnamed SIS agent was working simultaneously for American intelligence and for his true masters, the NKVD. Unbeknown to himself Owens was being used as a conduit for Soviet-inspired intelligence to the Germans. Much of his information was gained from an acquaintance, a fellow Welshman recently dismissed from the Royal Air Force on the grounds of his 'political unreliability'. Owens regarded this source of information as a windfall, but his handlers in the Abwehr were more circumspect. The former RAF officer, known simply as 'Mr Brown', was persuaded, via Owens, to visit the Abwehr in Lisbon and ultimately in their headquarters in Hamburg, where he was questioned in depth by expert debriefers.

Suspicious of the sheer parameters of 'Mr Brown's' knowledge, which extended far beyond the scope of a conventional RAF technical officer, the Abwehr had him drugged and, while asleep, searched. A complex NKVD cipher was discovered in a signet ring. Unaware of the discovery, 'Mr Brown' was allowed to continue his debriefing until the due date for his return to Lisbon. However, some unconscious change in Abwehr attitudes must have made the Soviet spy suspicious. En route back he left his flight during a refuelling stop at Madrid, evaded his German watchers, and was never seen again.

News of Brown's double identity broke when Owens was still in Lisbon. Owens asked for permission to emigrate to Germany but, instead, was ordered back to Britain. But, by now starved of information by the Soviets, his usefulness to the Abwehr diminished considerably. He received a final payment of £500, through contacts in the Japanese Embassy in London, during the Christmas festivities of 1940. He continued to transmit sporadically until the spring of 1941. His last transmission to his masters in Hamburg, 'Help me, my life is in danger,' went unacknowledged.

Hans Schmidt

During the summer of 1940, while still actively transmitting to Germany, Owens was ordered on a dangerous trip to Winchester. Hans Schmidt and Jorgen Bjornson, two Danish agents in the pay of the Abwehr, had been parachuted into England and Bjornson had severely damaged his ankle in the process. Owens met Schmidt in the waiting room of Winchester Station, passed him details of a safe house in Salisbury and made arrangements for the injured Bjornson to be treated by a sympathetic doctor. The agents split up soon afterwards. Bjornson was subsequently arrested and interned (it is said that the British authorities felt too sorry for him to execute him, though, again, he may have been turned), but Schmidt managed to avoid detection.

Schmidt began to move about the south coast reporting weather conditions, troop locations and damage assessments in his twice daily transmissions to Hamburg. Despite the omnipresence of his satchel transceiver and Ordnance Survey map, with the local RAF airfields marked with red pencil, he was never questioned.

Lest his remarkable luck ran out, Schmidt was ordered to cease transmitting in the autumn of 1940 and to move to the comparative protection of a safe farm in the Welsh mountains. He was reactivated in December 1940 and continued to transmit, albeit sporadically, for the rest of the war. He reported on Canadian troops near Southampton prior to Dieppe, on American dispositions prior to D-Day and was the last Abwehr agent to transmit before the Hamburg centre was overrun and captured. By now happily married with a family, Schmidt settled down in peacetime London, never caught, never compromised.

EARLY DISINFORMATION

German attempts to gain information through the medium of sympathetic neutrals was usually thwarted by British counter-intelligence. In October 1940, the Franco Government sought permission for a representative of the Spanish Youth Movement to visit Britain, ostensibly to study the Boy Scout movement but in reality to give a detailed report on the state of British defences and preparedness for invasion. Rather than reject the proposal out of hand, MI6 persuaded the Foreign Office to agree to the request and then, in cooperation with MI5, took charge of the plans for his arrival.

The Spaniard's room in the Athenaeum Court Hotel was bugged and one of the only three operational anti-aircraft batteries in London moved to Hyde Park, close to the hotel, from where it fired continuously throughout every air raid. Visits were arranged to Windsor Castle, where the spy was shown the Royal Family's 'ceremonial guard' (but was not told that it was the only fully equipped tank regiment in the country), and to Scotland, where his aircraft was passed en route by 'squadrons' of Spitfires (or, more precisely, by the same Spitfires passing several times in different formations).

Not surprisingly, the spy's report to Berlin counselled strongly against invasion, warning that British unpreparedness was a mere fiction promulgated by her secret services to lure a German expeditionary force into a trap. At a time when the bulk of the German intelligence services regarded Russia rather than Britain as their natural enemy, such assessments, however spurious, did much to counter the High Command's demands for an early invasion.

Alfred Wahring

Equally interesting in the annals of early disinformation is the story of Alfred Wahring, 'the spy who never was'. In October 1939, Captain Gunther Prien, commander of the German submarine U-47, entered Scapa Flow, sank the battleship *Royal Oak* and damaged the carrier support ship *Pegasus*. In 1942, Curt Reiss of the Philadelphia *Saturday Evening Post* published a fantastic story in which he suggested that the whole operation had been masterminded by a single agent. Captain Alfred Wahring, a World War I veteran who had witnessed the scuttling of the German Grand Fleet in Scapa Flow, had apparently vowed revenge. He had moved to Switzerland, applied for a passport under the name of Albert Oertel, and learned the trade of a watchmaker. In 1927, he moved to Britain, became a naturalised citizen and set up shop at Kirkwall in the Orkney Islands, close to Scapa Flow. At the outbreak of war he had somehow sent a message to the Germans, advising them of the lack of a boom or adequate anti-submarine nets protecting the eastern entrance to the Flow. When a U-boat had been dispatched, Wahring had guided it into position using the headlights of a motor-car.

The chief of German intelligence, Walter Schellenberg, enthused at the story. Allan Dulles of the CIA incorporated it into his lecture pack on the worth of the long-term sleeper, yet there was not a shred of truth in any of it. Neither German nor British records show any trace of a Captain Wahring, nor of a watchmaker named Oertel. Prien's log makes no mention of a signal from an agent ashore, but instead intimates that he entered Scapa Flow blind, with little idea of what to expect. Prien states that he did see the flash of a car headlight but assumed that it belonged to an alert motorist who had noticed the wake of the U-boat's conning tower in the water. The story of Wahring is undoubtedly a piece of fiction brilliantly planted in the United States by the Germans themselves.

THE VENLO INCIDENT

Prior to the outbreak of war Britain had one of the largest and most complex foreign intelligence networks in the world. Traditionally most agents were based in British embassies, usually in the guise of passport officers. Many were retired naval officers in search of a supplement to their pensions and few had any formal training or experience in espionage. They had little access to worthwhile information and were easily targetable by German counter-intelligence services. When Hitler annexed Austria in 1938, the SIS chief in Vienna was quickly arrested. The German occupation of Czechoslovakia destroyed a network based in Prague.

In 1936, Colonel Sir Claude Dansey, deputy head of the SIS, created Section 'Z', a third intelligence organisation beyond the scope of MI5 and MI6. Premises for the top secret Section 'Z' were established in Bush House in London. Commercial and business firms, even a film company, were established to give its agents anonymity. Within two months of the commencement of hostilities, however, Section 'Z' was closed down, a victim of one the greatest mistakes in the history of the British intelligence services.

During the last week of October two agents, Captain Henry Stevens, SIS head of station, and Captain Sigismund Payne Best, one of Dansey's 'Z' men, were dispatched from their offices in The Hague. They were ordered to Arnhem, where they were to meet two representatives of 'the German General Staff' eager to discuss the overthrow of Hitler. The British agents met Captain Schaemmel of the Transportation Corps and Captain Hausmann of the Medical Corps, verified their bona fides, and escorted them to MI6 headquarters in Amsterdam. While in Amsterdam the Germans were passed a compact wireless set and given instructions to contact London, using the call-sign ON-4, should there be further news of the anticipated coup.

About a week later ON-4 signalled requesting a second meeting, which took place on the Dutch–German border. The Englishmen were in violation of MI6 orders, which specifically forbade further meetings other than in the comparative safety of The Hague or Amsterdam. None the less a third meeting was arranged. The rendezvous was to be for 4 p.m. on 9 November at the Café Bacchus in Venlo, only a few paces from the Dutch–German border.

The British agents approached Venlo from The Hague in the company of Lieutenant Dirk Klop, a Dutch Army intelligence officer. As they arrived a German car screeched to a halt in front of theirs. Men standing on its running boards fired at the Dutch guards, fatally wounding Klop. The two Britons were bundled handcuffed into the car, which roared over the border into Germany.

'Hausmann' was in fact Max de Crinis, a psychologist from the University of Berlin. More crucially 'Schaemmel' was none other than Walter Schellenberg, chief of the Foreign Intelligence section of the SD. Unfortunately for the two agents, on 8 November—the eve of the Venlo meeting—Hitler had narrowly escaped death when he left a Munich beer hall only minutes before a bomb went off, killing seven Nazis and injuring 63 more. Quite erroneously he blamed the British secret services and, in a rage, ordered Schellenberg to abduct Stevens and Best.

The two were taken to the cellars at 8 Prinzalbrechtstrasse, Gestapo headquarters in Berlin, and kept in solitary confinement. Although rigorously questioned they were never tortured. They revealed a mass of detailed information, which included the identities of fellow agents and the structure of the SIS in Europe. Imprisoned in Dachau, repatriated and debriefed after the war, both admitted being quite open with their captors, but no action was taken against them. Stevens died in 1965, Best in 1978.

As a direct consequence of the Venlo affair, the 'Z' network and The Hague station had to be closed down. With Hitler's occupation of most of Europe, MI6 networks had to be shut down until the SIS had virtually no remaining agents active on the Continent.

SURVIVING SOURCES

Such intelligence networks as were left intact on the Continent continued to provide minimal, if often high-grade, information throughout the war. On 3 November 1939 an anonymous German scientist volunteered a ten-page document containing a mass of details relating to pilotless aircraft, radar and new bomb fuzes. Although initially discounted by SIS, this information was eventually passed to R.V. Jones of Air Intelligence, assessed and found to be of excellent scientific value. To the embarrassment of the neutral Swedish authorities the SIS station in Stockholm kept up a flow of reports on German shipping in the Baltic and along the Norwegian coast. Under the leadership of Commander Philip Johns the SIS station in Lisbon trained informants, debriefed refugees and compiled a list of 1900 known and 350 suspected German agents.

Spy networks left in place by the Czech, Polish and Dutch governments in exile provided a wealth of information on German intelligence and Wehrmacht and Luftwaffe strengths and dispositions. Even the Belgians and French, with their jealously guarded domestic networks, provided a fount of information to the SIS, though only because the latter controlled their radio networks.

THE DOUBLE CROSS SYSTEM

The Double Cross System was one of the earliest and most enduring of British secret service successes. German agents were arrested, held in secret in a centre in Richmond Park and either 'turned' or their places taken by British radio operators. The system was controlled by the Oxford academic Sir John Masterman at the head of the ad hoc 'Twenty (XX) Committee', which supervised the work conducted mainly by the B1A section of MI5.

In all there were some 120 double-cross agents on MI5 records, of whom 39 (with code-names as improbable as 'Mutt', 'Jeff', 'Lipstick' and 'Peppermint') were caught and controlled successfully from within the United Kingdom. In the early days of the war disinformation fed back to the Germans concentrated on troop dispositions, factory outputs and the strength of the localised defences. However, as the war progressed, agents began to feed false information on possible landing sites for the invasion, leading in no small part to Hitler's absolute conviction that the invasion would take place along the Pas de Calais.

The Double Cross System was most successful in the Middle East and North Africa. Working from its headquarters in Cairo, Security Intelligence Middle East (SIME) succeeded not only in keeping Turkey neutral but in forcing the Germans to keep tens of thousands of reserves needlessly in the Balkans. Ably assisted by Brigadier Dudley Clarke's 'A' force, SIME convinced German intelligence that Britain had several newly arrived divisions in North Africa poised for a strike across the Mediterranean. In reality the divisions comprised nothing more than a small team of hard-working radio operators sending routine radio messages to each other from relatively inaccessible parts of the Middle East. When tasked by German intelligence to investigate the source of this increased radio traffic, agents under SIME control reported completely fictitious troop build-ups in the transmission areas. Completely unaware of SIME's activities, German High Command in the area became obsessed with the idea of invasion through the Balkans, resisting pressure to release its reserves to France until several weeks *after* the Normandy landings.

When captured networks were unable to provide enough disinformation, SIME invented completely fictitious agents. One, a prostitute code-named 'Gala', was actually in prison in Palestine, but for the purposes of misleading the Germans was depicted as 'working' in Beirut.

She sent reports on a whole string of indiscreet, but wholly imaginary, lovers, including a motley series of Allied officers and a technician secretly working on the preparation of Turkish airfields for Allied occupation.

Not every double-cross was completely successful. When the Yugoslav brothers Ivo and Dusko Popov were recruited into the Abwehr in 1940, both offered their services to MI6 in Belgrade. When the Abwehr sent Dusko to Portugal in November 1940, MI6 gave him the telephone number of their Lisbon station. A month later he succeeded in flying secretly to the United Kingdom, where he was interviewed and recruited both by MI5 (code-name 'Scout') and MI6 (code-name 'Tricycle').

Returning to Lisbon he began to provide valuable intelligence for the British. However, one crucial piece of information was badly mishandled. From German sources he obtained detailed information of the proposed Japanese attack on Pearl Harbor. Inexplicably, rather than pass this information to the White House (the United States had no formal foreign intelligence service at the time) the British kept it to themselves. However, MI5's Guy Liddell (then a Soviet agent) informed J. Edgar Hoover of the FBI and arranged for the two to meet in Washington. Primed by Liddell that Popov was a double agent, and horrified by his code-name 'Tricycle' (which Hoover assumed to have sexual connotations), Hoover took an instant dislike to the Yugoslav, dismissing his completely accurate information out of hand.

SPECIAL OPERATIONS EXECUTIVE

THE BEGINNING

In the dark days of 1940 Britain stood alone, her espionage network shattered. Abwehr counter-intelligence had spent the months of the Phoney War painstakingly analysing the information obtained from Stevens and Best to piece together the names and addresses of all the Allied intelligence offices in France and the Low Countries. When the invasion had come none had survived, leaving Britain without a single agent between the Balkans and the English Channel.

The battered rump of the SIS had become defensive in nature. With the exception of Section D (for Destruction), set up in 1938 by Colonel Lawrence Grand to operate primarily in the Balkans, but now tasked with the formulation of plans for domestic subversion and sabotage in the event of a German invasion, little was being done to carry the war to the enemy.

In July 1940, the newly appointed Prime Minister, Winston Churchill, created the Special Operations Executive (SOE) to 'set Europe ablaze' through the medium of economic sabotage. The term 'economic sabotage' was deliberately left open to a variety of interpretations which broadened as the war progressed. Inevitably SOE and MI6 clashed, often bitterly, as the former began to grow in influence and encroach upon the latter's traditional responsibilities. SOE was empowered to extract staff from any government department at its sole discretion and without recourse to higher authority. It absorbed Department D (though not Grand, who returned to military engineering) and assumed responsibility for all acts of subversion by whomever generated. The Government Code and Cipher School (GC & CS) at Bletchley Park remained the jealously guarded domain of MI6, but all other radio traffic passed to SOE.

SOE was headed by Dr Hugh Dalton, the Minister of Economic Warfare, assisted by

Bletchley Park was headquarters of the Government Code and Cipher school throughout the war.

Topham

Gladwyn Jebb (later Lord Gladwyn), Philip Broad and the banker Leonard Ingrams. As Chief Executive Officer (CEO), Jebb divided SOE into three branches. SO1 under the command of Rex Lepper from the Foreign Office, was given responsibility for propaganda. SO2, under Jebb himself, supported by Robin Brook and the former Conservative backbencher Sir Frank Nelson, handled operational matters, while SO3, headed by Brigadier van Cutsem of the War Office, dealt with planning.

In November 1940, Major-General Sir Colin Gubbins MC, a larger-than-life veteran of the Royal Flying Corps, became effective director of operations and training. Wholly without experience in the field of espionage, Gubbins suffered indifference and occasional hostility from the Foreign Office, especially regarding operations in France, and often clashed with MI6.

SOE did not have a conventional headquarters but rather spread itself over a number of buildings. Its 200 telephone lines were distributed over three exchanges, Abbey, Ambassador and Welbeck, and did not carry addresses. Correspondence was usually sent without attribution or on Ministry of Economic Warfare letter headings, although occasionally fictitious commercial or service addresses were employed. MO1 (SP) at the War Office, NID (Q) at the Admiralty, AI10 at the Air Ministry and the Inter-Services Research Bureau were among the more popular covers. When SOE's original headquarters at 2 Caxton Street proved too small in October 1940 the organisation decamped to 64 Baker Street, a large complex of offices in Marylebone close enough to the hub of events to be convenient yet divorced enough to remain discreet.

As the war progressed sub-offices mushroomed until, by the winter of 1943-44, most of the western side of Baker Street as far as Gloucester Place had been requisitioned. Marks and

Major-General Sir Colin Gubbins, photographed at Buckingham Palace at his investiture as a Companion of the Order of St Michael and St George (CMG), 8 March 1944. Popperfoto

Spencer's new head office housed the cipher and signals branches while 1 Dorset Square, the peacetime headquarters of Bertram Mills Circus, became the home of the Gaullist RF Section.

SECURITY

As the SOE empire grew, internal security became a nightmare. Civilian maintenance and building workers with little if any vetting were allowed almost constant access to the buildings. Equally the multitude of inter-service and international uniforms crowding the Baker Street pavements made it obvious to the most casual onlooker that the area was anything but a quiet commercial backwater. Yet domestic SOE security seems not to have been breached by the Abwehr, who, unlike the Soviets (see Chapter Three), failed to plant a single agent within any of its headquarters or training schools. Desk officers operated a strict 'need to know' policy, living the lie of a cover story when away from the office. Many must have been sorely tempted to tell at least part of the truth to their loved ones, especially when, as occasionally happened, they were roundly criticised for not playing a larger part in the war effort. However, there is little evidence that any did, and certainly nothing suggests that German counter-intelligence benefited in any way from such leaks.

Operational code-names were allotted in blocks, by an inter-service committee in White-hall, to formations that needed them and were supposed to be at random. Once used, and finished with, code-names were reallocated. Although blocks of code-names were used by particular countries: N (Netherlands) used vegetables and F (France) English occupations, the categories were seldom kept distinct as an exercise in damage limitation in the event of compromise.

FIELD SECURITY

By contrast, SOE field security was atrocious. Petty rivalries and jealousies between it and MI6 caused each organisation to starve the other of information with occasionally lethal consequences for the agents on the ground. Agents were taught to keep their address and cover name a secret when operational, even from their closest contacts, and to make a point of moving house as often as possible, ideally every night or two. They were taught to counter routine police questioning, even when exhausted, and were provided with cover stories that would hopefully not collapse under initial investigation. They were trained to answer all questions in a brief, dull, uncomplicated manner and in no way to draw attention to themselves. However, no amount of training, however brutally realistic, could compensate for the 'shock of capture' inevitably sustained by a network when one of its agents was arrested. The temptation for the others to close ranks, perhaps even to attempt to contact a neighbouring, though totally independent, network, was at times overwhelming. Occasionally the consequences of so fundamental, if human, a breach of security were disastrous.

Inevitably a wartime organisation formed as hastily as SOE was unable to screen its recruits fully. Among the influx of French, Belgians, Dutch, Norwegians and Poles who sought sanctuary in Britain were some whose aim was to infiltrate British intelligence to the benefit of their Nazi masters. Refugees who volunteered for work in British intelligence, and whose cover stories passed peripheral examination, were usually passed on to SOE. Lacking both the experience and resources to vet such applicants further, SOE accepted most at face value.

DISASTER IN HOLLAND

The most dangerous of these refugees were the Dutch, with their historical propensity for producing double agents. When Queen Wilhelmina fled to London in 1940 she left Holland in a state of bewilderment and disarray, a country almost wholly devoid of leadership. Dutch intelligence had made no provision for clandestine organisations, not even secret radio stations, leaving the Queen and her advisers in exile completely isolated. To compound the problem, during his hasty departure from the capital an SIS agent had abandoned an attaché case containing the names and addresses of all his Dutch associates. This was discovered by the Germans with fatal consequences for all involved.

German intelligence was undoubtedly aided by the unpreparedness of the Dutch for clandestine war. Ultimately, however, their very considerable success turned on the three hinges of deciphering, deception and double agency. Hans Zomer, a Dutch intelligence operator working for SIS as well as SOE, was captured in possession of a complete radio post, including a pile of back messages, codes and their keys. Zomer steadfastly refused to divulge information to his interrogators, even under Gestapo torture. However, an SD sergeant, Ernst May, acting on his own initiative, succeeded in breaking the SIS cipher system. On 13 February 1942 two more SIS agents, Ter Laak and a former Royal Dutch Navy radio operator, William van der Reyden, were captured in possession of a second set of codes. Angry and disorientated after his capture, van der Reyden gave a large amount of information to the gentle and sympathetic May, enabling the latter to increase considerably his knowledge of British codes. Disastrously, May also learned of the existence of the security checks and test questions used by SIS and SOE agents to prevent impersonation, thus setting the stage for a deception exercise of massive proportions.

With the help of George Ridderhof, a pro-Nazi double agent (or 'V-Manner'), the Germans next closed in on an SOE group. Thys Taconis, a trained saboteur, and Huburtus Lauwers, his radio operator, had been parachuted in on 6/7 November 1941. Despite some startling irregularities in their forged identity papers the two men had successfully settled down to work, Lauwers in The Hague, Taconis at Arnhem. Under the guise of a road haulier, Ridderhof befriended Taconis, providing him with transport to remove supplies from his drops. He also supplied the agent with wholly inaccurate intelligence for transmission to London. Gradually, from snippets of information carelessly divulged, Ridderhof succeeded in unravelling crucial details of the SOE network, including the location of its radio. On 6 March 1942, while preparing to transmit to London, Lauwers was arrested. Taconis was taken a few days later. Both men were told that their lives would be spared if they cooperated with 'England Spiel', an operation involving the transmission of disinformation on Lauwers's captured radio set. Taconis refused, even under torture, and was eventually executed at Mauthausen in the early winter of 1944.

Lauwers agreed, though solely in the belief that London would realise from the lack of his security checks that he was operating under duress. Tragically London did not, and for two years continued to act upon Lauwers's messages despite their continuous lack of checks and the constant inclusion of netting-in signals (NIS) and other paraphernalia calculated to warn the receivers. On one occasion he even succeeded in signalling, in open language, the message 'CAUGHT CAUGHT CAUGHT' within a standard transmission, but to no avail. The listeners working for Bletchley simply chose to edit out what they did not want to hear as superfluous. After a few weeks the fact that Lauwers was omitting his security checks was not even relayed to SOE headquarters in London.

After only a few days' transmission Lauwers was advised by London that an agent named Lieutenant Arnold Baatsen (code-named 'Watercress') would be parachuted into a drop zone north of Assen on the night of 27 March. Baatsen, a professional photographer, dropped on schedule to be arrested by the waiting Germans. The *resistant* was furious and talked openly to his captors adding to their increasing knowledge of SOE ciphers and personnel. Lauwers was ordered to notify SOE that Baatsen had arrived safely, after which other agents followed in increasing numbers. Piet Homberg arrived in the autumn of 1941, followed by Lieutenant Leonard Andringa on 10 March 1942. On 29 March, another team, Hendrich Jordaan and Gerard Ras, was parachuted in to be followed a week later by Hendrick Sebes and Berend Kloos. Two weeks later, Lieutenant Hendrick van Haas arrived by boat.

By late 1942 SOE believed that it had no fewer than ten agents safely operational in Holland. In reality all were prisoners. In all 'England Spiel' netted 51 SOE agents, nine from MI6 and one, Beatrix Terwindt, the only woman in the party, from MI9. She survived Ravensbruck and Mauthausen, but almost all of her male companions were shot. Lauwers himself was spared and five agents escaped from the concentration camp at Haaren, north-east of Tilburg. Two of these, Sergeant Dourlein and Lieutenant Ubbink (code-named 'Cabbage' and 'Chive'), ultimately escaped to Switzerland, where they made contact with the local head of SIS in Berne.

With complete contempt for SOE, SIS then sent a damning message to all its agents warning of N section's insecurity. The message, which read 'Sister service totally infiltrated by Germans. We therefore urge you to break off all contact with their agents and keep clear of them,' was immediately intercepted by the Germans, who finally realised the game was up.

As a final twist of the knife Dourlein and Ubbink were arrested when they reached Britain and incarcerated in Brixton prison. During their laborious journey along an escape route from Switzerland they were denounced as Gestapo agents by the Abwehr, using a captured SOE radio set. After a few months both men were eventually released and ultimately decorated by the Dutch authorities.

When the Germans realised that 'England Spiel' had run its course they sent a gloating message in clear to the heads of N (Netherlands) section of SOE:

> TO MESSRS BLUNT BINGHAM AND SUCCESSORS LTD STOP YOU ARE TRYING TO MAKE BUSINESS IN THE NETHERLANDS WITHOUT OUR ASSISTANCE STOP WE THINK THIS RATHER UNFAIR IN VIEW OUR LONG AND SUCCESSFUL COOPERATION AS YOUR SOLE AGENT STOP BUT NEVER MIND WHENEVER YOU COME TO PAY A VISIT TO THE CONTINENT YOU MAY BE ASSURED THAT YOU WILL BE RECEIVED WITH SAME CARE AND RESULT AS ALL THOSE YOU SENT US BEFORE STOP SO LONG STOP

N section's response remains unknown, and was probably unprintable. What is clear is that 'England Spiel' represented one of the major catastrophes in the history of secret intelligence. It need never have happened—an object lesson in security.

AGENT RECRUITING AND SELECTION

As a secret organisation, SOE had to recruit by stealth, which meant by word of mouth and by some gentle subterfuge in official channels. SOE had informal arrangements with HM Customs, the immigration services and the RAF to pass on information of personnel with connections to occupied countries. Vaguely worded appeals or advertisements were also placed, asking people who spoke foreign languages to contact the War Office.

Few potential recruits knew the significance of their initial interview. Most had received rather uninformative letters, asking them to present themselves for an initial interview in connection with possible war work. Even those who had been introduced through personal contacts had no more than a vague idea that they were interviewing for high-security work. More than a few were women. Indeed, as the Germans began to rely increasingly on slave labour to maintain their war effort, and the sight of a fit young man on the streets of occupied Europe drew suspicion in itself, women became preferred.

Typical of the SOE assessors was the author Captain Selwyn Jepson, the recruiting officer for F, the independent French section. Regarded by Maurice Buckmaster, head of F section, as being 'far ahead of anyone as a talent spotter' it was his task to size up the potential recruits and to decide from the outset whether they would make good agents. Through questioning the interviewees in depth on their past and present lives he was able to establish their levels of worldliness. Inexperience was not in itself a disqualification if matched by potential. Nor were striking good looks and a vibrant personality. However, most agents preferred to blend into the background, grey men and women indistinguishable from the disillusioned and subjugated populace of occupied Europe. Agents had to pass as Continentals, so a markedly British appearance was a drawback, as was a markedly Jewish appearance, given the persecution of the Jews at the time. A perfect French accent was sought, although a strong dialect could occasionally be explained away by a clever cover story.

Despite the most rigorous of checks mistakes were occasionally made. Potential agents incapable of speaking a language other than their own, or who spoke with undisguisable Scots or Geordie accents, were accepted. On one occasion F section even sent an agent to occupied France who was so obviously Jewish that when the Germans arrested him they could not believe he was an agent until they saw his transmitter.

The initial interview for F section would take place either in the Northumberland Hotel or in Room 321 in the War Office itself. The room was always bare and bleak, two folding chairs, a naked light bulb and a blackout screen comprising the only furniture. Jepson made a point of always being on time. To conduct the interview he would wear civilian clothes, a plain army battledress, the service uniform of a Major in the Buffs (to which he was entitled) or the uniform of a Royal Navy captain (to which he was not).

After a sentence or two in English he would switch to French, a language in which he was fluent. For from 30 to 40 minutes he would probe the applicants for motive and character, discounting those of an impulsive or reckless nature. Those demonstrating prudence, an inner courage, a degree of introversion and a propensity for forward and objective planning under pressure were invited back for a second interview a few days later. Before their return they were vetted by MI5 to confirm as far as possible their loyalty. During the second interview Jepson would be more explicit, ultimately explaining the true nature of the work. Potential agents who showed an interest in volunteering were sent away to consider the idea overnight, having first been warned to discuss the matter with no one, not even their parents, husband or wife.

At a third meeting applicants were asked to take the plunge or finally withdraw. Those who hesitated were rarely given a second opportunity.

From June 1943, SOE adopted a new recruiting system. Candidates were no longer interviewed on a one-to-one basis but were instead assessed over several days by a board comprised largely of psychologists. Those who succeeded were then passed on to basic training. Failures were politely returned to their parent units or to their civilian lives without ever learning the true purpose of the board.

Many women were recruited from the First Aid Nursing Yeomanry (FANY), one of the least known, most socially exclusive yet effective of the services. FANYs, most of them still in their late teens, manned the wireless stations on which the SOE networks depended. A few, such as Violette Szabo (code-name 'Louise'), worked in the field. Most of her companions who did likewise were, as was she, commissioned as junior officers before they left, if not in FANY then in the Women's Auxiliary Air Force (WAAF).

Initially it was considered improper to employ women in active operations. They were expressly banned from carrying weapons in the conventional armed forces and it was felt that this prohibition might extend to irregular warfare. Churchill was asked to adjudicate and deferred on the side of reality. Of the 52 female agents sent by SOE into France, 17 were arrested, of whom 12 died in concentration camps.

Unlike MI5 and MI6, SOE recruited foreigners when it felt the need to do so. Some of its best agents enjoyed dual nationality, a few were even citizens of enemy states. Noor Inayat Khan, best known by her code-name 'Madeleine', was among the bravest. Born into an affluent family, with an Indian father and American mother, she had lived in both Germany and France. Her family had left France for England in 1940 and she had joined the RAF as a radio operator. Her radio skills and knowledge of France, if not her frailty, made her of interest to F section. She began her training in late 1942, was later inserted into France and captured. A beautiful and gentle girl, she died in the horrific death camp at Dachau.

The exact size of SOE has never been revealed. However, in its heyday in the summer of 1944 it is likely to have peaked at just under 10 000 men and 3200 women of whom some 5000 in total were trained, or under training, as agents. The rest, some retired veterans of field work, were involved in planning, intelligence, operations, signals, transport and administration.

TRAINING AND MISSION ALLOCATION

Volunteers who were accepted for training were subjected to a long and gruelling assessment programme to ensure their suitability as agents. Those who failed were offered alternative employment within SOE or, if unsuitable, were sent on other courses for different work. Security risks were posted somewhere distant and insignificant, typically to a series of workshops in the remote Highland village of Inverlair (said to be the inspiration for the television series *The Prisoner*).

No records were kept of how many recruits were rejected, and at what stages, although it is known that Baker Street received detailed weekly progress reports on each student. Most reports were destroyed after the war together with the vast majority of SOE records. However, from those which remain it is clear that many instructors clashed in their assessments, particularly of women candidates. Ultimately section heads had the last word and were free to ignore conflicting or adverse assessments. Indeed, there were many instances in which the initial intuition of men such as Buckmaster and Jepson proved superior to the views of more orthodox minds.

The entire training programme took place in a series of schools, many of them located in country homes requisitioned for the purpose. All were staffed by FANYs and, despite the rigidity of the training, were relatively palatial, causing some insiders to wonder whether the true meaning of SOE was not in fact 'Stately 'omes of England'.

Preliminary training was in physical fitness, with considerable time dedicated to cross-country runs, elementary map reading and rudimentary weapons handling. Where practical, theoretical lessons were conducted in the trainee's 'field' language. Students were known by code-names as a confidentiality measure, and to instil a sense of security. As a safety measure

Wanborough Manor near Guildford, one of many country houses loaned to the SOE during the war. Mark Lloyd

for the future they were told not to discuss their personal lives with each other, although it seems that many did. Supervision was constant. Each house had a well-stocked bar which the recruits were encouraged to use to test their security under the influence of alcohol. On a few occasions discreet 'companions' were even provided to ensure that agents did not talk in their sleep and, if they did, in which language!

The best known of these schools, Wanborough Manor, was situated in a secluded spot near the Hog's Back, south-west of Guildford. Run for F section by Roger de Wesselow, a retired Coldstream Guards officer who believed in leading from the front, it quickly attained a reputation for excellence. Locals were advised that the house had been commandeered for commando training but nothing else and were left to decide for themselves why so many of the students appeared to be middle-aged men or attractive young women.

Those who passed out from the first stage were sent up to the west coast of Scotland, to a site close to director of operations Gubbins's own home, to master the physical aspects of resistance. Intensive physical training, endurance exercises and rock climbing were interspersed with lessons in advanced weapons handling. Students were expected to master not only the Sten, Thompson and Bren guns but to learn to strip and reassemble all types of French and German light and medium machine-guns under pressure and by day or night. Unarmed combat, silent killing (always a contentious subject), demolitions and sabotage were also taught as the course progressed, as was basic Morse code for use on the drop zone.

Those who failed the course, or felt that they lacked the aptitude, were returned to normal life, perhaps after a short period in Inverlair. Survivors were sent to a fresh set of country houses in the Beaulieu area of the New Forest. Here the students were taught the defensive aspects of espionage; how to recognise the enemy by uniform and rank, how to avoid the attention of collaborators and how to behave when stopped at a routine road block. As their time at Beaulieu progressed their ability to resist interrogation was tested to the hilt by unknown instructors dressed in Gestapo or SD uniforms. Shaken awake in the middle of the night the students were taken to cells and questioned for hours, perhaps days (though never tortured), to test the strength of their cover story under duress. Students who failed were subjected to yet further training or, if necessary, transferred to other duties.

Nothing was left to chance. The Axis order of battle, message writing, the art of agent meets and the use of cut-outs were all taught. Returned agents thoroughly briefed their successors on local matters of crucial importance such as which cafes it was safe to visit, whom among the locals could be trusted to be discreet and which back roads were most liable to military spot checks.

However, no amount of training could prepare the agent for the numbing shock of seeing so many enemy uniforms on the streets. Nor could it quell the feeling of sheer terror experienced when first presenting a set of forged identity papers for inspection.

More technical courses were needed once a student had passed out of Beaulieu. Parachuting was taught by Department STS 33 from a large house at Altrincham, near Manchester, with drops into the grounds of Tatton Park from Whitley aircraft based at Ringway, now Manchester's civil airport. Wireless operators were sent to Thame Park, near Oxford, where they were given a thorough grounding in Morse code, the theory and practice of transmission and reception and coding and ciphering techniques. Research and training into sabotage techniques were undertaken by Departments IX and XVII in Hertfordshire. Under the watchful eye of George Rheam, agents were taught to identify the Achilles' heel of an industrial complex and to establish when and how it might most easily be attacked.

Morse keys were deliberately made as small as possible to facilitate concealment.
IWM

Each resistance group, or 'reseau', required a small number of specialist agents at its heart; an organiser in overall command, a courier to liaise between the organiser and the different groups within the 'reseau' and a radio operator to keep up communications with Baker Street. Once in the field responsibilities tended to merge. Couriers in particular would tend to work closely with their radio operators, finding them safe houses, providing them with lookouts and arranging for transportation for their sets from place to place. The more resilient might also deputise for the organiser in his dealings with local groups, help organise the reception of arms drops and even take an active part in sabotage operations.

Many couriers were women, and as such they were able to move about the towns and countryside without attracting undue attention. However, their gender brought with it its own peculiar disadvantages. Female agents in F section were reminded that they were entering a male-dominated society which still denied French women the vote. They were advised to be extremely circumspect when giving local (all-male) resistance groups advice and were warned to give direct orders only when absolutely necessary. To the dismay of many, they were told that French women did not receive a cigarette ration and were warned to be extremely careful when smoking in public.

Couriers were encouraged to memorise messages wherever possible. When these were simply too long or complex the trainees learned to transcribe them in minute handwriting on to tiny sheets of rice paper which could be easily hidden and even swallowed in an emergency. Couriers were taught to manufacture 'sympathetic', or invisible, inks usually from non-prescription drugs easily obtainable on the Continent. Typically one part of alum, used widely for tanning rabbit skins, might be mixed with 100 of parts water to make an invisible ink developed by passing a hot iron over the sheet of paper.

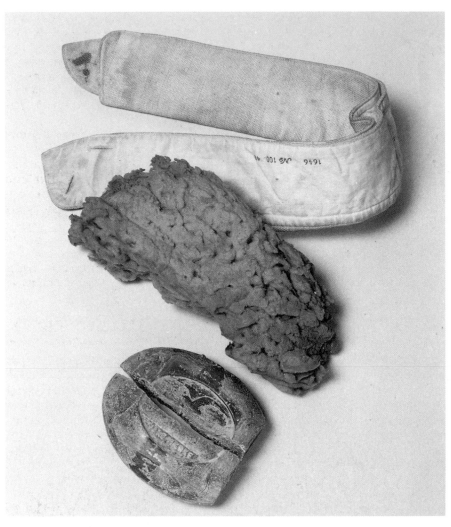

The soap, sponge and soft collar were part of a secret writing kit. The ink was concealed in the collar or sponge and mixed with the soap.   IWM

Agents were taught to hide short messages, or 'barn codes', in ordinary letters. Although this system was virtually impervious to analysis it required a great deal of time and effort to formulate a plausible letter and was therefore of necessity confined to the passage of urgent yet simple messages.

AGENT INSERTIONS
In the early days agents could only be inserted into enemy territory by parachute or boat. However, SOE's options were increased in 1943 when squadrons of Lysander reconnaissance

aircraft and Hudson bombers were made available to land on secretly prepared fields, taking agents in and picking up fugitives for the return journey. Landings were made at night and were wholly dependent on the weather. Coastal insertions required total darkness, whereas parachute drops could be made only on a still, near cloudless night with the assistance of bright moonlight. Timings were always uncertain. Drop zones could be compromised or become the subject of a completely unrelated sector security search, causing last-minute cancellations. Resistants awaiting transportation were kept in a series of Section holding-houses with other agents, whom they were allowed to know only by nickname.

During the period immediately prior to embarkation, agents were provided with clothing compatible with their cover story. Local labels were sewn into continental-style suits and dresses and teeth checked for signs of British dentistry. Where necessary agents were provided with large sums of money to pay for the formation of new networks, although occasionally this ended in disaster. There were instances of SOE agents in the Balkans being murdered for their bank rolls, while Nigel Low, an F section recruit with a known record of embezzlement, was inserted into France never to be seen again.

THE COVER STORY

Once an agent's mission was agreed a cover story was invented and papers forged in support of his or her newly assumed identity. Cover stories had to satisfy the initial scrutiny of a curious

This cigarette lighter is not all it seems; a compass has been hidden in a false compartment at the bottom. A reverse thread protects it from casual discovery. IWM

policeman and not lead to the agent being held for further questioning, as few papers would withstand detailed analysis. The names of parents had to appear on the identity card, as did the place and date of birth and the address of the town hall where the fictitious birth was registered. As a simple check of the town hall register would lead to compromise, agents invariably purported to come from areas in which the records had been destroyed by Allied bombing.

Male agents had to have a cover which explained why, if they were of service age, they were not working in Germany. Many were given 'jobs' as salesmen, often with bona fide work permits supplied by firms involved in the production of war materials. Others claimed to be itinerant tradesmen bombed out of their places of business and now seeking casual work wherever they could find it. Women agents required no special exemption from service and could more easily pass as refugees or war widows. Papers in occupied Europe were constantly changed by the authorities in an attempt to frustrate forgeries and it was no easy task to ensure that agents were supplied with the latest documentation.

The British Type 3 Mark II transceiver entered service with the SOE in 1943.   IWM

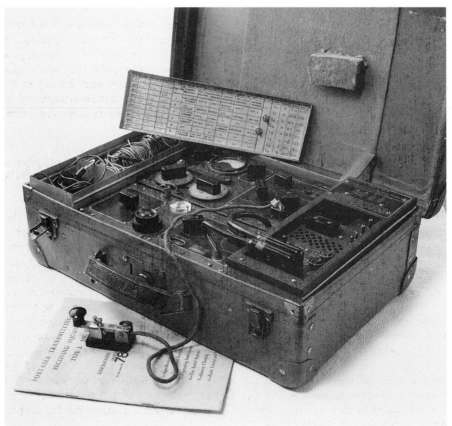

Final briefings took place at the very last moment and where possible were conducted with the assistance of recently returned agents. Drop zones, passwords, safe houses and contacts were only now disclosed and the cover story checked for the very last time. Security remained strict, with strenuous efforts made to ensure that agents destined for different operations did not meet. Every effort possible was taken to lessen the agent's sense of isolation. Promises were given to write periodically to relatives, who had no idea of the agent's activities, and, in the case of women leaving behind young children, arrangements were finalised for their schooling and general welfare.

However they were due to enter the Continent, agents invariably left England by aeroplane. Those due to enter southern Europe by boat would fly to Gibraltar, where they would board a submarine or fast patrol boat for the final dash through the Mediterranean. Flights took off in darkness from either Tangmere airfield in Sussex or Tempsford airfield in Bedfordshire. Before boarding, agents were given two things: a good-luck gift in the form of a cigarette case, a pair of cufflinks or a brooch, which they could sell on the black market in an emergency; and a cyanide pill for use *in extremis*. Several agents refused even to carry the pill; none is known to have used it.

RADIO OPERATORS

Women made ideal radio operators. Their patience, care, manual dexterity and steady temperament were ideally suited to the long, alternating periods of tension and boredom associated with the careful maintenance of a radio net. Operators, or 'pianists', had to pass an exacting six-week course designed to turn them into dedicated experts. They were taught the importance of schedules, or 'skeds', the imperatives of speed and accuracy when transmitting and the need to keep constantly on the move. They also had to learn to maintain and repair their sets and to improvise when they found themselves in poor transmitting conditions.

COMMUNICATIONS

Communications between home base and the resistance groups in Europe was by radio. The radios the agents used were modified as the war progressed, but basically comprised a receiver, transmitter and about 20 m (65½ ft) of aerial. They were tuned with slices of quartz, known as crystals. Cut to a precise dimension, which determined the wavelength, the crystals were about the size of a postage stamp. Each was mounted in a small rectangular Bakelite box, with a pair of prongs to plug it into the set. Crystals were notoriously fragile, and prone to loss, yet without them the set was useless. Sets had to be capable of operating by day or night over ranges from as little as 160 km (100 miles), for a clandestine station located in northern France, to a maximum of 1600 km (1000 miles) for stations in Czechoslovakia and the Balkans.

Because power had to be subordinated to the design imperatives of weight and space, most transmitters were of no more than 1 to 10 watts. The siting and positioning of the outdoor aerial was essential. If bent or tangled a clandestine aerial would beam most of the transmitter's energy into the surrounding walls. If not perfectly aligned with the home station it would beam its message away from the intended receivers, possibly into the waiting antennae of an enemy direction finder.

THE HOME STATION

Initially SOE sets, crystals, codes and operating schedules were controlled by SIS from its centre at Bletchley. They were passed from Bletchley to Baker Street by dispatch rider, which added a further hour or two to the sending of a message and its receipt, although secure teleprinters were later introduced. As SOE and SIS grew in size and rivalry it became clear that the one could no longer assume responsibility for the communications network of the other. On 1 June 1942, SOE was at last authorised to take over the running of its dedicated nets. It was allowed to build its own sets according to its particular specifications, devise its own crypto systems and administer its own home stations.

SOE home stations were manned by dedicated radio operators, many of whom had volunteered as agents but for some reason had failed to make the grade. Of necessity, station locations were secret but tended to be in rural areas as far away as possible from prying eyes. Many were disguised as the country annexes of perhaps fictitious government departments evacuated in the face of the enemy bombing threat.

The first two home stations were set up between Bletchley and Thame—at Grendon Underwood and Poundon, on the Oxfordshire–Buckinghamshire border. Both stations normally transmitted on 250 watts, but had a 15 kW transmitter in reserve if any operator reported severe difficulties in reception.

Reception was dependent on atmospheric conditions and could not be guaranteed. Schedule timings and transmission frequencies were allotted according to 'ionospheric propagation forecast charts', regularly updated to anticipate forthcoming climatic conditions, but were no more than 75 per cent accurate. Recording devices were therefore attached to each home base receiver and activated as soon as a signal was heard to ensure minimum loss through message 'break up'.

As a matter of routine security, recorded messages were regularly compared with sample tapes deposited by each agent. Morse operators tend to develop a personalised 'shorthand', perhaps in the form of a dot a little too short or a dash a little too long in a particular letter, which makes them instantly recognisable to a trained analyst. It was therefore considered possible to establish whether or not an operator was being impersonated or, in theory at least, was being forced to transmit under duress.

However, few theories are perfect. Just as handwriting can be forged, so can Morse styles. As has already been seen, German intelligence was able to mimic no fewer than ten N-section operators simultaneously during 'England Spiel'. In France, several operators were imitated with equal success, including Macalister, a luckless Canadian arrested near Orléans in possession of his security checks even before he had a chance to operate his set. Taken to Fresnes prison, south of Paris, Macalister was 'befriended' by a sympathetic warder and given a Morse key to play with in an attempt to alleviate his boredom. Unknown to the Canadian his 'transmissions' were monitored by a signals corporal stationed in an adjacent cell.

As soon as the corporal felt capable of aping his style the Germans activated Macalister's ('Archdeacon') circuit, running it for nine months without SOE realising the true identity of the radio operator. During that time the network received drops of arms, money and, on one disastrous occasion in March 1944, no fewer than six operators, who were immediately arrested or killed.

Unaware of such failures and freed from SIS constraints, SOE radio traffic proliferated. Taking F section as an example, in May 1941 it had only two clandestine stations operational, both in Vichy-France. By May 1942, this number had increased to seven, and by December

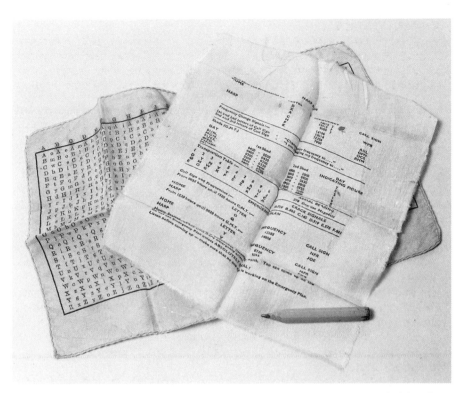

The transposition table and transmitting 'sked' were printed on uncrushable silk and were capable of being folded up very tightly for concealment.   IWM

1943 to nearly 30. At its peak in August 1944, F section operated no fewer than 53 networks servicing hundreds of radio operators, cipher clerks and teletypewriter operators in four home receiving stations.

COMMUNICATION PROCEDURE

During the early stages of the war, the clandestine operator was forced to carry a heavy suitcase containing his radio set and quartz crystals around with him. He would spend several weeks, even months, living at a safe house arranged for him by Baker Street. When he wished to establish contact with his home station, which remained constantly manned in anticipation of his call, he would leave the security of his base to find a suitable site for transmission. He would set up his radio, position his aerial and attempt to establish contact using his personal call-sign. If reception was poor, the base might ask him to repeat several groups or even the entire message. After acknowledgement, the home station transmitted any messages it might have for the network.

It was not unusual for the collective operation to take several hours. Although sophisticated monitoring equipment had yet to enter service, the procedure remained extremely hazardous. Aware that a transmission was taking place, the enemy would swamp the area in the hopes

ONE-TIME PAD

One-time pads may vary in detail and size but all are basically numbered pages of random numbers, usually in groups of five. For espionage use they may be photographically reduced on to easily burned nitrate film. A magnifier is required to read it. (See also p.120)

```
TRANSMISSION TABLE          PAGE   3

15783  15789  45775  54213  04267  14578  14587

12450  15736  10458  45973  05871  34892  04578

58710  39456  91042  30759  48526  24798  21486

18753  94586  35054  17423  05605  47852  90068

58742  36452  04895  99421  68423  47895  02458

57889  24567  54770  94562  14578  04264  01598

34587  02459  42970  35941  31477  26479  71478

11472  85955  59641  48630  94513  68824  65423

87542  02694  56897  71200  12456  98756  32101

45789  96542  89745  60125  44978  52345  01267

89520  14720  56879  74531  52678  45912  45687

10012  34589  90726  45389  12485  24875  24785

21862  35530  14587  52097  41002  45522  36587

41565  58663  44587  91255  46842  00475  42112

45789  12356  42025  38691  58001  16457  98253

46854  69824  51046  79800  21346  79859  63168

64421  56825  97015  48394  01487  01245  65724
```

```
TRANSMISSION TABLE       PAGE   3
15783 15789 45775 54213 04267 14578 14587
12450 15736 10458 45973 05871 34892 04578
58710 39456 91042 30759 48526 24798 21486
18753 94586 35054 17423 05605 47852 90068
58742 36452 04895 99421 68423 47895 02458
57889 24567 54770 94562 14578 04264 01598
34587 02459 42970 35941 31477 26479 71478
11472 85955 59641 48630 94513 68824 65423
87542 02694 56897 71200 12456 98756 32101
45789 96542 89745 60125 44978 52345 01267
89520 14720 56879 74531 52678 45912 45687
10012 34589 90726 45389 12485 24875 24785
21862 35530 14587 52097 41002 45522 36587
41565 58663 44587 91255 46842 00475 42112
45789 12356 42025 38691 58001 16457 98253
46854 69824 51046 79800 21346 79859 63168
64421 56825 97015 48394 01487 01245 65724
```

Approximate Actual Size

of catching the operator on the ground. Spot checks and road blocks would be increased and strangers treated with more than usual suspicion.

As the war progressed, and radio direction finding techniques improved, it became necessary to introduce more sophisticated security procedures. Radio sets were reduced in size and weight until they could fit comfortably into a small suitcase easily transportable on the luggage rack of a bicycle. Operators were issued with a series of variable call signs and frequencies, ciphers were improved and transmission schedules introduced.

In 1944 transmission and reception were split into two hermetic compartments and were no longer carried out from the same location. SOE introduced minute receivers which enabled the operator to receive and decipher messages at night in the comparative security of his safe house. Transmissions were still sent in daylight, when atmospheric conditions were better. Ideally a large number of operators in the same general region would swap call signs and frequencies and send simultaneously to swamp the direction finders. Each operator maintained as many as five transmitters secreted within his area from which he would choose one at random for his broadcast. Once a set had been used three times its frequency would be reset and it would be moved to a new location known only to the operator and his bodyguard.

SECURITY CHECKS

During the formative years of SOE espionage, routine and random security checks were inserted into all messages to verify that the sender was not transmitting under duress. Routine checks often comprised a particular error, such as the fifth and twentieth letter of each message misplaced by five places of the alphabet. It was soon known by the enemy that such checks existed, so agents learned to carry two codes; one for divulgence to the Germans, the other for insertion in messages to friends.

Random checks were more secure but harder to memorise. A three-letter word, which would be changed on a regular basis, would be inserted at the beginning and end of each message if the operator was still able to transmit freely. The word would be disguised by advancing its letters by an agreed number of letters in the alphabet. Thus, if the word were 'bin' it might appear at the beginning of the message advanced by three letters to read 'elq' and, at the end of the message, advanced by five letters to read 'gns'. Two letters would be added at random to the codes 'elq' ('ielqy') and 'gns' ('tgnso') to camouflage them as standard five-letter transmission packs.

The random check system was backed up by a series of seemingly innocuous questions which might be asked by the home station in the case of persistent doubt. Thus, if to the question 'Do you require cigarettes?' the agent replied 'Yes', he was no longer free. If, however, he replied 'My shoes are black' his network was operating normally.

Regretfully security checks were only as good as the covert and home base operators employing them. In too many instances, when checks were omitted, the home base chose to assume that the agent had simply forgotten to add them. Indeed, there were several instances of captured agents who were transmitting under duress, omitting their safety codes only to be sharply reminded by home base to include them in future messages. Not surprisingly routine and random checks were phased out in 1942.

DIRECTION-FINDING TECHNIQUE

The Germans, like the British, kept a constant watch on every wireless wavelength, and it took only 20 or 30 minutes for a team of their armed direction-finders to get within a few yards of

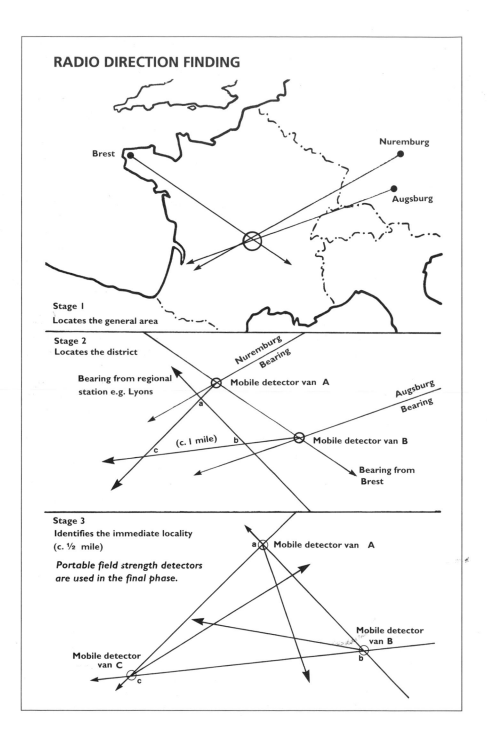

RADIO DIRECTION FINDING

Nuremburg

Brest

Augsburg

Stage 1
Locates the general area

Stage 2
Locates the district

Nuremburg Bearing

Bearing from regional
station e.g. Lyons

⊗ Mobile detector van **A**

a

Augsburg Bearing

c (c. 1 mile) b

⊗ Mobile detector van **B**

Bearing from
Brest

Stage 3
Identifies the immediate locality
(c. ½ mile)

a⊗ Mobile detector van **A**

Portable field strength detectors
are used in the final phase.

Mobile detector
van **B**

b

Mobile detector
van **C**

c

an operator who was foolish enough to remain on the air too long. Some of SOE's early organisers insisted on sending messages which were so verbose that their operators had to remain at their Morse keys for literally hours on end. Inevitably most were caught.

It did not take long for Gubbins, as head of operations, to identify this weakness and for the signals school at Thame to begin to impress the need for brevity. Even so, it was not until the winter of 1943–44 that all transmissions were reduced, as a matter of policy, to less than five minutes. This made life difficult for the enemy, though not impossible, unless the agent moved often and kept varying the frequency he used. In mid-January 1944 the Swiss operator Jolande Beekman was arrested during a transmission after she insisted on sending from the same attic in St Quentin, at the same hour, on the same three days of several consecutive weeks.

German direction-finding operations in France were centred on Gestapo headquarters in the Avenue Foch in Paris. Relays of 30 clerks monitoring up to 300 cathode-ray tubes kept up a continuous watch on every conceivable frequency between 10 kilocycles and 30 megacycles. When a new set opened up it showed up at once as a luminous spot on one of the tubes. Alerted by telephone, large goniometric stations at Brest, Augsburg and Nuremburg started to take cross-bearings. Within 15 minutes they were able to establish a triangle with sides about 16 km (10 miles) across into which detector vans from a mobile regional base could be moved to pinpoint more precisely the area of transmission.

Typically, a mobile regional base would be equipped with two front-wheel-drive Citroën 11 light vans, each crewed by four civilians carrying machine guns, and two four-seater Mercedes-Benz convertibles with fake French licence plates. If the transmission had ended the vehicles would move to the intersection points of the triangle and wait in the hope that the unknown station would acknowledge a reply to its message. An acknowledgement of a mere three to four seconds would allow an experienced team to reduce the sides of the triangle to no more than 800 m (0.5 mile). If the transmission were longer, the operator would almost inevitably be compromised.

Attentive agents were often able to evade capture at this stage. Armed protection teams would ring the transmitter constantly on the lookout for unmarked vans or suspicious strangers glancing at their watches (localised direction finders were worn on the wrist). These teams would fight if necessary to save the operator. However, operators usually elected to slip away unobtrusively, abandoning their schedule and, if the worst came to the worst, their set.

CIPHERS

SOE ciphers were crucial to the security of its clandestine networks. They were also complex and, to many of its operators, unintelligible.

The Playfair Code

Initially operators were taught the Playfair Code, named after the English scientist and Parliamentarian Sir Lyon Playfair, but in fact invented by the physicist, Charles Wheatstone.

Agents were told to learn a memorable line from a favourite song or poem. Their chosen line was then transposed into blocks of five letters, omitting any letters used already. Thereafter the rest of the alphabet was used to fill the 5 × 5 square in an agreed order, the letters I and

J counting as one. By way of example, the line 'A Nightingale Sang in Berkeley Square' appeared as:

A	N	IJ	G	H
T	L	E	S	B
R	K	Y	Q	U
W	C	F	D	M
O	V	P	X	Z

The message to be sent, in this instance 'Marie Safe', was divided into bigrams (groups of two letters). Thus MARIE SAFE became MA RI ES AF EZ, the final Z being added at random to fill the blank space. Each bigram was then encoded by taking the two opposite corners of the rectangle it formed in the word square. MA became WH and RI became YA. If both letters of the bigram were in the same line then the next letters to the right were used; if both were in the same column, the next letters below. Thus ES became YQ, AF became IW and EZ became BP. The message, simply encoded, became WH YA YQ IW BP and was transmitted in two five-letter groups as WHYAY QIWBP. If necessary, the final group was made up to five letters by the addition of duds chosen at random.

Although Playfair had the advantage of simplicity it was relatively easy to break and required the memorising of a large number of lines. In late 1941 it was gradually replaced by the more intricate, though still not impenetrable, double transposition system and, in 1942, was banned completely.

The Double Transposition System

The double transposition system required the agent to memorise two random numbers of between six and nine figures long. Agents were ordered to memorise their numbers, but many chose, despite the obvious security risk, to write them down rather than forget them. The message was written under the first random number. Each vertical column was then taken in numerical order, transcribed to the second random number, and again taken off by numerical order of vertical column. Taking 763152 and 8513427 as the random numbers and 'Marcus taken Saturday' as the text, the message was written out under the first number:

7	6	3	1	5	2
M	A	R	C	U	S
T	A	K	E	N	S
A	T	U	R	D	A
Y					

The columns were then read off in numerical order, CER SSA RKU UND AAT MTAY, and written out under the second number:

8	5	1	3	4	2	7
C	E	R	S	S	A	R
K	U	U	N	D	A	A
T	M	T	A	Y		

Again the columns were read in numerical order, RUT AA SNA SDY EUM RA CKT, and the result put into groups of five letters, RUTAA SNASD YEUMR ACKT, for transmission. Upon receipt, the home station wrote out the message under the second key, vertically by numerical order of columns. The message was then read off horizontally, split into groups and put under the first key in numerical vertical columns. The message was then read horizontally and processed.

In practice messages included a serial number, two or more pre-arranged dummy letters, the operator's code and possibly a date/time group. Not only did this make them more difficult to prepare but easier for German counter-intelligence to decipher. To overcome this inherent weakness agents were encouraged to change their random numbers as often as possible.

In the early days the number groups were determined by reference to a book. Both agent and home station held identical copies of the same book. Messages began with two groups indicating the page number, the line, and the number of letters to be used for the two tables. The agent had to memorise a table for converting the letters composing these two groups into numbers and a far more complex number-to-letter conversion table for translating the letters from the text of the book into numbers. Hopelessly complex, almost impossible to memorise and prone to human error the book system became deeply unpopular with all who attempted to operate it.

The Poem

In 1942, the book was abandoned in favour of the poem. Every agent was asked to memorise a series of lines containing no fewer than 26 words and taken from a poem popular in the area in which he or she was to operate. Once chosen, each word of the poem was represented by a letter of the alphabet. Taking, by way of example, a poem by W.B. Yates:

AND	THOUGH	I	WOULD	HAVE	HUSHED	THE	CROWD	THERE	WAS	NO
A	B	C	D	E	F	G	H	I	J	K

MOTHER'S	SON	BUT	SAID	WHAT	IS	THE	FIGURE	IN	A	SHROUD
L	M	N	O	P	Q	R	S	T	U	V

UPON	A	GAUDY	BED
W	X	Y	Z

Six consecutive letters were then chosen at random, for example PQRSTU.

The six letters were then numbered and divided as between odd and even to enable the odd letters to form the first group of the code and the even numbers the second.

Thus PRT, the first group, became WHAT THE IN and QSU, the second group, IS FIGURE A. The letters forming the two potential keys were then numbered in alphabetical order:

W	H	A	T	T	H	E	I	N
9	3	1	7	8	4	2	5	6

I	S	F	I	G	U	R	E	A
5	8	3	6	4	9	7	2	1

The two codes therefore became: 931784256 and 583649721.

To conceal the chosen groups during transmission dud letters were first added to each: thus PRT became, for example, PARPT and QSU QNSTU.

To further garble the codes the letters were then replaced by, say, the third letter following in the alphabet: P A R P T and Q N S T U were thus transmitted as: S D U S W and T Q V W X.

The system remained difficult to use, particularly under pressure, and remained prone to error. The Gestapo quickly became aware of the importance of an agent's poem and went to any lengths to extract it from captured resistants. To counter enemy deciphering, messages had to contain no fewer than 100 letters and were ideally longer. This meant that an operator had to transmit at least 30 groups, however brief his actual real message; an ingredient for disaster in an environment of improving direction-finding techniques.

The Delastelle System

In an attempt to reduce the very real human error factor of the double transposition, SOE introduced the Delastelle System in 1943. Essentially a return to the 5 × 5 Playfair letter square, it was rendered less vulnerable to enemy counter-intelligence by the introduction of numbers along the upper and left-hand sides:

	1	2	3	4	5
1	G	M	P	S	D
2	Q	A	W	C	K
3	N	H	B	T	U
4	E	V	Y	IJ	R
5	Z	F	L	X	O

A message, such as SEND ARMS NOW, was broken into groups of five letters with dummies added if required. Thereafter, each letter was broken into its coordinates as if it were an Ordnance Survey map. Thus V became 42 and T 34.

The message was then transposed in its five-letter groupings with its coordinates written vertically below. The coordinates were then read horizontally in pairs to produce fresh letters based on the original square:

S	E	N	D	A		R	M	S	N	O		W	X	X	X	X
1	4	3	1	2		4	1	1	3	5		2	5	5	5	5
4	1	1	5	2		5	2	4	1	5		3	4	4	4	4

The numbers were then read horizontally in pairs to give:

14 31 24 11 35 25 55 54 11 52 52 41 53 44 44

Each number was then recoded using the original code block:

14	31	24	11	35		25	55	54	11	52		52	41	53	44	44
S	N	C	G	U		K	O	X	G	F		F	E	L	I	J

Deciphering was carried out by reversing the operation. The transmitted letters were written horizontally, the coordinates determined by the known code and the message deduced in clear at the bottom:

S	N	C	G	U		K	O	X	G	F		F	E	L	I	J
1	4	3	1	2		4	1	1	3	5		2	5	5	5	5
4	1	1	5	2		5	2	4	1	5		3	4	4	4	4
S	E	N	D	A		R	M	S	N	O		W	X	X	X	X

The Delastelle System was good but not perfect. It was still mathematically solvable. In September 1943, SOE introduced the one-time pad, so effective that it remains operational with every major security organisation to this day. As such it is described in detail in Chapter Three.

ENIGMA

The Enigma coding device constituted perhaps the greatest breakthrough in the transmission of secret information during World War II. It was a German invention which turned messages into an unintelligible scramble before sending them in Morse. Under the personal supervision of Colonel Stewart Menzies, then deputy head of MI6, a number of British agents helped to obtain the secrets of the Enigma coding device through Polish intermediaries in 1939.

One of Britain's most valuable contacts in Warsaw who helped to obtain the Enigma secrets was Charles Proteus Steinmetz, a Jewish scientist who had worked in the German factory where the Enigma machine had been built. Expelled from Germany for his socialist-democratic views, he had returned to Warsaw, where he had immediately made himself available to Polish intelligence. Thereafter, a young an impressionable aide of the Polish Foreign Secretary

Bletchley Park even built replica enigmas to help with the massive decrypting task.
Topham

Colonel Beck quickly succumbed to the amorous attentions of Amy Elizabeth Brousse, the British agent 'Cynthia', and agreed to assist in the passage of the top secret codes to MI6.

Britain's possession of the Enigma codes remained one of the great secrets of the war. Administered first under the code-name BONIFACE and later ULTRA, messages were decoded at GC & GS headquarters at Bletchley Park, Buckinghamshire. Their contents remained top secret, although it seems likely that Menzies of MI6 informally passed the contents of certain relevant but no doubt sanitised signals to Gubbins of SOE at their weekly meetings.

In September 1940, four months after he became Prime Minister, Churchill ordered that he be given 'daily all Enigma messages'. This proved impractical, but by the summer of 1941 he was getting each day a selection of several dozen, together with reports on the progress of cryptanalysis, brought to him in a special dispatch box, buff-coloured to distinguish it from the black boxes for other official papers. The box was to be unlocked only by Churchill, who carried the key on his key ring.

Extremely conscious of the need for security, and constantly worried by the number of people with access to the Enigma secrets, Churchill urged restrictions. The solutions of the Enigma intercepts were, however, exploited widely by those few in the know.

In an attempt to mislead the Germans about the vital work of the Bletchley team, MI6 conspired to make the Vichy French appear responsible for the leakage of German intelligence. The services of the ubiquitous 'Cynthia' were once again sought. Posing as a journalist she targeted Charles Brousse, a public relations officer at the Vichy Embassy in Washington. Discovering him to be an ex-navy fighter pilot, something of an Anglophile and unrelentingly anti-Nazi she took him as a lover and in due course became the recipient of a considerable amount of high grade intelligence.

Obtaining the French ciphers, however, proved more difficult as they were locked in an embassy vault to which Brousse had no access. A typically French solution was found by the enterprising 'Cynthia' when she and Brousse pretended to the embassy night watchman that they were lovers with 'nowhere to go to make love'. During one of their nightly assignations they gave the watchman champagne laced with drugs. As he slept Brousse and 'Cynthia' let in a second Allied agent, a Canadian locksmith known as the 'Georgia Cracker', who had been let out of jail after he had volunteered for the dangerous task of cracking enemy safes. The Mosler safe with its click-click combination lock posed no problems for this expert and within 45 minutes the ciphers were safely in British hands. When British Intelligence, with considerable support from the FBI, leaked the news of the break to the Germans, the latter became convinced that they had located the source of a major breach of security.

RADIO SETS

Prior to gaining its operational independence in June 1942, SOE was forced to employ transcievers designed for general SIS use. Some of these were mere prototypes used for a single operation. Others proved wholly impractical and were not even taken into the field. As the war progressed, sets became smaller and lighter, but more complex and prone to breakdown.

Early SOE operators were trained to use the Mark XV transceiver. Introduced for the commercial telegraphy market and issued to SIS agents from 1938, the Mark XV was designed primarily for transmission. Although it had an excellent quiet micro key, and was capable of remote transmission by means of a separate key connected by a long cable, its abilities as a receiver were sadly lacking. Its poor selectivity, delicate tuning and sheer bulk (it weighed 20.45 kg [45 lb] and required two suitcases to transport it) made it far from ideal.

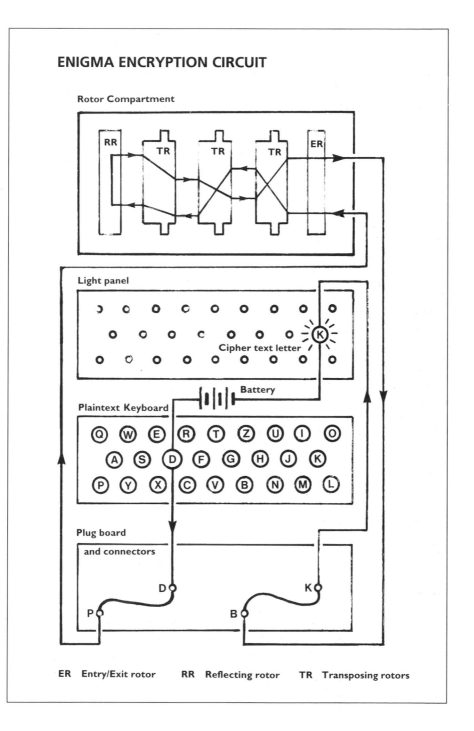

ENIGMA ENCRYPTION CIRCUIT

Rotor Compartment

RR

TR   TR   TR   ER

Light panel

Cipher text letter

Battery

Plaintext Keyboard

Q W E R T Z U I O
A S D F G H J K
P Y X C V B N M L

Plug board

and connectors

D   K

P   B

ER   Entry/Exit rotor   RR   Reflecting rotor   TR   Transposing rotors

The Paraset transceiver, which was purpose-built for the security services, began to replace the Mark XV in late 1939. Tiny in comparison, the entire transceiver, less batteries, weighed no more than 1.47 kg (3¼ lb) and fitted into a single cadmium steel box. Designed to transmit by day or night over ranges in excess of 800 km (500 miles), its emergency receiver was equally capable of picking up short messages sent by a powerful home station in all but the worst of atmospheric conditions. When set to receive, however, it would interfere with the other wireless sets within a 100 m (328 ft) radius, a distinct disadvantage in a densely populated urban environment.

In 1941, a remarkable group of Polish refugees began to manufacture clandestine transceivers far in advance of those in British service. From their discreet workshop in Letchworth they succeeded in producing a series of ten different models in increasingly substantial quantities.

In 1942, MI6 purchased 24 of the Polish B.P.3 transceivers to equip its secret bases in Paris, Lyons, Bordeaux and Rheims. The great power of the B.P.3 virtually guaranteed communications throughout Europe, however unfavourable the installation and whatever the atmospheric conditions. However, the sheer weight of the B.P.3 (the batteries alone weighed 7 kg [15½ lb]) made the set difficult to carry and therefore less popular with SOE.

In June 1942, SOE was given leave to design sets dedicated to its own peculiar aspirations. It at once gathered together a team of expert technicians, physicists and radio hams sympathetic to the needs of its user-agents. The original preference was for a set that could be carried in a small attaché case similar to those in everyday use in occupied Europe. SOE's first effort, the A Mark I, was introduced in August 1942, but proved as obsolete, bulky and temperamental as the MI6 sets it was designed to replace. The A Mark II model, however, was a distinct improvement. Introduced in October 1942 it comprised three metal boxes each 264 × 96 × 76 mm (11 × 4 × 3 in) packed side by side in their case with a little space at the end for the operator's accessories. Sending at 5 watts on 3–9 Mc/s, the Mark II was somewhat weaker than the Polish sets. However, it was the first British transceiver to use the latest generation of sturdy and compact American Loctal valves and as such was more reliable.

Its successor, the B Mark II (known commonly as the B2), was more popular with the operators. Capable of transmission between 3 and 16 mc/s, and with an output of 30 watts, it was considerably more powerful. It was also the first set designed with a built-in fail-safe to counter the German interception services. When the search for a clandestine set had been narrowed to a particular area the Gestapo tended to cut the electricity, block by block, while the set was transmitting, and then close in on whichever block fell silent. The B2 was capable of accepting power either from the mains or from an emergency 6-volt battery. If the Germans cut the supply to the building the operator had simply to throw a switch to transfer to battery power. The set would continue to transmit after a one- or two-second delay, leaving the operator comparatively safe.

The B2 weighed 14.5 kg (32 lb) and was housed in a small suitcase divided into four compartments. The upper of the two central compartments contained the transmitter—dimensions 228.6 × 177.8 × 127 mm (9 × 7 × 5 in) and weighing 3.18 kg (7 lb)—the lower compartment, the receiver—228.6 × 114.3 × 127 mm (9 × 4½ × 5 in), weight 3.18 kg (7 lb). The combined house current/battery supply was located in the right-hand compartment and the Morse key in the left.

Ironically, the B2's weakness lay in its disguise. Many residents in the Baker Street area came to recognise the agents-in-waiting by their identical attaché cases, a potentially lethal oversight of which SOE (and by and large the Gestapo) surprisingly remained seemingly unaware.

The SOE A Mark III Suitcase Transceiver which followed was the smallest transceiver conceived during World War II and was completely miniaturised save for its 'lock-in' American tubes (thermionic valves). Air-droppable by parachute in two separate containers, the A Mark III weighed 11.11 kg (24½ lb), inclusive of a 6-volt battery and had a range of 800 km (500 miles).

In the final stages of the war, SOE introduced a transmitter that could fit into a large pocket. The 51/1 had three miniature valves, weighed only 567 gm (1¼ lb) with battery fitted, and measured a mere 146 × 114 × 38 mm (5¾ × 4½ × 1½ in). Despite its small size the set was capable of maintaining contact at ranges in excess of 965 km (600 miles).

LOGISTICS, TRANSPORTATION AND WEAPONRY

BLACK SQUADRONS

Clandestine operations rarely find favour with senior officers of the conventional armed forces. It is perhaps not surprising, therefore, that during the early stages of the war the RAF did everything in its power to block the release of its aircraft to MI6 and SOE.

In his excellent book, *SOE The Special Operations Executive 1940–46*, M.R.D. Foot quotes a particularly poignant example of RAF intransigence. On the very first occasion when SOE sought the RAF's help to put a party into Europe, for the specific purpose of killing the Luftwaffe's pathfinder pilots, the Chief of the Air Staff protested. In a secret and personal letter of 1 February 1941 he wrote:

'I think that the dropping of men dressed in civilian clothes for the purpose of attempting to kill members of the opposing forces is not an operation for which the Royal Air Force should be associated. I think you will agree that there is a vast difference, in ethics, between the time-honoured operation of the dropping of a spy from the air and this entirely new scheme for dropping what one can only call assassins.'

Notwithstanding RAF hostility, two obsolescent Whitley bombers were formed into 419 Flight, RAF, and made available to SOE in September 1940. They were joined by a third Whitley on 9 October and by a fourth in February 1941, when the Flight moved to Newmarket racecourse. Disaster struck on 10/11 April 1941, when the only one of the four Whitleys capable of dropping containers as well as personnel crashed on landing when returning from an abortive mission, killing a number of its crew and wounding all the Polish agents on board.

On 25 August 1941, the Flight was expanded to form 138 Squadron, RAF, and was re-equipped with ten Whitleys and four larger and newer Halifax bombers. In March 1942, the squadron redeployed to Tempsford, Bedfordshire, where it formed a close association with 161 Squadron, its sister special operations squadron which specialised in pick-ups. No. 138 Squadron grew steadily throughout the war until, by May 1943, it boasted 20 Halifaxes. These were replaced by 22 Stirlings in July–September 1944. For its part, 161 Squadron was formed with seven Lysanders. It later used Whitleys, Halifaxes and Hudsons, and added Stirlings from September 1944.

Obsolete as a bomber, the Armstrong Whitworth Whitley was usefully employed in dropping agents and equipment into occupied Europe.   Popperfoto

OPERATIONAL AIRCRAFT
Whitley Bomber

The Armstrong Whitworth Whitley entered service with the RAF as a long-range night bomber in 1937. The first models were powered by two 795-horsepower engines. Subsequent models followed with increased engine power and performance, but, by 1939, the then operational Mark V was outclassed. Its armament, speed, ceiling and useful load were simply insufficient.

Notwithstanding its shortcomings the Whitley served with Bomber Command in 1940 and 1941. It was then handed over to Coastal Command and ultimately ended its career as a transport aircraft.

The Whitley's great cruising range, particularly with auxiliary fuel tanks fitted, made it ideally suited to clandestine work. It entered service with MI6 in August 1940 and with SOE in March 1941, providing both services with their principal carriers until gradually phased out in the summer of 1943. The angular lines of the long and flat fuselage were made all the more sinister by the coat of matt black paint applied to avoid reflecting searchlight beams and moonlight.

Powerplant:	Two Rolls-Royce Merlin X 1140-horsepower engines
Maximum Speed:	367 km/h (228 mph)
Cruising Speed:	290 km/h (180 mph)
Service Ceiling:	5365 m (17 600 ft)
Empty Weight:	8777 kg (19 350 lb)
Loaded Weight:	12 792 kg (28 200 lb)
Wing Span:	25.6 m (84 ft)

Wellington Bomber

The Vickers Wellington medium bomber was an excellent aircraft, ideally suited to the many purposes for which it was employed during World War II. Based on 1932 specifications, its geodetic structure and great strength enabled it to be regularly updated without weakening the airframe or compromising the cleanness of its lines. An IFF (Identification Friend or Foe) aerial enabled the aircraft to utilise the protection of the Allied radar surveillance umbrella to maximum effect.

The Wellington passed from Bomber Command to Coastal and overseas commands in 1943 and was used extensively as a transport aircraft. It was effectively employed, though in small numbers, by the clandestine services and was used to train agents for parachute jumps. One Wellington was attached to 138 Squadron and two to 161 Squadron in February 1942.

Powerplant (Mark III):	Two Bristol Hercules XVIII 1500-horsepower engines
Maximum Speed:	410 km/h (255 mph)
Cruising Speed:	290 km/h (180 mph)
Range:	3540 km (2120 miles)
Service Ceiling:	6005 m (19 700 ft)
Empty Weight:	11 941 kg (26 325 lb)
Loaded Weight:	14 288 kg (31 500 lb)
Wing Span:	26.26 m (86 ft 2 in)

Halifax Heavy Bomber

The Handley Page Halifax heavy bomber first flew in October 1939 and was regularly updated throughout the war. Between August 1941 and January 1944, 20 Halifaxes saw service with 138 and 161 Squadrons, dropping agents and supplies into occupied Europe. Each aircraft was fitted with an array of tiny radio aerials under the nose which enabled the crew to converse on a secret frequency with the resistance reception committee awaiting the agents at the drop zone.

Powerplant (Mark III):	Four Bristol Hercules XVI 1640-horsepower engines
Maximum Speed:	454 km/h (282 mph)
Cruising Speed:	350 km/h (215 mph)
Range:	3194 km (1985 miles)
Service Ceiling:	7315 m (24 000 ft)
Empty Weight:	17 346 kg (38 240 lb)
Loaded Weight:	29 484 kg (65 000 lb)
Wing Span:	31.75 m (104 ft 2 in)

Stirling Heavy Bomber

The Short Stirling heavy bomber first flew with Bomber Command in August 1940. However, due to its inadequate performance and low operational ceiling it was dropped from service in early 1943. Underpowered and overweight, the Stirling was prone to accident on take-off, but, once airborne, was remarkably manoeuvrable.

Between October 1943 and September 1944, 22 Stirling transports served as supply planes for SOE, flying most of their sorties during the three months immediately prior to D-Day.

Powerplant (Mark III):	Four Bristol Hercules VI or XVI 1650-horsepower engines
Maximum Speed:	418 km/h (260 mph)
Cruising Speed:	346 km/h (215 mph)
Range:	950 km (590 miles)
Service Ceiling:	5029 m (16 500 ft)
Empty Weight:	21 273 kg (46 900 lb)
Loaded Weight:	31 750 kg (70 000 lb)
Wing Span:	30.21 m (99 ft 1 in)

Lysander

Affectionately known as the 'Lizzie', the Westland Lysander, with its braced high-set monoplane wing, was one of the most distinctive aircraft of the war. It entered RAF service in June 1938 and subsequently operated in the artillery fire-support and reconnaissance roles in Egypt, Greece, India, Burma and Palestine as well as occupied Europe.

Despite the Lysander's comparatively short range (it was forced to carry out many of its operations from Tangmere, on the south coast, and could still only reach Lyons), the aircraft's outstanding sturdiness and manoeuvrability, coupled with its ability to take off and land in a small field, made it a favourite with the clandestine services. Usually stripped of its armament and fitted with a detachable external tank and metal ladder for rapid passenger boarding, it operated a regular agent-passenger service between England and occupied Europe for four years. The pilot sat in the small front cockpit (he was also the navigator); two passengers could be carried with ease (sitting side by side, facing aft) in the rear cockpit, three with less comfort and four in a crisis.

Originally developed for Army co-operation, modified matt-black painted Lysanders flew regularly into France and the Low Countries. Popperfoto

Powerplant:	Bristol Mercury XXX 870-horsepower engine
Maximum Speed:	338 km/h (210 mph)
Cruising Speed:	266 km/h (165 mph)
Service Ceiling:	7929 m (26 000 ft)
Range (Mk III/SD):	2253 km (1400 miles)
Empty Weight:	2336 kg (5150 lb)
Loaded Weight:	4536 kg (10 000 lb)
Wing Span:	15.24 m (50 ft 0 in)

Hudson Bomber

The Lockheed Hudson light bomber needed an open space twice as large as that required by a Lysander for landings and take-offs, ideally 1 km (1091 yds) in length. It could, however, fly faster, had a greater range and could carry ten passengers in comfort. Hudsons attached to 161 Squadron retained their Boulton Paul dorsal turret, giving the aircraft a modicum of protection against ambush on the ground.

Powerplant:	Two Wright Cyclone R-1820, 1100-horsepower engines
Maximum Speed:	357 km/h (222 mph)
Cruising Speed:	249 km/h (155 mph)
Range:	2181 km (1355 miles)
Service Ceiling:	6400 m (21 000 ft)
Empty Weight:	5484 kg (12 091 lb)
Loaded Weight:	8845 kg (19 500 lb)
Wing Span:	19.96 m (65 ft 6 in)

COVERT FLIGHTS

Covert flights flew beneath the German radar umbrella and thus attracted little interference from enemy anti-aircraft fire. To mask the true purpose of their mission many aircraft carried propaganda leaflets as well as their clandestine loads. Once the drop had been made, or on the way to it, the aircraft would scatter the leaflets over the nearest undefended town. Not only did this provide a reason for the aircraft being in the area but distracted the local police, who were forced to confine their energies to collecting the leaflets before anyone read them.

Various ruses were employed by London to advise resistants when and where drops were to be made to them. From the autumn of 1941 prearranged messages, mixed in with genuine news or family information, were broadcast by the BBC. Depending on circumstances these might be repeated hourly to confirm to the organiser that the sortie had not been cancelled before he mobilised his reception committee. Given that the German authorities regarded listening to the BBC as a serious offence, and even banned ownership of receivers in certain areas, waiting for such messages was not without risk.

Missions were often cancelled at the very last minute (Tempsford was particularly liable to fog) or even aborted after take-off. Equally, an arms find, an escaped prisoner of war from a local camp or even a random area search could all result in the location being suddenly swamped with troops, making a drop impossible.

Navigation in the early stages of the war was far from precise, particularly for lone low-flying aircraft. It was not at all unusual for sorties to reach the area of a drop only to return, their loads intact, because they could not locate the precise drop zone. During the first year of SOE operations 55 per cent of its flights failed to end in a drop, either because the crew could not find the drop zone or some hitch prevented the reception committee getting to it.

A number of aides to navigation did exist to make the task of the pilot/navigator easier. The S-phone, SOE's own invention, was a variant of the portable radio-telephone used by soldiers and civilians alike before the war. It comprised a small transceiver with five or six valves, according to the model, five canvas pouches holding two miniature rechargeable cadmium-nickel batteries each, a sixth pouch containing the vibrator power pack and a seventh for the headset, microphone and collapsible aerial. The entire set could be carried on a single belt supported by two cross straps, was easily transportable by one man and weighed a mere 6.75 kg (15 lb).

Both the headset and mouthpiece were soundproofed to enable the user to operate unheard yet the conversations were clear enough to allow friends to recognise each other's voices, a crucial factor when a number of sets fell into enemy hands. Provided the ground set was pointed in the direction of its flight path the operator could speak to an approaching aircraft at 3050 m (10 000 ft) at a range of about 65 km (40 miles) or to one at 150 m (490 ft) up to 10 km (6¼ miles) away. The S-phone's minimal use of power—its output was as low as 0.1 to 0.2 watts—made it virtually immune to ground monitoring interception at ranges in excess of 1.6 km (1 mile).

'Eureka-Rebecca', the brain-child of the Telecommunications Research Establishment (TRE), was less well received by SOE field agents. 'Eureka' was designed for use on the ground and comprised a slim 1.52 m (5 ft 0 in) metal mast, positioned above a 2.13 m (7 ft 0 in) tripod and connected to a closed box below it. Once set up by the reception team it required no attention although the batteries needed to be changed regularly. 'Rebecca' was carried in the delivery aircraft. However, its 7.62 m (25 ft 0 in) aerial was too large for the diminutive Lysander, limiting the system's usefulness within SOE to missions employing the Hudson bomber.

Once in range 'Rebecca' transmitted to 'Eureka' in a prearranged radar code on 214 megacycles. 'Eureka' responded at 219 megacycles, advising the aircraft of its precise location, ultimately guiding it in to the landing or drop zone.

Although lauded by the RAF, the embryonic airborne units and the SAS, the sheer bulk of the 'Eureka' made it unpopular with SOE's agents. The whole package weighed some 50 kg (110 lb) and fitted into a box 76 × 38 × 25 cm (30 × 15 × 10 in)—far too large to be disguised should its unfortunate courier fall victim to a random spot check. Despite the secrecy surrounding 'Eureka' the Germans were aware of it from 1943, but were unable to find a counter.

CONTAINERS

Resistance groups were regularly resupplied from the air. With the exception of particularly delicate items such as radios, which had to be specially packed in kapok packages or lined wicker panniers, supplies were dropped in metal containers. Of these by far the most popular were C-type containers. Each was 35 cm (1 ft 2 in) in diameter and 175 cm (5 ft 9 in) long, weighed up to 100 kg (220 lb) when full and was fitted with four carrying handles for relatively easy transportation from the drop zone. The C container could be divided into three variable compartments to prevent load movement during the drop, but, even so, loads occasionally exploded on impact.

The Polish-designed Type H container was lighter but less robust and liable to disintegration on impact with the ground. It was essentially a series of five sheet-metal drums, piled one on top of the other and held together by two steel rods. Two extra compartments were fitted to the container ends, one to act as a shock absorber, the other to hold the static line, which automatically opened the parachute.

Containers were usually loaded into an aircraft's bomb bay and released conventionally by the bomb aimer. A Whitley could hold 12, a Halifax 15 and a Stirling 18. Packages and wicker panniers were stacked inside the aircraft's fuselage and released by a dispatcher through a hatch specially cut in the floor.

Agents due to drop by parachute would use the same means of exit. They learned at the parachute school at Altrincham to shuffle on their hands and bottom towards the metre-wide hole until they were in a position to swing their legs into the void below. Then, as the red light turned to green and as the dispatcher signalled the 'go', they pushed themselves forward into space. As they fell they adopted the position of attention until the static line straightened, took the strain and forced the canopy of the parachute to deploy.

Occasionally the static line malfunctioned or more often snarled, or the parachute canopy failed to open, causing the luckless agent to plummet towards the ground. As the war progressed, experience, augmented by the sheer professionalism of the parachute packagers at Ringway, reduced parachute failure rates in the European theatre from five in a thousand to one in a hundred thousand, odds considered acceptable by agents reconciled to the fact that the hours following their landing would be infinitely more risky than the jump itself.

CLANDESTINE WEAPONS

In order to 'set Europe ablaze' and take the war to the enemy, SOE had to be well armed. Between 1940 and 1944 sub-machine-guns represented 47 per cent of all firearms dropped into occupied Europe. A further 30 per cent were rifles, 15 per cent pistols, 5 per cent automatic rifles, 2 per cent carbines and 1 per cent anti-tank weapons. Early attempts to equip SOE teams with the United States Thompson sub-machine-gun were frustrated due to the sheer cost of manufacture. However, the ubiquitous Sten gun proved far easier to obtain. Designed by R.V. Shepherd and H.J. Turpin and manufactured by the Royal Ordnance factory at Enfield (and later under licence at a number of factories), the Sten proved as resilient as it was easy to manufacture.

Although wartime stories that the Sten could be bought for '7s 6d (37.5p) from Woolworths' or that it cost less than a full magazine of ammunition to produce were untrue, at £1 10s per weapon it was indeed cheap to manufacture. About three and a half million Stens were produced throughout the war, of which over a million were distributed by SOE to its various guerrilla groups. Each gun was normally dropped with three or four magazines pre-loaded with their normal complement of 28 rounds. The Sten was designed specifically to accept the 9 mm Parabellum ammunition used by the German Schmeisser MP 40 to make replenishment from stolen or captured stores easier.

The commonest Sten to be deployed with SOE was the Mark I, distinguishable by its skeleton frame butt. It arrived in three pieces—barrel, body and butt—with simple multi-lingual instructions for assembly. It could be easily disassembled for carriage in any type of rucksack or suitcase. The later Mk II had a tubular butt; so did the III, which could only be disassembled into two parts, but was in all other respects similar to the Mark II. The Sten Mark V, the last of the Sten models, was designed specifically for Airborne forces and only saw service

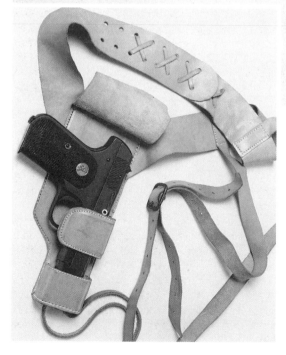

(Top left) Colt automatic; (top right) Wellrod single-shot silenced pistol; (bottom left) The Liberator single-shot pistol; (bottom right) High Standard .22 silenced automatic. IWM

(left)
The Colt .32, although less powerful, was easier to conceal than the larger Colt .45. IWM

with SOE in limited numbers. Equipped with two pistol grips the Mark V could easily be operated without the butt, which made it an excellent close-quarter weapon. Uniquely for a sub-machine-gun the Mark V was designed to accept the new British bayonet, a wholly impractical weapon taking into account the diminutive dimensions of the Sten itself.

Notwithstanding its popularity with SOE, the Sten had a number of disadvantages. Its ultra-short barrel—only 19.05 cm (7½ in) long—made it inaccurate at ranges in excess of 50 metres. It was prone to blockage and jamming and had a tendency to misfire if knocked or dropped when cocked.

When United States parachute drops began in July 1944, SOE substituted M3s and Thompsons for Stens whenever possible. The M3 was heavier and more expensive to produce than the Sten. It was completely manufactured out of sheet steel, would accept 9 mm or .45-calibre ammunition (with the aid of an interchangeable barrel) and would only fire automatic.

Colonel Maurice Buckmaster states that of the 418 083 weapons delivered to France during the war, 57 849 were automatic pistols or revolvers. Automatics were far more popular with the resistants, who accepted less sophisticated (though far more reliable) revolvers only grudgingly.

Where possible Remington-manufactured Colt .45 automatic pistols were distributed. In general use with the French, American and (to a lesser extent) British armies, Colts were sturdy and thoroughly reliable. Yet their small magazines and large-calibre rounds made them heavy and outmoded.

The Canadian 9 mm Browning High Power pistol was far more practical, but so scarce that its distribution was limited to SAS, Commando and Airborne units. A few were delivered as a status symbol to resistance network organisers. However, the jealousy which often ensued within the group when such a weapon was produced tended to make its presence counter-productive. Designed in 1935, the Browning was of Belgian origin but manufactured under licence in Canada during the war by the John Inglis Company of Toronto. Capable of holding 13 rounds of 9 mm ammunition it had a comparatively short range, limited stopping power and was prone to jam unless properly maintained. None the less it was light, relatively easy to strip, hide and reassemble and well suited to covert warfare. As a testament to its versatility the Browning remains in service with the British Army today.

The Smith & Wesson 0.38/200 typified the revolvers issued to the resistance. Produced in the United States to a British specification, the weapon was completely conventional in its design yet robust in the extreme. The weapon was opened by pushing the six-round cylinder to the left, after which the spent cartridge cases could be cleared quickly with the aid of a sprung plunger rod. The trigger action could be converted to double-action for speed shooting if necessary, although a constant shortage of 0.380-calibre rounds forced resistance groups to husband their ammunition where possible.

Although of limited use in the cut-and-run warfare in which guerrilla units excel, rifles were dropped to the resistance in large numbers, particularly in the final stages of the war. Of these the most common was the Short-Magazine Lee Enfield, the standard weapon of the British infantry in World War I and during the early stages of World War II. Reliable and deadly accurate, in the hands of a trained shot it had a lethal range in excess of 1.5 km (0.93 mile). A few of the better-equipped networks received the Bren light machine-gun in limited numbers. Arguably the best weapon of its kind in the war, the Bren accepted rimmed 0.303-in ammunition identical to that fired by the Lee Enfield. It had a rate of fire of 500 rounds per minute and was accurate to 750 m (2460 ft).

SILENCED FIREARMS

Small-arms silencers work by controlling the expansion of the propelling gases, in a manner similar to a car exhaust silencer. To eliminate the crack caused by the bullet, sub-sonic ammunition must be used.

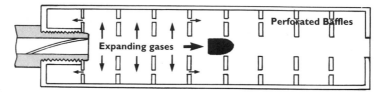

Perforated metal discs form expansion chambers. The silencing effect is directly proportional to the number of expansion chambers.

Type 2

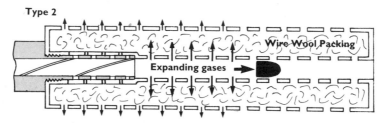

Wire wool packing slows the expanding gases.

In 1993 Russia revealed a silent cartridge design. A captive piston pushes the bullet out of the cartridge. As no propellant gases reach the atmosphere it is truly silent.

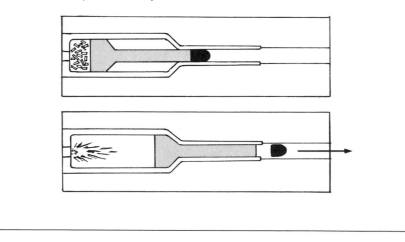

The American M1 carbine was a favourite with resistance networks everywhere. Short, light and easy to handle, its relatively short range and the lack of stopping power of its ammunition proved no real disadvantage.

THE AGENTS

No single individual neatly epitomises the agents of World War II. The following individuals have been chosen, almost at random, to demonstrate the sheer bravery and versatility of the men and women who volunteered for hazardous duties in occupied Europe. One in four of the agents employed by SOE failed to return, and in many cases suffered hideous fates at the hands of the enemy.

It is becoming increasingly acceptable to question the effectiveness of covert warfare in occupied Europe. Whether or not such criticism is justified will probably always remain a matter for conjecture. What can never be disputed, however, is the sheer bravery of those often superficially very ordinary people who risked their lives in the spirit of resistance.

AMY ELIZABETH BROUSSE—'CYNTHIA'

Amy Elizabeth Brousse so enthusiastically coupled the activities of the world's two oldest professions that she became one of the most successful sex spies in modern history. She was born Amy Elizabeth Thorpe in Minneapolis, USA, and at the age of 20 married Arthur Pack, a taciturn somewhat pompous commercial secretary at the British Embassy in Washington. Despite the vast difference in their ages and the wholesale difference in their characters Amy stuck with her husband as his job took him to Chile, Spain and finally Poland.

During the Spanish Civil War she helped a number of Franco supporters to escape, but it was not until she went to Poland that she became a secret agent in earnest. Now working for MI6 she gained the confidence of a young aide to the Foreign Secretary, Colonel Beck. From him she gleaned considerable intelligence, some of which led directly to Britain gaining possession of the top secret German Enigma cipher machine.

When war broke out a few months later, Amy was summoned to New York and given the code-name 'Cynthia' by William Stephenson, head of the British Secret Service in the United States. She was established in a comfortable home in Washington and introduced to the diplomatic cocktail set. She renewed the acquaintance of an ex-lover, Admiral Alberto Lais, Mussolini's naval attaché in the United States, seducing from him a detailed set of codes and ciphers which were to prove invaluable in the prosecution of the war in the Mediterranean. Lais was besotted by Cynthia, but once he had served his purpose she dumped him, reporting him to the FBI and having him expelled as an undesirable.

Cynthia's next target was Captain Charles Brousse, a press officer at the Vichy French Embassy in Washington. Her orders were to obtain as much detail as possible on all correspondence passing between Vichy and Washington and, if possible, to obtain copies of the French ciphers. So irresistible were Cynthia's charms that she soon won over the young man completely. He gave her details of a secret cache of French gold buried on the island of Martinique and arranged for her to move into his hotel, where he lived with his third wife.

Unlike later sex spies Cynthia made no secret of her intentions, and when she told Brousse of her aims towards the ciphers he readily agreed to assist in their theft. Later Cynthia was sent to London and attached to an SOE office in Dorset Square. She volunteered for further service in Europe, perhaps not surprisingly as an assassin, but was kept in England. In 1945, Arthur Pack committed suicide in Argentina and Brousse divorced his wife. The couple subsequently married and lived in a castle in southern France until Cynthia's death in 1963.

When asked if she were perhaps a little ashamed of her wartime sexual activities, Cynthia is reputed to have replied with almost simplistic naivety: 'Ashamed? Not in the least. My superiors told me that my work saved thousands of British and American lives.'

ODETTE SANSOM

Born and bred in France, Odette Brailly married an English friend of her father's, Roy Sansom, at the age of 18 and moved with him to London. In 1942, with her husband away in the armed forces, she moved with their three young daughters to Somerset. Her not untypical recruitment into the ranks of SOE followed soon thereafter when she answered a War Office appeal for French speakers. Instead of being offered a job as a translator as she had expected she was interviewed by a member of F section and told something of its covert role in France. Initially, a lack of faith in her own abilities compounded by a very natural fear for her children's future caused her to decline to help. However, the worsening situation on the Continent coupled with the knowledge that her family were suffering invasion and occupation led to a change of heart.

Odette was readily accepted for initial training, but only for field work after considerable misgivings on the part of her assessors. Jerrard Tickle, the author of a 1940s book on Odette, quotes from one of her few course reports to have survived the immediate postwar period:

> 'Celine (her training code-name) has enthusiasm and seems to have absorbed the teaching given on the course. She is, however, impulsive and hasty in her judgements and has not quite the clarity of mind which is desirable in subversive activity.
> 'She seems to have little experience of the outside world. She is excitable and temperamental, although she has a certain determination.
> 'A likeable character and gets on well with most people.
> 'Her main asset is her patriotism and keenness to do something for France; her main weakness is a complete unwillingness to admit that she could ever be wrong.'

Notwithstanding this somewhat subjective analysis, F section decided to accept her and in October 1942 landed her with four other agents on the coast of Vichy-France. The agents were taken to a safe house in Cannes, where they were introduced to the head of the local reseau, a young Cambridge blue called Peter Churchill.

Within days of Odette's arrival the Allies invaded North Africa and Germany occupied Vichy-France in retaliation. Churchill now asked Odette to abandon her plans to move north to form her own reseau in Auxerre and to remain with him as his courier. Having gained agreement from London, Odette began to travel regularly along the coast to Marseilles with messages and codes. She quickly became fiercely loyal to Churchill and to Adam Rabinovitz (code-named Arnaud), the group's radio operator, whom she kept fed and supplied with new addresses from which to transmit.

Disaster was only narrowly averted in early 1943, when Churchill was recalled to London for talks. The disused airfield chosen for his pick-up was compromised and the Lysander due to fly him to England nearly captured. Although Odette and Churchill managed to evade arrest they and Arnaud were forced to quit the Cannes area immediately for the comparative safety of the Haute-Savoie mountains 300 km (186 miles) to the north.

Odette Sansom being toasted by her three daughters and captain Peter Churchill DSO, after her investiture with the George Cross. Popperfoto

Once settled into their new home the trio began tirelessly to offer assistance to the local reseaux. After a few months, however, under circumstances which have never been fully clarified, Odette and Churchill were betrayed by a double agent and captured. In an attempt to save the man whom she by now loved, Odette claimed to be Peter Churchill's wife. More dangerously, she claimed that he was a distant relative of Winston Churchill's. After a short period in Italian custody the couple were moved to Fresnes, the notorious Gestapo prison to the south of Paris. Although tortured for information by the Gestapo, and ultimately sentenced to death, Odette divulged nothing. In May 1944, a full year after coming to Fresnes, she was moved to Karlsruhe prison in Germany and from there to Ravensbruck concentration camp. There she was incarcerated below ground in complete darkness in a room furnished with nothing but a plank to sleep on. After a few weeks she was moved to a tiny cell above ground, where she remained in isolation until her liberation in May 1945. Odette was awarded the GC and MBE, and married Peter after the war. However, their wholly different personalities could not withstand the different tests of peacetime co-existence and they subsequently divorced.

VIOLETTE SZABO

Violette Szabo is best remembered as the heroine of the romanticised book and film *Carve Her Name With Pride*. She was described by Maurice Buckmaster as 'really beautiful, dark haired

79

Violette Szabo with her husband Etienne, of the Free French forces. It was his death in North Africa which spurred her into volunteering for SOE service.
Popperfoto

and olive skinned, with a porcelain clarity of face', and it is clear that she had an effect on everyone with whom she came into contact, yet her background was far from exotic. Born Violette Bushell, the daughter of an English father and French mother, she spent much of her early youth in Paris, where her father drove a taxi. She returned to Brixton in South London for her education, leaving school at 14 to become first a hairdresser's assistant and then a sales assistant in a local department store.

In 1941, in a parade of the Free French Army in London, she met an officer of the French Foreign Legion, Etienne Szabo. The couple married soon after, when Violette was 20, but were almost immediately parted when Etienne received orders to sail with his unit to North Africa. In the autumn of 1942, a few months after Violette gave birth to his daughter, Etienne was killed at El Alamein.

Smitten with grief and hatred of the enemy, Violette volunteered at once when she was approached by SOE a few months later. Despite the misgivings of many of his subordinates, and after a period of doubt himself, Selwyn Jepson of F section eventually cleared Violette for field work. In April 1944, she was flown by Lysander into the Rouen area, where she was tasked with assessing the state of local resistance effectiveness after large-scale arrests in the district. She completed her task successfully, despite twice being arrested by suspicious French police, and was flown back to London.

Her second incursion into France, this time by parachute, took place almost immediately after the Normandy landings. On 10 June 1944, just three days after landing, she drove into an advance party of SS troops while escorting the maquis leader 'Anastasie'. As the couple tried to escape, Violette tripped and twisted her ankle. She begged the Frenchman to go on and complete his crucial mission without her, giving him covering fire until she ran out of ammunition. After capture and interrogation she was taken from a French prison to

Ravensbruck concentration camp, where she was executed. In recognition of her great bravery and selflessness, Violette Szabo was posthumously awarded the George Cross in 1946.

NANCY WAKE

Nancy Wake has been described as a strongly built girl with an exuberance and a zest for living. This is an understatement. Nancy Wake was born, and indeed now resides, in Australia. In her youth she had worked as a journalist in Sydney and as a nurse in a country mental hospital. In her early twenties she began a world tour, supporting herself by freelance journalism. Just before the war she moved to Marseilles where she subsequently met and married Henri Fiocca, a wealthy steel industrialist 14 years her senior.

With the advent of the phoney war Nancy Wake volunteered her services as an ambulance driver, but retired in anger and frustration to Marseilles when France fell. Soon after her husband's repatriation from the Army, Nancy became involved in helping British prisoners of war to escape. She travelled regularly between Marseilles and Cannes to organise escape routes, using the family flat as a safe house for escapers.

The Fioccas became a crucial part of the PAT escape line (named after the Belgian Albert Guerisse, also known as Patrick O'Leary). Nancy Wake was arrested by the French police, but, by employing a combination of femininity and arrogance, handled the situation so well that she was released. However, she was considered too compromised to remain much longer in France and, when Pat himself was captured, was forced to flee across the Pyrenees. She succeeded in crossing the Spanish frontier at the fifth attempt. She got back to England after a long delay in 1943, not knowing that her husband had been captured soon after her flight and tortured and shot.

Nancy Wake was recruited almost immediately by SOE and after a period of training as a courier, which apparently her instructors found far more exacting than she did, was parachuted into the Auvergne late in February 1944. Under the command of John Farmer, a regular army officer parachuted with her, she set about assisting in the training and arming of the 22 000 potential resistants in the area. Although the local leader, Gaspart, was happy to accept SOE arms he was less willing to tolerate interference in the daily running of his organisation. Indeed, the first maquis group that Nancy and Farmer approached proved so hostile that the couple found themselves actually arguing for their lives.

It was not until the pair were joined by a radio operator, the highly experienced Denis Rake, a few days later that they became safe from the very real threat of murder at the hands of their dubious allies. With the establishment of a dedicated radio link the agents were able to organise supervised parachute drops. Nancy began to cycle from group to group taking their orders, assessing their needs, finding drop zones and arranging reception committees.

When the Germans sent 22 000 troops into the Corrèze and Haute-Loire to flush out the maquis, Nancy drove back and forth across the battlefield carrying ammunition forward and evacuating the wounded to the comparative safety of the rear. A lull in the battle brought no rest for Nancy. Discovering that Denis Rake's radio codes had been destroyed in the fighting she set out upon an epic cycle ride of 36 hours' duration across the mountains to the site of the nearest working radio. Having delivered her messages and placed her orders for resupply with London she turned for home at once, reaching her base, tired, bleeding and sick, another 36 hours later.

After the war Nancy returned to Marseilles, where she learned the tragic news of her husband's death. She moved to England in the early 1950s and thence to Australia, where she stood for parliament and became something of a celebrity. She subsequently married John Forward, with whom she now lives as quietly as a woman such as she is capable.

WING-COMMANDER FOREST FREDERICK YEO-THOMAS

Wing-Commander Yeo-Thomas was 38 when the war broke out. A Welshman, he had served in World War I and thereafter had fought for Poland against the invading Bolsheviks. Captured at Zhitomir and sentenced to death, he had escaped the night before sentence was due to be carried out. Yeo-Thomas spoke perfect French. His family had settled in France in the mid-19th century and he himself had obtained pre-war employment with the haute couture house of Molyneux in Paris.

When France fell, Yeo-Thomas returned to England and was commissioned into the RAF. Too old for flying, he gravitated naturally towards the world of espionage and was accepted into the RF section of SOE. Early in 1943 Yeo-Thomas returned to France in the company of André Dewarvrin, head of RF section, and Pierre Brossolette, a journalist, broadcaster and propagandist for the pre-war Socialist Party. Yeo-Thomas's role was largely that of an observer.

On his return to London he was able to advise De Gaulle that there was a growing spirit of resistance within France. Enraged by the German policy of conscripting young men at random for forced labour, increasing numbers of young people were forming themselves into armed, though otherwise disorganised, bands in the woods and mountains of the French interior. For his efforts Yeo-Thomas received the Croix de Guerre with palm from de Gaulle, but was ordered by the RAF not to wear the medal as the Frenchman was not then a recognised Head of State!

During a second covert visit to France, Brossolette and Yeo-Thomas spent eight weeks in the Arras area, assessing the weaknesses of the newly formed groups of maquis, establishing their needs and trying desperately to instil within them the basic safety rules for survival. When

Wing-Commander Yeo-Thomas. Although an RAF officer, he was awarded the Military Cross for his exceptional bravery on the ground.
Popperfoto

Yeo-Thomas was ordered home by Lysander he travelled to the landing site hidden under flowers in a funeral hearse, gripping a Sten-gun to defend the secrets he was carrying home concealed in the coffin.

Obsessed by the RAF's refusal to release more aircraft in support of the maquis, Yeo-Thomas went over the heads of his service superiors and invoked the assistance of Churchill direct. In less than an hour the Welshman convinced the Prime Minister of his case, forcing the RAF to increase substantially the number of aircraft for dropping supplies to France.

When Yeo-Thomas heard that Brossolette, who had remained in France, had been captured he decided to return to rescue him. Adopting the identity of Squadron-Leader Dodkin, shot down over France, he hatched an ingenious plan involving a number of colleagues disguised as German guards. However, the plan never materialised, and Brossolette ultimately committed suicide by jumping through a fifth floor window at Gestapo head-quarters in Avenue Foch.

Yeo-Thomas was betrayed and arrested at a pre-arranged rendezvous on the steps of the Passy Métro station in Paris, just below his father's flat. He was thereafter subjected to appalling tortures, which precipitated his death in 1964. With the collusion of a guard he escaped first from Buchenwald, Germany then, after recapture and posing as a French Air Force prisoner, from a POW camp. For his 'exceptional gallantry' Yeo-Thomas was awarded the Military Cross and the George Medal.

THE LUCY ENIGMA

It has been claimed that, without the 'Lucy' spy network in Switzerland, the Soviet Union might not have won the war on the Eastern Front. The network took its title from the code-name of its leader, Rudolf Roessler, a Bavarian anti-Nazi publisher who fled to Geneva after Hitler came to power. Roessler's impressive intellect was put to use by Brigadier Masson, head of Swiss military intelligence, who employed him as an analyst within Bureau Ha, ostensibly a press clippings agency but in reality a covert department of the Swiss Security services.

When France fell Roessler was ordered to assess military intelligence relating to a possible German invasion of Switzerland. While providing excellent information for the Swiss he began sending out information to the Soviets. Aided by the Englishman Alexander Foote and the Hungarian Sandor Rado (then NKVD head in Switzerland), Roessler fed the Soviets with highly accurate intelligence for over two years. Operating from three independent transmitters the trio supplied Stalin with German High Command plans down to brigade level on a daily basis.

No one has ever discovered precisely how Roessler obtained such high-grade intelligence. Before his death he claimed that he was fed information by a mysterious group of ten Bavarian anti-Nazis high in the German command. Although he may well have obtained a limited amount from sympathisers within the Abwehr, the substance of this explanation seems unlikely.

It is far more likely that the Lucy ring obtained the bulk of its information from top secret Enigma material deliberately disseminated by the British from intercepts of German radio traffic. Britain realised that it was crucial to keep the Germans hard pressed on the Eastern Front yet appreciated that Stalin would almost certainly discount as untrue any information passed direct from MI6. More fundamentally, Churchill, who was completely unaware of the existence of the Cambridge spies within British intelligence, had no desire to share the secrets of Station X and Ultra with Stalin. It is known that Masson had discreet contacts with MI6 and it seems highly probable that he acted as a conduit between Bletchley and Roessler.

The Lucy Ring continued its activities until late in 1943, with the Swiss authorities turning a diplomatic blind eye to the activities of the 'Rote Drei' (Red Three). However, as it became clear that Hitler was losing the ascendancy, the Swiss reverted to their traditional neutrality. Lucy was wound up and the three agents given jail sentences of a few months each and deported.

Rado, who had defied Stalin's orders not to share secrets with the Allies by telling the British about the V2 rockets at Peenemünde, was reluctant to return to the USSR. When his plane arrived in Cairo en route for Moscow he immediately tried to defect. The Russians pressed for his arrest, alleging that he was an army deserter. Maurice Oldfield, then MI6 station head in Egypt, sought instructions from London and was ordered (by Kim Philby) to reject Rado's request for asylum. Rado was sentenced to ten years in a Siberian prison camp, where he remained incarcerated until after the death of Stalin in 1953.

Roessler never revealed his true sources, taking his secrets with him to the grave in 1958. Foote was ordered by Moscow to move to Mexico to work against the United States. However, when he reached East Berlin he defected back to the British, and after a period of debriefing accepted a minor post in the Ministry of Agriculture.

In the arms of the black-clad Mrs Odette Churchill (formerly Sansom), Tania Szabo seeks her mother's name on the memorial tablet to Britain's war heroines after its unveiling at St Paul's Church, Knightsbridge. Popperfoto

T H R E E

A WARY PEACE; COLD WAR ESPIONAGE

THE WORLD'S MAJOR SECRET SERVICES

FRANCE

France has one of the oldest, most single-minded and effective security services in the world. Its weakness lies in its propensity for breaking the law, both national and international, when it feels the interests of France are under threat. The widespread reports of kidnapping and torture during the Algerian War were hardly denied. More recently, the French government was forced to concede secret service complicity in the sinking of the *Rainbow Warrior* in Auckland Harbour. Although defence minister Charles Hernu resigned and Admiral Lacoste, head of the security services, was sacked, France remained largely unrepentant. When two agents, Major Alain Tourand and Captain Sophie Turenge, were arrested, France threatened New Zealand with economic sanctions to secure their release. As a result they were transferred to French military custody and deported to the Pacific island of Hao to complete their sentences. Tourand and Turenge were returned to France on the grounds of ill health and released well before their sentences were completed. Both made surprising recoveries.

DGSE

The modern security services can trace their antecedents to the Gaullist Colonel Passy's wartime Central Bureau for Information and Military Action (BCRAM). Whereas Passy was content to operate with the tenuous support of SOE and later the American OSS, de Gaulle yearned for autonomy. In 1943 he established the Direction Générale des Services Spéciaux (DGSS) under the control of Jacques Soustelle, moving its headquarters to Algiers. After the liberation of Paris, Soustelle moved his headquarters to the city, renaming the service the Direction Générale des Etudes et Recherches (DGER).

After the war de Gaulle recalled Colonel Passy to take over and reorganise the DGER. The service once again underwent a change of name, this time to the Service de Documentation Extérieure et de Contre-Espionnage (SDECE). More fundamentally it shed its wartime excesses. Over 10 500 staff were dismissed, 100 buildings derequisitioned and 400 vehicles returned to civilian ownership.

The SDECE was reorganised by de Gaulle in 1958 and yet again by President Mitterrand, who gave it its present title, Direction Générale de Sécurite Extérieure (DGSE). Arguably the organisation's greatest head was Count Alexandre de Marenches, a friend and appointee of President Pompidou. A strict disciplinarian, Marenches purged the DGSE of its post-Algerian criminal element while improving relations with the CIA and SIS. However, he was dismissed by Mitterrand, and his deputy, Colonel Alain de Gaigneron de Marolles, was forced to resign, following allegations of a joint DGSE-CIA plot to overthrow Libya's Colonel Gaddaffi.

France's counter-espionage organisation, Direction de la Surveillance du Territoire (DST), has an equally good, if far less controversial, reputation. Controlled by the Minister of the Interior it is fully computerised with a retrieval system the envy of the world. In the early 1980s it disclosed the names of 50 Soviet 'legals', 47 of whom were subsequently accused of spying and expelled in 1983.

It seems likely that France has recently adopted a concerted policy of aligning intelligence with diplomacy. In 1987, head of the DST Bernard Gérard visited Damascus to discuss bombings in Paris with the Syrian authorities despite evidence that the latter were then heavily involved in the sponsorship of anti-Western terrorism. Equally, it has been suggested that both the DGSE and DST are presently liaising closely with French armament manufacturers to ensure the smooth sale of military equipment to the Third World.

GREAT BRITAIN

The traditions of espionage in Great Britain date back to Walsingham and the Court of Queen Elizabeth I. Military intelligence was gathered and successfully exploited by Marlborough in the 17th century and by Wellington in the Napoleonic Wars. However, it was not until 1911 that the fabric of the modern service was established.

Century House has served MI6 as its headquarters for many years. The organisation will shortly be moving to a new building.
Guy Taylor

MI6

The history of the Secret Intelligence Service (SIS), or MI6 (originally Military Intelligence, Department 6), has been somewhat erratic. It enjoyed some considerable successes during World War I, but became somewhat complacent during the inter-war years, making it an easy prey for German intelligence during the early days of World War II. Its European network was almost completely destroyed by 1940 and several of its agents captured. However, it remained a potent force in the eyes of the Abwehr, a crucial factor in convincing the German High Command that stories of Britain's unpreparedness were nothing more than an involved SIS ruse to lure an invasion fleet to destruction.

MI6 rebuilt its networks after the war, but suffered a series of crushing rebuffs when it was discovered that a number of its key operatives were in fact KGB agents. However, it also enjoyed a number of successes, including 'Operation Gold' (tunnelling under East Berlin to tap the Soviet Army communications to Potsdam) and the recruiting of Colonel Oleg Penkovsky.

MI6 was severely criticised for its failure to foretell the invasion of the Falkland Islands by Argentina. The Franks Commission, set up in the wake of the fiasco, made a number of recommendations, most of which have now been implemented. Although recruitment remains by invitation, the methods of selection have greatly improved in recent years, relying more on professionalism and less on the 'old-boy network'. More fundamentally the Joint Intelligence Organisation (JIO), the liaison between MI6 and the Government, is no longer automatically chaired by a Foreign and Commonwealth Office appointment. Instead it is now headed by a Prime Ministerial nominee from the Cabinet Office, ensuring (it is hoped) a far greater level of government accountability.

GCHQ

The Government Communications Headquarters (GCHQ) at Cheltenham was established in 1952 and today intercepts communications from all over the world. Its 12 000 personnel operate from a number of international stations and enjoy close cooperation with the Americans, Australians and Canadians. GCHQ played a key role during the Gulf War. Working closely with the American National Security Agency, it gathered much of the intelligence from one of its bases in Cyprus. It also spearheaded the long and frustrating hunt for the hostages in Lebanon.

But the Gulf War made it clear that such technology could provide only part of the picture: it was unable to predict accurately the Iraqi invasion of Kuwait, nor could it predict Saddam's strategy thereafter. It was accepted that the lack of a reliable mole within Saddam's inner circle was a fundamental lapse, given the hundreds of Iraqi officers who had trained in the West and were approachable for recruiting. Accordingly MI6 is now leading the return to 'humint', or human intelligence, proving that the day of the spy is far from over.

MI5

Britain's counter-intelligence organisation, MI5, was formed in 1906 by the expatriate Polish count Major General Sir Vernon Kell. It proved highly successful in rounding up enemy suspects on the outbreak of the two World Wars and played a crucial part in World War II in helping to 'turn' enemy agents as part of the 'double cross' system. However, more recent attempts to detain suspect 'terrorists' during the Gulf War proved disastrous when a number of wholly innocent Iraqis and Palestinians were detained on the strength of outdated intelligence and often unsubstantiated rumour.

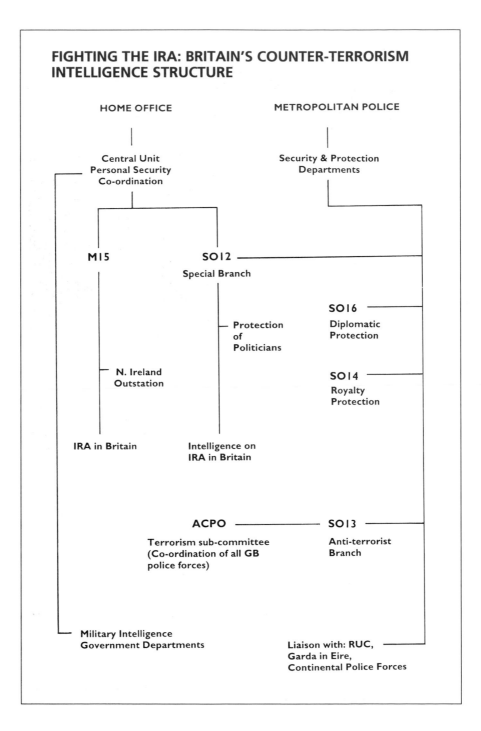

FIGHTING THE IRA: BRITAIN'S COUNTER-TERRORISM INTELLIGENCE STRUCTURE

HOME OFFICE

METROPOLITAN POLICE

Central Unit
Personal Security
Co-ordination

Security & Protection
Departments

MI5

SO12

Special Branch

SO16

Diplomatic
Protection

Protection
of
Politicians

N. Ireland
Outstation

SO14

Royalty
Protection

IRA in Britain

Intelligence on
IRA in Britain

ACPO

SO13

Terrorism sub-committee
(Co-ordination of all GB
police forces)

Anti-terrorist
Branch

Military Intelligence
Government Departments

Liaison with: RUC,
Garda in Eire,
Continental Police Forces

This non-descript office building on the Euston Road houses the headquarters of MI5 until it moves to new buildings near Lambeth Bridge.   Guy Taylor

Since 1945, MI5 has suffered from frequent changes in leadership. Kell retired as Director General after 37 years to be succeeded by Sir David Petrie, Sir Percy Sillitoe, Sir 'Dick' White, Sir Roger Hollis, Sir Martin Furnival Jones and Michael Hanley. When Hanley retired in 1979 he was replaced by Sir Howard Smith, a professional diplomat nominated for the first time from outside the service. In February 1992, MI5 became the first major Western intelligence agency to appoint a woman as its head, when Stella Rimington assumed the mantle of Director General.

During the 1980s, MI5 suffered from revelations of infiltration compounded by allegations of ineptitude in its higher echelons. Officially non-existent, it fell easy victim to politically motivated smear campaigns. However, since the passage of the Security Service Act, 1989, MI5, perhaps the worst-kept secret in modern British history, has officially existed. Unlike her predecessors Stella Rimington is now able to defend her organisation publicly.

MI5 is being heavily restructured. It is now concentrating less on its former Cold War adversaries and has recently taken over responsibility for the war against the IRA. Both MI5 and SIS are in the process of moving into new headquarters and are likely to be seen in higher profile in the future.

ISRAEL

The Israeli Intelligence and Security Services were conceived during the years immediately preceding the United Nations mandate of 1948, and have since been honed to near perfection by over four decades of constant insecurity.

Mossad

Mossad Le Aliyah Beth (The Institution for Intelligence and Special Services) was formed in 1949. Inspired by Eliahu Golomb and Shaul Avigur, the founders of the 1940s Haganah intelligence service Shai, it quickly developed a remarkable reputation for ruthlessness and unorthodoxy. From the outset Mossad regarded its brief as international. Isser Harel, the organisation's first permanent head, had suffered badly at the hands of deep-rooted Communist anti-Semitism before emigrating from the USSR in 1931. Consequently he regarded the Soviet Union, rather than the neighbouring Arabs, as Israel's greatest threat. Espionage cells were set up in Tehran and Istanbul and disclosed early attempts by the Soviet NKVD to infiltrate non-Zionist Jews from Bulgaria and Romania. In October 1952, Mossad gained an early success when Hagop Antaryessian, an expatriate Armenian living in the Old City of Jerusalem, was arrested and charged with spying for Stalin.

Mossad suffered a series of reverses in 1954 when a number of sabotage operations within Egypt and Syria ended in disaster. However, with limited, and at the time top-secret, CIA support Israel was able to rebuild an embryonic espionage network within both countries. The Mossad agent Elie Cohen, an Egyptian Jew who had fled to Israel in 1956, was infiltrated into Syria via Argentina and quickly became accepted by the Damascus government. Prior to the Six Days' War he sent masses of intelligence on Syrian military dispositions and preparedness to Tel Aviv. In 1965, Cohen's luck finally ran out. He was discovered transmitting to Israel, arrested and publically hanged.

Today Mossad receives help and support from the CIA and MI6 as well as the French and German security services. However, it is probably fair to say that none of these institutions fully trust it. In 1960, completely unknown to the Argentinians, Harel sent a secret team into Buenos Aires to carry out the kidnapping of Adolf Eichmann. The sheer horror and immensity of Eichmann's crimes against humanity led most to support Israel's actions, at least publicly. Privately, however, many began to question the ethics of carrying out so blatant a clandestine operation in the sovereign territory of a friendly nation. When, a few months later, Swiss newspapers reported that Otto Joklik had been expelled from Switzerland for attempting to coerce Swiss scientists into working for the Israelis, Harel was forced to resign.

In 1985, relationships between Mossad and the CIA reached a low point when Jonathan Pollard, an American intelligence analyst, was arrested and charged with spying for Israel. Subsequent revelations indicated that Brigadier Rafael Eitan, a former head of operations for Mossad, had visited a United States nuclear plant in Pennsylvania that year to arrange for quantities of weapons-grade uranium to be diverted to Israel. Despite strong representation from Washington, Israel refused to punish Eitan, ultimately appointing him head of the nationalised Israeli Chemicals Company.

Shin Beth

Shin Beth, the Security and Counter-Espionage Service, was also formed in 1949. Although primarily concerned with counter-espionage, it retains an interest in the collation of military information with links to the Directorate of Military Intelligence.

Shin Beth has three sections: Arab, Eastern European and Anti-Terrorist. All work closely with Mossad and Aman, a smaller organisation responsible for the external collection of purely military intelligence. Counter-espionage within Shin Beth is undertaken by 'Sheruth Bitakhon Klali', more usually known as Shabak, and political surveillance by 'Reshud'.

The head of the Israeli civilian secret service, the Memuneh, is directly responsible to the

Prime Minister for all matters relating to national security. As a safeguard, and in marked contrast to the heads of MI5 and MI6, the Memuneh is also answerable to the Knesset, the Israeli parliament, which has ultimate powers of dismissal if necessary.

PEOPLE'S REPUBLIC OF CHINA

The People's Republic of China boasts one of the most secretive and secure intelligence services in the world. Communist tradition has it that the service was introduced by Mao Tse-Tung before World War I. In fact the first real director of intelligence was K'ang Sheng, the son of a wealthy Shantung landlord. While studying at Shanghai University K'ang developed a personal espionage network, supplying the local Communists with a wealth of local intelligence.

In 1934, K'ang was elected a member of the Central Executive Committee of the Chinese Communist Party and a year later became one of the Chinese delegates to Moscow. Although willing to learn their security and intelligence techniques, he shunned too close a liaison with the Soviets, whom he never trusted fully. In 1951, his suspicions were proven correct when it was discovered that the KGB had infiltrated the Chinese Institute of Mathematics, acquiring control of its computer techniques in engineering, aerodynamics and nuclear physics. K'ang Sheng remained an influential figure in the field of Chinese intelligence until his fall from grace after the Cultural Revolution of the early 1960s. He died quietly in 1975.

In modern China all government and civic departments have their own dedicated intelligence organisations which feed into the Central Control of Intelligence via three distinct conduits. The Party, with its own investigation department, provides one source of information, the Central External Liaison Department (CELD) another and the States Council, with its direct links to Military Intelligence and the Ministry of External Trade, the third.

Internal security within the People's Republic of China is undertaken by the Cheng pao k'o (Political Security Section), responsible for counter-espionage and the control of expatriates, the Chi pao k'o (Organisational Security Section) focusing on government, municipal, corporate and academic personnel and the Social Order Section dealing with daily administration.

China's greatest intelligence successes were gained legally in the fields of nuclear and scientific espionage. During the early 1960s, K'ang Sheng ordered a register of all known Chinese scientists living in the West, gaining from them a huge quantity of nuclear secrets. Discreet efforts were made to lure the very best scientists back to China. One, Dr Ch'ien Hsue-shen, having worked on United States rocket programmes for 15 years, returned to head the Chinese nuclear programme.

Chinese attempts at espionage in Europe have been extremely limited. The rift with the Soviet Union effectively denied them use of the Warsaw Pact embassies, while Albania, their only true ally on the Continent, was too isolated to offer any realistic assistance. Two Chinese (one a Taiwanese national) were expelled from Switzerland in 1966 and another, Liao Ho-shu, sought political asylum in Holland three years later.

RUSSIA

Modern Russia's security services are inextricably interwoven with her Communist past. In 1917, Lenin ordered the liquidation of the Tsarist Intelligence and Security Police, the Ochrana. Most agents were executed, although a few were recruited to the new Extraordinary Commission for Combating Counter-Revolutions and Sabotage—the Cheka. Under the leadership of the Pole Felix Dzerzhinsky, a nationwide sub-culture of informers was recruited by the Cheka and terrorised into informing on its friends, neighbours and relatives. In an orgy of blood-letting, anyone even suspected of counter-revolutionary thought was liquidated.

In 1922, the Cheka was changed into the State Political Administration (GPU) and brought under the control of the People's Commissariat of Internal Affairs (NKVD). When Trotsky created a Chief Intelligence Administration (GRU) within the Red Army, the GPU, fearing that its absolute authority was being threatened, retaliated. Dzerzhinsky insisted that the GPU should have the power to screen GRU personnel (but not vice versa) and demanded the right to place GPU nominees in key positions within the GRU. In 1923, the GPU was streamlined, reorganised and renamed the Unified State Political Administration (OGPU).

Rivalry between the civil and military intelligence organisations remained fierce until the Soviet Union's early defeats in the Great Patriotic War (1941–45). Political officers were removed from combat units and the GRU allowed unbridled control of military intelligence. In 1944, however, with ultimate victory assured, Stalin recalled the political officers, placing the Red Army once again under NKVD supervision.

KGB

On 13 March 1954, the NKVD was replaced by the Komitet Gosudarstvennoi Bezopastnosti, the Committee of State Security or KGB. Under the leadership of men such as Yuri Andropov (1967–82), Vitali Fedorchuk (May–December 1982) and Viktor Chebrikov (1982–88) the KGB became a potent force, infiltrating the vast majority of Western intelligence and counter-intelligence agencies while suffering relatively few breaches in its own security.

At its zenith the KGB comprised four chief directorates and a number of subordinate departments and services. The 1st Chief Directorate, formerly the Foreign Department (INO), incorporated the Passport and Press Sections and the somewhat more sinister Executive Action Section responsible for espionage missions involving assassinations. The 2nd Chief Directorate covered internal security, counter-intelligence, Department D (disinformation) and the Secret Political Department. The 8th Chief Directorate dealt with communications and cryptography and the last major directorate the Border Guards.

Military counter-intelligence was dealt with by the smaller 3rd Directorate, transport by the 4th, economic counter-intelligence and industrial security by the 6th, surveillance by the 7th and KGB archives by the 10th. The somewhat more sinister 6th and 12th Departments dealt with the interception and inspection of correspondence and eavesdropping respectively.

In the 1970s, the KGB is estimated to have employed some 350 000 full-time officers, ranging from diplomats, journalists and Aeroflot pilots to collective farmers. The largest KGB formation, the Border Guards, had some 175 000 soldiers, many of them conscripts undertaking three years' national service.

Modern Russia

The old KGB simply did not survive the disintegration of the Soviet Union. Its leadership's ill-conceived bid to topple the Gorbachev regime, and the KGB rank and file's refusal to support the coup, brought the entire apparatus to a halt. After the failure of the coup, Vadim Bakatin, the liberal former Minister of the Interior hounded from office by a KGB-backed conspiracy, was placed at its head with the brief to dismantle and democratise it.

Many of the former Soviet Union's KGB facilities were transferred to the new republics, leaving the rump to be broken into three distinct and administratively separate services. The

Inter-State Security Service was formed to deal with counter-intelligence matters, the Central Intelligence Service was given responsibility for intelligence and the State Border Protection Committee many of the political duties of the former Border Guards. The Border Guards themselves have been removed from KGB jurisdiction to become a demilitarised customs service. A total of 56 senior commanders were sacked or arrested for their role in the coup and a staggering 25 per cent of lesser KGB personnel forcibly retired.

SOUTH KOREA

Since its birth South Korea has been a country under siege. Accordingly, the South Korean Central Intelligence Agency, formed with United States aid in 1953, has had to learn to be both ruthless and efficient. The Agency is more correctly titled the Korean Intelligence and Security Service, or KISS, and is closely linked to the National Security Planning Service and the Defence Security Organisation.

KISS gained one of its most significant successes in 1969, when it successfully uncovered a small but active Chinese spy ring at Cambridge University. The network organiser, Pak No-su, was induced back to Seoul with the offer of employment in the President's office and arrested. He was accused of recruiting Korean intellectuals in Europe for the North Korean cause, tortured for information, tried and executed two years later.

The Korean Security Service retains intimate links with the United States CIA. On 1 September 1983 the Korean Airlines flight 007 was intercepted in Soviet air space over the highly sensitive Sakhalin Island and shot down with the loss of all 269 passengers and crew aboard. The aircraft's captain, Chun Byung-in, was one of KAL's ablest pilots and a former military air ace, on the face of it far too experienced to make so fundamental a navigational error in so dangerous an area.

It has been strongly suggested that the aircraft was in fact flying a civilian surveillence mission to obtain intelligence for the CIA on the new Soviet radar station then being constructed at Krasnoyarsk. Others feel that the aircraft was simply probing the Soviet's defensive radar network. Whatever the truth, the CIA gained considerable information by monitoring the Soviet response to the unravelling tragedy.

SWITZERLAND

Switzerland is not a member of the United Nations. Both politically and economically she is neutral and has invested a considerable amount of time and energy in remaining so. As a consequence she has succeeded in attracting a large number of international headquarters and enjoys an influence in world affairs far greater than her relatively diminutive size would ordinarily merit.

Switzerland's wartime military intelligence was set up in 1937 by Brigadier Roger Masson. Originally tasked by no more than ten men, divided into three bureaux, D (Germany), F (France) and I (Italy), it grew within three years to 120 staff. When it seemed that Germany would win the war, and would almost certainly invade Switzerland, a second, covert intelligence agency was set up under a well-known anti-Nazi officer, Captain Hans Hausmann. With Masson's agreement Hausmann formed and privately financed the Bureau Ha, ostensibly a press-clippings agency but in reality a conduit for the gathering of German military intelligence.

Masson also recruited Rudolf Roessler, an ardent anti-Nazi German who had recently fled to Switzerland. As has been described in detail in the previous chapter, Roessler provided excellent intelligence directly to the Swiss and indirectly to the British. However, an ardent

Communist, he worked primarily for the Soviets. It has been suggested that Britain used Roessler to pass Ultra-produced intelligence to Stalin without disclosing its source. Whether or not this is true, it is certain that the Red Army owed many of its victories to Roessler's brilliant analysis of the enemy's potential.

After the war several United Nations organisations moved to Geneva, bringing with them an inevitable group of wholly unrelated agents. Typically, GRU Colonel Gregori Miaghov posed as a railways expert in the International Labour Organisation until accused of espionage against the Swiss railways and removed.

Even countries as law-abiding as the Swiss have their rogues. In 1979, the Austrian police arrested a Swiss junior intelligence officer, Lieutenant Karl Schilling, for allegedly spying on Austrian military exercises. Schilling was given a suspended sentence and deported. Colonel Albert Bachmann, head of the Swiss Intelligence Service, was suspended and subsequently sacked. It transpired at a subsequent inquiry that he had organised a private espionage service within the government organisation. His precise motives for so doing were never ascertained.

UNITED STATES OF AMERICA

The United States of America is protected by one of the youngest of the major intelligence services. Prior to the Pearl Harbor catastrophe the country had no coordinated foreign intelligence service at all. The Federal Bureau of Investigation (FBI) dealt successfully with internal matters of security, allowing the White House to pursue a wholly isolated foreign policy. After the outbreak of war, President Roosevelt set up the Office of Strategic Services (OSS) with a brief somewhat akin to Britain's MI6 and SOE. Although the OSS proved a quick learner, and by 1945 was ideally placed to counter the growing incidence of Soviet espionage in Europe and USA, it was disbanded by President Truman soon after the Allied victory.

Within months it was conceded that this had been a tragic error. Despite its protestations to the contrary, the FBI had neither the experience nor the manpower to protect United States' interests abroad. Furthermore, many in Congress began to question the motives of its over-ambitious head and were less than willing to grant J. Edgar Hoover an opportunity to spread the growing tentacles of his FBI empire abroad.

CIA

In 1947, the jurisdiction of the FBI was once again confined to internal matters and the Central Intelligence Agency (CIA) was established to meet the increasingly aggressive attentions of the NKVD. The early days of the CIA, or C.I.Group as it was initially known, were less than auspicious. It had three different directors within its first 20 months; Rear-Admiral Sidney W. Souers, USAF General Hoyt S. Vandenberg and Rear-Admiral Roscoe H. Hillenkoetter. The Agency was almost wholly unprepared for the Korean War, but, before that, had already been heavily censured for its failure to warn of a revolution in Colombia.

The Agency began to streamline its affairs when Hillenkoetter was replaced as director by General Walter Bedell Smith in 1950. A former ambassador to Moscow, Bedell Smith was alarmed by much of what he found within the CIA administration. Convinced of the existence of an internal Communist plot, he ruthlessly purged the Agency of its misfits, including many veterans of the OSS days. Ably assisted by his deputy, Allen Dulles, he tightened entrance qualifications and vetting procedures, making the CIA one of the most secure organisations of its kind in the world.

In 1952, Bedell Smith left the Agency to become Under Secretary of State for Political

Affairs at the White House. Dulles became director and at once introduced a policy of infiltrating expatriate Russians into the Soviet Union. Although the success, or otherwise, of this policy has never been made public, the Soviets subsequently stated that some 23 agents were caught attempting to penetrate its borders in 1951 and 1952.

Under Dulles the CIA enjoyed a number of successes, several of them at its Allies' expense. It uncovered the Anglo-French plans to invade Suez in 1956, and subsequently proved MI6 wrong in its pronouncement that there would not be a coup in Algeria. However, it also made mistakes. It was heavily implicated in the incident which led to Francis Gary Powers's U-2 spyplane being shot down over Soviet territory prior to the East–West summit in 1960. The Bay of Pigs fiasco, the CIA plan to land Cuban exiles in Cuba to depose Fidel Castro, which ended in disaster, finally forced the resignation of Dulles.

The CIA suffered by implication as a result of the Watergate scandal. Admiral Stansfield Turner, a former naval colleague and close friend of President Jimmy Carter, was appointed director in 1977 and at once set about a disastrous purge of the service in which 2000 personnel were dismissed. Morale foundered, causing many of the highly experienced Old Guard to resign in disgust. The CIA recovered in the 1980s, and was generally considered to be in excellent shape until the Gulf War. Although technologically without peer, when Saddam Hussain invaded Kuwait the CIA simply did not have enough agents on the ground to provide the White House with up-to-date human intelligence (Humint). Quite simply it had forgotten the fundamental necessity of the spy on the ground.

James Adams, the present director of the CIA, is currently changing the very fundamentals of the Agency by forcing it to accept the realities of the post-Cold War world. The bureaucracy is being slashed, while many more spies are being put back into the field to provide timely intelligence in a potentially chaotic world. The CIA's traditional secrecy is being replaced by an internal Glasnost, in which Gates and his senior deputies are now declaring themselves available to the press and politicians.

FBI

Intelligence-gathering within the United States of America is undertaken by various agencies. The National Security Agency, with its headquarters at Fort Meade, Maryland, employs over 100 000 personnel and is responsible for communications intelligence. Counter-espionage is controlled by the FBI with its 15 000 full- and part-time agents. The Army, the US Navy and the Atomic Energy Commission all have their own intelligence networks subordinated to the National Security Council.

It is perhaps worh noting that the United States Secret Service itself has nothing to do with the CIA. Formed during the Civil War to deal with counterfeiting, it is now solely responsible for Presidential security.

THE MODERN AGENT

THE 'LEGAL'

Agents fall into the twin categories of 'legals' and 'illegals'. 'Legals' are accredited diplomats and as such are immune from prosecution. If caught in the act of espionage they simply claim

Oleg Gordievsky was an accredited diplomat in London and therefore a 'legal' resident.
Associated Press/Topham

diplomatic immunity and return to the safety of their embassies to await the inevitable expulsion order. Traditionally Soviet 'legals' worked under the control of a KGB head, or Resident, completely divorced from the conventional embassy chain of command. Residents had their own top-secret codes and teams of KGB cipher clerks, but were able in addition to call on the full resources of the embassy's mainstream diplomatic staff.

Although Residents were theoretically clandestine, few were able to attain so important a position without becoming known to the counter-intelligence services. They were therefore closely monitored and rarely became actively involved in espionage.

East–West intrigue did not die with the Cold War. As recently as December 1991, UK Foreign Secretary Douglas Hurd, during a visit to Moscow, made an official protest about London-based spying to Vadim Bakatin, the new chairman of the reorganised KGB. He was concerned that the KGB's 1st Chief Directorate, the state security foreign espionage wing, had kept up full pressure against the West. He estimated that there were up to 50 KGB and GRU 'legals' still working in London and threatened mass expulsions unless their activities ceased.

More recently, however, the hub of international terrorism, and with it espionage, has shifted to the Middle East. Iran in particular has moved teams of trained 'legals' to its European embassies. According to Israeli intelligence sources, more than 20 of the 70 full-time staff at the Iranian embassy in Bonn in April 1993 were linked to intelligence, terrorism training and arms procurement.

A few Iranian 'legals' have become involved in conventional espionage. Others have taken responsibility for tracing dissidents, locating Eastern European arms and nuclear experts and instructing 'students' in the arts of assassination. Three Iranian diplomats, reportedly operating for the head of national intelligence Ali Falshian, were expelled from Britain in July 1992 on suspicion that they had been sent to assassinate the author Salman Rushdie.

THE MILITARY ATTACHÉ

A small but crucial minority of 'legals' comprise relatively high-profile career servicemen (or, these days, servicewomen) holding appointments within the military attaché's department. As such they are entirely overt, frequently wearing uniform in public. They are closely monitored on all visits to military installations and superficially offer little real threat. Inevitably, however, they carry 'shopping lists' of kit and equipment of particular interest to their intelligence departments and often prove surprisingly adept at taking close-up clandestine photographs in prohibited areas.

Although much of the information gleaned from these relatively primitive methods is comparatively low grade, in large enough quantities it may prove of great value to technical intelligence analysts. Vehicle and (where possible) engine numbers are photographed as are suspensions and tyre pressures to establish the actual, as opposed to stated, weight of individual equipment pieces.

If caught the attaché often suffers little more than a rebuke from his military hosts, if only to preserve the status quo and minimise the possibility of retaliation.

VERIFICATION TEAMS

Under the terms of the Conventional Forces in Europe (CFE) Treaty, elements of the former Soviet Union are now exchanging verification teams with the major NATO powers. Teams of high-ranking specialist officers are being allowed into the very core of once top-secret installations to confirm to their own satisfaction that weapons systems allegedly deactivated under the treaty have in fact been neutralised.

There is no suggestion that the verification teams of any country contain active spies. However, there can be no doubt that these experts have been probing to the very limits of their authority.

In March 1991, the forces of Saddam Hussain were comprehensively defeated by a United States-led Coalition army. In less than 100 hours of fighting his divisions, dug in along the Kuwaiti–Saudi border, simply ceased to exist as coherent military entities. As part of the subsequent ceasefire agreement Saddam agreed to neutralise his NBC (nuclear, biological and chemical) facilities and to allow United Nations scientific teams qualified access to monitor their destruction.

Almost from the outset Saddam reneged on the agreement. Accusing the verification teams of espionage (an accusation which he was never able to substantiate) he began to make it increasingly difficult for them to work. Transportation was withdrawn at short notice and access to key buildings suddenly denied. On occasions the teams were even taken to the wrong site in an attempt to frustrate their investigations. However, with the assistance of Navstar they were invariably able to establish their true position and register a protest.

THE MILITARY MISSIONS

The Treaty of Potsdam, signed by the victorious powers in 1945, heralded the division of Germany and the advent of the Cold War. Under its provisions the United States, Britain, France and the Soviet Union each formed a series of military missions. Superficially the missions were tasked with nothing more onerous than monitoring the state of war graves in the sectors controlled by the other three powers. In reality, however, they became responsible for monitoring military exercises. Inevitably, the United States, British and French missions quickly allied themselves against the Soviet mission, or 'Soxmis'. Under the terms of the original agreement, when operating out of their own sector mission members had to travel in uniform. They were confined to vehicles clearly identified by special number plates and were banned from the most sensitive military areas.

In reality, mission vehicles had a marked propensity for getting 'lost', usually on the outskirts of a prohibited area. Undoubtedly mission teams provided a vast pool of useful illicit military intelligence. Although their vehicles enjoyed diplomatic status, mission members were not immune from retaliation, and injuries caused by ramming were not uncommon. Occasionally mission members went well beyond the scope of their stated authority. A United States Army major, challenged while trying to breach the perimeter surrounding a tank base on the outskirts of Berlin, was shot dead by a Soviet sentry. With the coming of Glasnost the missions were gradually reduced and were scrapped completely on German reunification.

THE COMMERCIAL ATTACHÉ

The demand for industrial information became paramount in the Soviet Union in the 1950s. Khrushchev introduced the State Committee of Science and Technology and began to expand his espionage targets beyond the purely military. The role of the Soviet commercial agent grew unabated for the next decade and a half until, in 1971, Whitehall at last declared that it had had enough and expelled 105 Soviet officials.

The vast majority of 'legals' are in reality full-time intelligence agents working under the guise of clerks, drivers or junior commercial attachés. Although inevitably a few will be known to the security services, the majority will not. As such they are able to mix comparatively freely with the local population without arousing undue suspicion. The number and grade of 'legals' attached to each embassy depends entirely upon its political and strategic importance.

Viktor Suvorov, a medium-level Soviet defector of the 1970s, states that in the height of the Cold War up to 40 per cent of the entire staff of an average Soviet embassy were directly employed by the KGB, whilst a further 20 per cent were answerable to the GRU. Although the Soviet Union has now collapsed, Russia continues to operate a reduced KGB and certainly retains agents in the West.

THE TALENT SPOTTER

'Legals' become experts in the art of spotting and assessing potential spies, particularly in the armed services and defence industries. However, talent spotting is not limited to active servicemen. Reservists, civilian employees, contractors, outside consultants, even retired government officials will be targeted. Civil servants are prime targets if they have present or future access to classified or sensitive material. Even those on the periphery—family or friends—may be viewed as useful conduits in gaining access to targeted persons, activities or information.

Occasionally agents will be spotted while abroad. Russia, China and a few Eastern European republics require visitors to obtain visas. Visa applications, which contain full details of the visitor as well as the nature of his visit, are invariably processed by intelligence agencies (the KGB still undertakes this duty in the Russian Embassy). A relatively simple cross-reference against the commercial files routinely held in the embassy will enable the agent to assess the would-be visitor's strengths, weaknesses and potential for compromise.

The majority of agents are targeted in the comparative security of their home or working environment. Once a potential target has been spotted he will be approached by an experienced recruiter. The first approach will appear thoroughly innocent and will almost certainly be social. The target will have no idea that he is being assessed, nor will he know the true identity of the recruiter. Thereafter a friendship may be fostered and the target possibly put under some small moral obligation to the agent. The 'friendship' will be developed over years if necessary until a usefulness for the victim can be established. By then the recruiter will have a full portfolio of his target's likes and dislikes, virtues and faults, strengths and weaknesses.

Occasionally the target will become suspicious and report his fears to the authorities. When this happens the recruiter, who will have been careful not to have broken the law in any of his approaches, will simply withdraw to concentrate on a new victim.

Some of the most successful talent-spotting sweeps are undertaken at random. In 1962, the Soviets made a detailed survey of all radio hams serving in the British military. They noted from his lifestyle that one, Douglas Britten, a Chief Technician in the RAF, had potential.

Britten was recruited by a man whom he simply knew as Yuri. The Soviet 'legal' approached him while he was strolling through the Science Museum in South Kensington, London, and addressed him by his amateur call-sign 'Golf Three Kilo Foxtrot Lima'. Yuri asked Britten to obtain a model 1154 wireless transmitter. Unaware that the set was considered obsolete by the RAF, and was generally available on the open market, Britten complied and was rewarded

An electrically-fired pistol, firing cyanide coated dum-dum bullets, issued to Soviet Assassins. Popperfoto

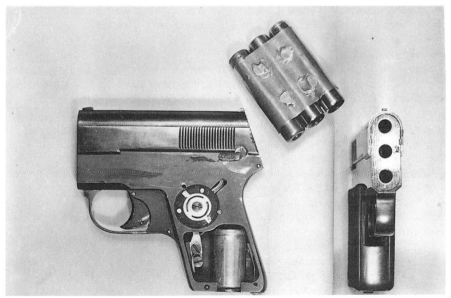

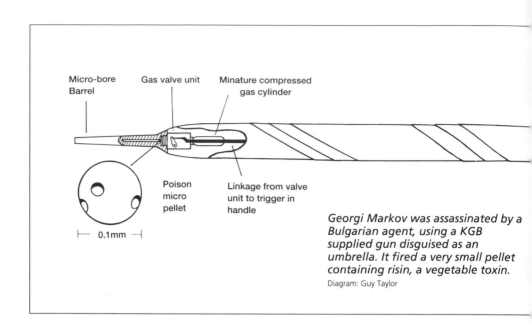

Micro-bore Barrel
Gas valve unit
Minature compressed gas cylinder

Poison micro pellet
Linkage from valve unit to trigger in handle

0.1mm

Georgi Markov was assassinated by a Bulgarian agent, using a KGB supplied gun disguised as an umbrella. It fired a very small pellet containing risin, a vegetable toxin.
Diagram: Guy Taylor

handsomely. When Britten was posted to Cyprus shortly thereafter the Soviets appointed a local case officer who had him photographed receiving money in exchange for low-grade intelligence. Thereafter, Britten was constantly blackmailed. Upon his return to Britain in 1966 he came under the control of Alexsandr Borisenko, a First Secretary at the Soviet Embassy, and was arrested two years later, having compromised himself by a fundamental breach of security. He was sentenced at the Old Bailey to 21 years' imprisonment.

THE ASSASSIN

Assassination is not within the remit of this book. None the less it is important to remember that murder is becoming an increasingly acceptable weapon of diplomacy in certain quarters. More than a dozen prominent opponents of Iran have been killed in Europe over the last six years and translators of Salman Rushdie's *The Satanic Verses* attacked in both Italy and Japan.

In September 1978, Georgi Markov, the dissident Bulgarian writer, was murdered on the streets of London. Markov's execution belongs to the world of spy fiction. He left his office at the BBC's Bush House in central London and was walking across Waterloo Bridge when he felt a sharp jab in his thigh. When he turned round he saw a man picking up an umbrella. The man mumbled, apologised, and walked off.

Markov soon developed a high temperature. Within three days he was dead. An autopsy discovered a tiny, poisoned pellet in his thigh. A similar pellet was used unsuccessfully against another Bulgarian dissident in Paris.

Although probably known to the authorities in Sofia and London, the name of the assassin has never been formally divulged. The KGB defector Oleg Gordievsky claims that the KGB provided the poisoned umbrella and Bulgaria the assassin. Whatever the truth, the assassin would almost certainly have enjoyed diplomatic status.

THE MARKOV UMBRELLA GUN

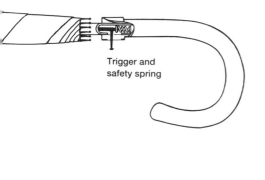

Trigger and
safety spring

*(Above) Georgi Markov,
Bulgarian emigré, killed on
Waterloo Bridge by the
Bulgarian secret service.*
Topham

*An almost silent poison
bullet projector, disguised as
a cigarette case, issued for use
by Soviet assassins.*
Popperfoto

THE SUPPORT AGENT

Support agents provide the operational and administrative back-up without which an espionage network cannot hope to operate effectively. They rarely break the law and are never tasked with the collection of secret information direct. Instead they enable others to operate by providing them with a false background. Support agents occasionally target the criminal world, possibly masquerading as fraudsters or smugglers to buy stolen passports and credit cards on the black market. Usually, however, they prey on completely innocent citizens.

Typically, a Soviet support agent working in Britain used a completely unsuspecting charity as a cover. Feigning genuine compassion he visited a number of terminally ill patients in hospital, gaining their trust by sending them cards and presents at Christmas. Once he had established which patients did not hold current passports he obtained their birth certificates from the Registrar of Births, Marriages and Deaths. Forged applications were then made to the Passport Office, quoting the patients' true personal particulars but with false addresses and photographs.

Although the advent of computerisation has made the exercise more difficult, it is still quite possible for a good support agent to supply an 'illegal' with a completely false identity. If that 'illegal' then chooses to travel on his false papers, for the sake of argument from one European Community country to another, and then settles down, his anonymity is almost certainly guaranteed.

THE 'ILLEGAL'

Domestic agents targeted to commit acts of espionage or sabotage against their own country are commonly referred to as 'illegals'. They live a wholly different and far more precarious existence than their 'legal' masters. Denied diplomatic immunity, they are subject to the laws of the land and can expect long prison sentences, or worse, if caught. To compound their problems, 'illegals' will invariably be disowned if apprehended and may be discarded, or even compromised, once their limited usefulness is over.

Once an 'illegal' has been recruited he or she must be put to work. Some will be given immediate tasks. Others will be told to infiltrate themselves into ordinary society and await instructions. All will have to be trained, protected, paid (if necessary) and administered.

THE IMMEDIATE AGENT

'Illegals' who spy for money, particularly those who volunteer their services, are invariably impatient. Whether broke or merely greedy, they know that they will be paid only by results and are eager to be put to work at once. If money is not forthcoming they will simply offer their services elsewhere. Wholly immoral and invariably careless, by their actions they are a danger to themselves and their 'legal' handlers. They will often give themselves away by their sudden change in lifestyle as they acquire new affluence. They will begin to work late, often into the night, as a means of gaining covert access to classified areas. They will start to show an unusual, often probing, interest in matters which do not concern them and may begin to take an unusual number of foreign holidays to facilitate meetings with their controllers.

The greatest ally of an immediate agent is inertia. It is not in the European or American psyche to question the activities of friends or workmates too deeply. The vast majority of commercial organisations have facilities for monitoring unusual behaviour in employees, but these can be effective only if individuals are willing to report their suspicions. Too often unusual behaviour is noticed but goes unquestioned for weeks if not months.

George Blake being welcomed home by his mother after his release from North Korea.   Topham

Immediate agents are given little training, beyond the possible use of a miniature camera, and are exploited fully from the outset. Eventually most are noticed, watched, caught and prosecuted. All are regarded as expendable. Indeed many agents working for East German intelligence were deliberately compromised by their former Stasi controllers after German reunification.

A few 'immediate' agents are ideological. They spy out of a sense of duty to a cause and rarely require payment. As such they can be relied upon not to draw suspicion upon themselves by a sudden change in lifestyle.

George Blake, née Bahar, was a typical 'immediate' agent of conscience. He was born in Rotterdam the son of a naturalised British father (of Sephardic Jewish origin) and Dutch mother. During World War II he served successfully in the Dutch Resistance and the Royal Navy before transferring to Naval Intelligence. In 1947, Blake spent a year at Downing College, Cambridge, learning Russian before joining MI6 in 1948. In 1949, he was posted to South Korea, working under cover as a Vice-Consul in Seoul. In 1950, shortly after the outbreak of the Korean War, he was interned by the North Koreans, interrogated by their Soviet advisers, and turned. By the time of his release in 1953 he was fully committed to the Communist cause.

While enjoying a short period of convalescence in London, Blake became engaged to a former MI6 secretary. In 1955, he was offered the post of Deputy Director (Technical Operations) in Berlin, under local head of station Peter Lunn; he was activated by the Soviets, and at once began to pass high-grade intelligence. During his four-year tour of duty Blake betrayed many British and American agents, among them Lieutenant-General Robert Bialek of the East German State Security Service (SSD). Bialek defected to the West in 1953, living under an assumed name in West Berlin. One evening in February 1956, whilst walking his dog, he was bundled into a car, taken back to SSD headquarters in East Berlin and executed. Blake was also responsible for the betrayal, show trial and execution of Lieutenant-Colonel Popov, a GRU agent in the employ of the CIA. More drastically for MI6, he compromised 'Operation Gold', the top-secret excavation and maintenance of a 500 m (547-yard) tunnel under East Berlin used to intercept telephone landlines running between Moscow and the Soviet military and intelligence compound in Karlshorst.

When Blake returned to London in 1959 to take up an appointment at MI6 headquarters he came under the control of KGB Resident Nikolai Borisovich Rodin. For the next 18 months he continued to pass valuable information until posted to Beirut. Blake was eventually compromised by a Polish double agent; he was recalled to London on the pretext of being offered promotion, but instead was charged with espionage. He was eventually tried at the Old Bailey and sentenced to a record 42 years' imprisonment—reputedly a year for the life of every agent lost through his treachery. Blake served only a small part of his sentence before escaping. He now lives, a free man, in Moscow.

THE SLEEPER

When ideologists are young and upwardly mobile it is often considered wiser to save their services for the future than risk their compromise at an early stage. They are given every assistance to advance in their chosen professional field but are otherwise left alone until the need should arise to activate them. Known as sleepers, many will suffer the frustration of awaiting a call which never comes. During the decade immediately prior to German reunification, the HVA (Hauptverwaltung für Aufklärung), the espionage agency of the East German State Security Service, maintained an estimated 20000 agents in the West. Most were sleepers, the majority of whom would only have been activated in case of war.

Sleepers are rarely, if ever, obvious. Indeed they do all in their power to blend into the social, political and economic background of their chosen environment. Most hold secure and respectable, though far from outstanding, jobs, enabling them to live relatively comfortably within their means. Many are married (often to spouses totally ignorant of their double lives) and a number have families. In a society that regards discretion and loyalty as paramount, sleepers neither spread nor allow themselves to become the subject of gossip. Most importantly they do nothing to break the law or draw themselves to the attention of the security services until activated.

Very occasionally sleepers are employed in the gathering of low-grade, minimal-risk intelligence whilst awaiting activation. They may be asked to report breaches of security at their place of employment, or even repeat bar-room gossip from the local pub. Residents of garrison towns may be asked to befriend servicemen in the hopes of gleaning information about weapons systems or troop states.

Although sleepers may occasionally be used as photographers, messengers, couriers or guides, until activated they will never be asked to carry out acts of disruption or sabotage against their own employers. If coincidentally their employer is being infiltrated by a

(Opposite) The original Cambridge four: (top left) Anthony Blunt; (top right) Guy Burgess; (bottom right) Donald Maclean; (bottom left) Kim Philby. Topham

sympathetic fringe movement, neither the infiltrator nor sleeper will know of each other's existence.

High-grade sleepers are watched constantly. When Kim Philby was recruited by the Soviets and ordered to infiltrate British intelligence 'in his own time', he was subsequently called to numerous secret meetings by Samuel Cahan, the pre-war Resident in London, to monitor his progress and assure his continued loyalty.

AGENT IDENTIFICATION

Agents become involved in the betrayal of their country for many, often complex, reasons. As such they do not form a discernible pattern. Most seem outwardly respectable, with an often banal approach to daily life.

The Ideologist

Ideologists operate from political conviction. As such they rarely, if ever, seek financial gain and are therefore not easily compromised by a sudden change in lifestyle. Ideologists were common before the war, when many academics came to regard Communism as the only realistic counter to the growing threat of Fascism. They are, however, rarer today, although the recent growth in Islamic fundamentalism has proved a dangerous breeding ground for a whole new generation.

The most notorious ideologists were the so-called Cambridge spies—Guy Burgess, Donald Maclean, Kim Philby, Anthony Blunt and John Cairncross. Contrary to earlier suggestions it is now felt that their simultaneous connections with Cambridge University were purely coincidental. They never operated as a team, had limited knowledge of each other's existence and were spotted and recruited independently.

During and immediately after World War II the Cambridge five passed top-secret Western intelligence, much of it gleaned from the British Code and Cipher School at Bletchley Park, to the Soviets. Critically, none of these academics regarded himself as a traitor to his country. In the words of John Cairncross: 'They (the Soviets) were fighting a life or death struggle against the Germans and the military information was crucial. I was providing information at the time to help Britain's allies—the Russians—to win.'

The Agent of Conscience

The human conscience can be a dangerous intangible. In the post-war years an increasing number of trusted state employees have breached their codes of silence, bringing to the public attention secret government activities which they have regarded as wrong.

One of the most enigmatic of the Cold War agents of conscience was the GRU colonel Oleg Penkovsky. In the firm belief that he was helping to avert nuclear war, Penkovsky passed masses of critical information to British intelligence via the MI6 agent Greville Wynne. As a member of the State Committee for the Coordination of Scientific Research, Penkovsky was able to report on the true state of the Soviet missile programme. He revealed that the Kremlin was in no position to threaten the USA, even confirming that a Soviet missile had actually blown up on its launching pad, killing the head of the Soviet missile force with 300 of his officers.

Penkovsky continued to take tremendous risks in his highly subjective pursuit of world peace, refusing to defect when warned that he was under KGB observation. He was arrested, charged and reportedly executed in 1963. Some Soviet-watchers feel that Penkovsky's evidence was simply too good to be true and that he had to be a double agent. Certainly the Soviets pumped out massive disinformation in a subsequent attempt to discredit him. However, it is more than likely that this was simply to cover their own failure in not catching this most single-minded idealist earlier.

Perhaps the most famous agent of conscience imprisoned today is the Israeli Mordechai Vanunu. A senior nuclear technician and former government employee at the secret Israeli nuclear plant at Dimona, Vanunu divulged highly classified intelligence relating to his country's atomic weapons programme to the *Sunday Times* newspaper in 1986. In his politically naïve and highly blinkered way Vanunu felt confident that his revelations would further the cause of peace in the Middle East. In the eyes of Tel Aviv, however, he became the greatest traitor in the history of modern Israel.

Retribution was swift. In September 1986, while sheltering in a series of safe houses in London, Vanunu became the victim of a classic honey trap. He was befriended by 'Cindy', a vivacious Jewish-American posing as a tourist. When a picture of him appeared in the *Sunday Mirror* Vanunu panicked. Fearing that his cover had been blown, he accepted an invitation from 'Cindy' to shelter in her sister's flat in Rome. On 30 September he was surprised in the flat by a team of Mossad agents working in conjunction with 'Cindy'. Drugged, chained and gagged he was returned on board ship to Israel. After a space of six weeks, during which time nobody knew whether he was alive or dead, the Israelis admitted his captivity but refused to

Mordechai Vanunu, photographed before his remand.
Topham

release details of his kidnapping. At a trial held in camera (during which Vanunu further angered his captors by attempting to leak details of his kidnapping) the court accepted that he had acted from purely ideological motives. None the less Vanunu was found guilty of treason, espionage and the passage of state secrets and was sentenced to 18 years' imprisonment. To date all pleas in mitigation to win him a lesser term have failed. Despite failing health he continues to be held in Ashkelon Prison in the most rigid conditions of solitary confinement.

The Non-Achiever

Occasionally agents will offer their services out of sheer frustration. In July 1991, Albert Sombolay, an American soldier of Zaïrian extraction, was sentenced to 34 years' imprisonment for spying for Iraq and Jordan during the Gulf War. Sombolay, who had been reduced in rank from sergeant to private for two disciplinary infractions, became disillusioned with army life. In December 1990, during the final build-up to 'Operation Desert Storm', he contacted the Iraqi Embassy in Bonn and the Jordanian Embassy in Brussels with offers to photograph his unit's activities in Saudi Arabia.

US Army investigators learned of his activities and set up a 'sting' operation. An investigator posing as an Iraqi consular official contacted Sombolay, who handed him low-grade information, none of it secret, in exchange for $1300. Sombolay was subsequently arrested, tried for treason and sentenced.

The Agent Under Pressure

Espionage, the second oldest profession in the world, will occasionally seek the services of the oldest. Many agencies run prostitutes, both heterosexual and homosexual, male and female, whom they will use to compromise the unwary. Victims occasionally 'volunteer' themselves through their obvious instability or well-known weakness for the opposite (or same) sex. Typically, however, the victim may be a businessman, happily married but far from home and bored. Perhaps flattered by the mildly flirtatious attentions of a strikingly attractive woman, he will accept her suggestion that they meet for a pre-dinner drink in the hotel bar. The drink will lead to dinner, the dinner to a night club and the night club to seduction. All will be photographed and possibly recorded.

Occasionally the drinks in the night club will be drugged. The unwary businessman, suddenly feeling the worse for alcohol, will return to his hotel room. Before long he will be joined in bed by a prostitute (possibly under age and male) and photographed in compromising positions. He will awake next morning with a hangover, but otherwise completely unaware of the events of the previous night. Later he will receive copies of the photographs . . . and with them the blackmailer's demands!

Blackmail does not always work. Targets will occasionally find the moral courage to tell their spouses, will express no great interest in their fate or will report the matter to the authorities. Legend has it that at the height of the Cold War the Soviets attempted to blackmail a South-East Asian president. Knowing the diplomat's weakness for young girls the KGB provided him with some particularly attractive examples while he was on a state visit to Moscow. When confronted with the pictures, thoroughly unabashed and far from agreeing to succumb to Soviet influence, the president allegedly asked if close-ups could be provided for the entertainment of his government ministers.

When it does succeed, blackmail can be devastating. Initially victims will only be asked for low-grade intelligence which they will be photographed handing over. As they become more deeply enmeshed, so the demands will increase. Invariably, when the hapless and wholly expendable victim is compromised or caught, he will find that the authorities have little if any sympathy for his dilemma.

During the 1960s and 1970s, Erich Honecker's German Democratic Republic was reputed to be operating in excess of 20 000 'illegals' in the West. Of these a number were tasked with seducing bored or lonely secretaries attached to the Government ministries in Bonn. They would wine, dine and if possible seduce the unwary women, sympathising with their predicament but never openly talking about their work. In so doing they would gain an immense quantity of low-grade intelligence, usually on personalities. On its own most of this information was useless. Properly assessed, however, it proved invaluable in targeting future blackmail victims.

Not all victims of sexual indiscretion divulge secrets. There has never been the slightest suggestion that Jack Profumo, as Minister for War, ever divulged any classified information, covertly or overtly, to Christine Keeler. However, the very fact that she was simultaneously having an affair with the GRU agent Yevgeny Ivanov was enough to guarantee his political ruin.

Financial Gain

The vast majority of modern 'illegals' act from no motive higher than avarice; most share two common characteristics. They relish the secret world of intrigue and enjoy the opportunity to show others up as fools. Some are psychopathic or sociopathic, incapable of loyalty either to an individual or group. Others demonstrate a peculiar mix of greed and ideology. The German 'Chaos' computer-hacking club was set up primarily to wreck commercial systems with viruses and logic worms. However, when its members discovered that they could break into the United States Department of Defense computer network several approached the Soviets.

United States reports suggest that many agents are egocentric, selfish, insincere, amoral and contemptuous of society. Most are living beyond their means. Of the 55 United States citizens known to have committed acts of espionage against the Department of Defense between 1948 and 1990, 31, well over half, were over the age of 30 when they began to spy.

A few 'agents for financial gain' are spotted or trawled. The majority volunteer their services. Of these many will have been vetted and cleared to work at the highest security levels. In 1970, Sub-Lieutenant David Bingham of the Royal Navy was recruited as a spy by Loriy Kuzmin, an Assistant Naval Attaché at the Soviet Embassy in London.

The incident began in February of that year when Mrs Bingham paid a visit to the embassy in Kensington Palace Gardens. Heavily in debt, she had previously left her husband and put her children into voluntary care. Now, desperate for money, she carried with her a letter from her husband setting out his naval credentials and offering her services as a spy. A few days later she was invited to a Ladies' Day function at the embassy. While her son listened to a children's choir she was given sealed instructions setting out the details for a meeting the next evening between Kuzmin and her husband.

At that meeting, which was held in Kuzmin's flat, the Soviet gave Bingham £600, telling him that £100 of it was for his wife. Having purchased a camera and light meter as instructed, Bingham met his GRU controller on the steps of Guildford Cathedral ten days later to receive some rudimentary lessons in dead letter box procedure (p. 116). For the next 18 months Bingham filmed secret documents at the Portsmouth naval base. However, he became greedy, demanding more and more money to placate his growing number of creditors. Eventually the

David Bingham, a former Royal Navy officer, who was sentenced to 21 years for selling secrets to the former Soviet Union.
Topham

Soviets began to lose their patience. On 31 July 1971, Bingham was ordered to photograph as many documents as he could during the next six weeks and to prepare himself for a journey to Moscow.

By now Bingham was ill, frightened to distraction and on the point of suicide. On 31 August 1971, he confessed his actions to his superior officer, was taken into Naval custody, and was formally arrested by the civil authorities on 5 September. He was subsequently tried for espionage and sentenced to 21 years in prison.

One of the most successful of the post war KGB 'illegals' to operate within the United States Department of Defense was Chief Warrant Officer John Anthony Walker. While serving as a communications watch officer on the staff of the Commander Submarine Forces Atlantic, Walker approached the Soviet Embassy in Washington demanding to see 'someone from security'. As a mark of his worth he brought with him a month's key settings for the ultra-secret KL-47 cipher machine.

Walker was in many respects an archetypal spy for money. Equally he was a person who should never have been allowed access to his nation's closest secrets. Walker joined the Navy as a high school drop-out to avoid prosecution for a series of burglaries. When he fell into debt after the collapse of a series of private business ventures, he attempted to restore his finances by forcing his wife into prostitution. When she refused, he became violent towards her.

During his staggering 17-year career as an 'illegal', Walker not only enlisted the services of his friend Jerry Whitworth as a sub-agent but recruited his son and elder brother. Walker was under suspicion for a number of years. However, he was arrested only when his ex-wife, by now alcoholic and alone, reported his transgressions to the FBI.

Walker's post-capture analysis estimated that cipher information provided by him had enabled the Soviets to decrypt a staggering one million US Navy messages, including many crucial to the operation of the nuclear submarine fleet.

It is perhaps refreshing to note that not every honest man can be bought. During a working visit to Sofia in 1982, *Morning Star* journalist Graham Atkinson was approached by agents of the Bulgarian State Security Committee, or KDS. Atkinson was offered £80 000 to establish the whereabouts of Major Vladimir Kuzichkyn, who had recently defected to the British Embassy in Tehran. Instead of complying, the loyal 36-year-old reporter made the offer public during a subsequent appearance on Channel 4 television. His less than happy newspaper bosses rewarded his integrity with summary dismissal.

RUNNING AN AGENT

THE CELL STRUCTURE

Not all agents feel comfortable working within the confines of a cell structure. A few prefer to work directly with a home-based controller. Others, notably John Walker, recruit their own sub-agents, whom they then task, pay and supply independently of their principal.

Where they do exist, most cells comprise a controller, a courier, technical support liaison, a radio operator and a number of field agents. To limit the potential damage to the cell should any single individual be arrested and interrogated, the agents are told as little as possible about each other and never meet. Information is transferred to the courier, whom again they never meet, via dead letter boxes.

Arguably the most successful of all post-war espionage cells was run by the Soviet Konon Trofimovich Molody entirely independently of the local 'legal' Residency.

One of the most gifted of all KGB 'illegals', Molody was born in Moscow but educated in Berkeley, California. He was taken to the United States by an aunt at the age of 11 bearing a Canadian passport in the name of a deceased Finnish-Canadian, Gordon Arnold Lonsdale. In 1938, the young Molody was taken to Finland and thence to Russia. During the war he saw service with the NKVD, the forerunner of the KGB, returning to the United States in 1950.

In 1955, Molody moved to Britain, where he utilised KGB funds to set himself up as the director of several leasing companies. Technical support for Molody's espionage activities was supplied by Morris and Lona Cohen, alias Peter and Helen Kroger, formerly key players in the United States' Rosenburg nuclear spy ring. Only two of the British agents recruited by Molody, Harry Houghton, an Admiralty clerk at the top-secret Admiralty Underwater Weapons Establishment at Portland in Dorset, and his mistress Ethel Gee, were ever caught. How many other agents existed, and indeed who they might have been, will almost certainly never be known.

Ironically the strength of Molody's cell was proved by his own arrest. He was noted meeting

The Kroger's bungalow, to which Molody was followed prior to his arrest.   Mark Lloyd

Houghton, who was already under suspicion, and was followed to the Krogers' house in Ruislip. After several such meetings he was arrested and the Krogers' property raided. At his subsequent trial Molody refused to give any information about his other agents. He was sentenced to 25 years in jail, but was exchanged for the MI6 agent Greville Wynne three years later.

Despite the length of his sentence Molody's morale remained high in prison, as if he knew that the KGB would do all it could to engineer his freedom. He played chess to a high standard, translated three books into Russian and started a Chinese-Russian dictionary while awaiting the outcome of prima-facie top-secret negotiations for his release. He died on 14 October 1970 at the early age of 48, reportedly while picking mushrooms in a field near Moscow.

COMMUNICATIONS
Espionage cells are efficient only if they are secure. It is imperative therefore that the controller is able to transmit instructions to, and receive information from, his agents without attracting undue attention.

MEETINGS
Face-to-face meetings will take place only when absolutely necessary, and then usually abroad, ideally in a neutral capital such as Vienna. Should a controller need to meet an agent regularly he will do so in as inconspicuous a manner as possible, and only when he can be absolutely

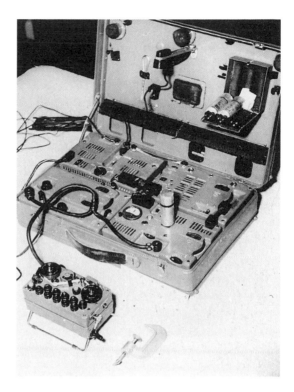

Londsdale's radio transmitter is remarkably similar to wartime sets, only a little less bulky.
Popperfoto

certain that neither he nor his agent is under suspicion. Meeting places will be changed regularly so as not to establish a traceable pattern and will be chosen for their blandness and normality. Typically they will comprise suburban high streets, thoroughfares, open parkland, indeed anywhere where individuals might be expected to meet and join in innocent conversation.

If the controller is an accredited 'legal', meeting places will usually be established within 30 miles of his embassy to preclude his having to obtain permission to leave the area. Crucially they will be accessible by at least two means of public transport. The controller will not wish to draw attention to himself by arriving at the scene in a car bearing distinctive consular or diplomatic plates, nor will he wish to run the risk of arriving or leaving by the same route as his agent. Contrary to popular opinion meetings are rarely, if ever, held in crowded pubs or restaurants.

When Douglas Britten returned home from his tour of duty with the RAF in Cyprus he was met by his new controller, Alexsandr Ivanovitch Borisenko, at Arnos Grove station in North London. Thereafter they met irregularly, largely to enable Borisenko to keep pressure on his wavering agent. It was agreed that, should either controller or agent be unable to keep a scheduled meeting, they would rendezvous at a fixed site on the first Saturday of the following month.

The fall-back meeting was to take place near the parish church in Pinner, Middlesex. Britten was to come to the bench beneath the church notice board. Having waited for five minutes

The parish church at Pinner, used by his Soviet contacts to meet Douglas Britten.

Mark Lloyd

(presumably to allow the controller or a member of his team a chance to sweep the area for potential MI5 tails) he was to proceed slowly along Church Lane. He was then to turn into Grange Gardens (a leafy, typically suburban road full of respectable semi-detached properties) and return to Pinner High Street. He was to carry a book and spectacles in his hand and, when asked the way to the library, apologise for the fact that he did not live in the area. He would then be met by his controller.

MEETING SIGNALS

Meeting signals, indicating whether or not a planned liaison will in fact take place, are occasionally planted along the agent's proposed route. Any one of a multitude of seemingly innocent objects may be used to confirm a meeting. A piece of chewing gum may be discarded under a particular bench or a can left in an agreed position. For a number of months John Walker left an empty 7-Up can against a telephone pole to indicate his willingness to meet his controller. Hundreds of people passed the spot, yet none became suspicious of so mundane a piece of litter.

Meeting signals may also be used to indicate the presence of a message in a dead letter box (see page 116). In the 1980s, the KGB employed seven London sites as DLBs, including the Brompton Oratory, a large and busy Catholic church in the heart of Knightsbridge. The Brompton box was filled and emptied within a few seconds using an intricate system of chalk marks as signals. The first agent would make a light blue mark on a lamp post in Audley Square, indicating that he was filling the box that day. Seeing this signal, the second agent would

A simple blue chalk mark on this street lamp (right) indicated that the DLB in Brompton Oratory contained a message. A chalk mark on the centre bench (below) acted as a signal from the second agent that the mark on the lamp post had been seen.

Guy Taylor

proceed some 250 m (840 ft) to a predesignated park bench which he would mark with a small chalk cross. The first agent would then proceed to the box, leave his container and return to and clean the lamp post. The second agent would then collect the package, remove the chalk mark from the bench and disappear. Brilliantly simple in its operation, the Brompton Oratory DLB was never discovered until compromised by the defector Gordievsky.

Agents are taught to return home normally and wait should a meeting not be kept and a back-up meeting fail. Douglas Britten, for one, was compromised when he failed to remember this simple rule. He was photographed during routine MI5 surveillance of the Soviet Consulate, when he panicked and attempted to hand-deliver a message after his case officer had failed to turn up for a rendezvous.

BRUSH CONTACTS

A brush contact is organised when a controller simply wishes to hand over or collect a small package from his agent. Unlike more formal meetings, contacts often take place in crowded department stores or in busy shopping precincts. Difficult to conceal, they rely on speed and the anonymity of the parties for success. If the object to be passed is small and incongruous enough the parties need not meet at all. Having agreed a contact by prearranged meeting signal the donor drops the object for the other to pick up a few seconds later. Should an unrelated third party inadvertently intervene by picking up the object, the attention of the 'rightful owner' can be drawn by the intended recipient and the package retrieved intact.

Where possible the controller will not attend a brush contact himself but will send an unrelated member of the embassy staff. As the embassy official will not be directly associated with espionage he or she will not be under suspicion and will therefore almost certainly not be under surveillance.

Colonel Oleg Penkovsky met Janet Chisholm, the wife of Rory Chisholm, an MI6 'legal' accredited to the Moscow Embassy, no fewer than 12 times. Although they often met in the crowded GUM department store in Red Square the couple never attracted KGB suspicion. It was only when Penkovsky subsequently met Chisholm himself, who unknown to British intelligence had been compromised by George Blake, that he was spotted on a routine surveillance check.

DEAD LETTER BOXES

Unless a meeting is necessary, bulky instructions and documents are passed between a controller and his agents by means of a dead letter box, or DLB. DLBs are always carefully researched before use. Unlike meeting points they are usually situated in remote areas where they cannot easily be compromised. Some consist of natural phenomena, such as a hole in a fence or tree trunk, large enough to secrete a document. Others comprise an everyday object, perhaps a drinks can, seemingly discarded at the side of the road or inside a rubbish bin. All large cities, however crowded, have areas of comparative tranquillity, ideal for the positioning of DLBs. During the 1980s, in London, the Soviets used not only a marble column in the Brompton Oratory but also Holy Trinity Church behind the Oratory and Coram's Fields off the Gray's Inn Road as boxes.

Controllers have a number of dead letter boxes available to them and are unlikely to use the same site for two or more agents. The agents themselves will be aware of only one, or occasionally two, DLBs assigned to them. If the controller can be certain that his agent is wholly

A hollowed-out base of a cross served as an impromptu DLB.　　　Mark Lloyd

above suspicion he may tell him to check for meeting signals on a regular (perhaps twice daily) basis. If not the agent will receive more specific instructions so as not to establish an obvious trend.

OPERATIONAL HOUSES

To enable him to maintain the pretence of a normal life it is imperative that an 'illegal' has a conventional home from which to operate. The property must reflect the agent's overt income and lifestyle and in no way betray the possibility of a second, more sinister, income. Ideally the property should be detached or semi-detached in the outer suburbs of a large city. Northern European and American families tend to keep themselves to themselves unless provoked. They show an interest in their neighbours, but tend to accept domestic situations at face value. They rarely pry deeply into others' affairs and as such provide no real threat to a discreet agent.

Operational houses may be either owned or rented. If owned they will be registered in the agent's name and often purchased with the assistance of a conventionally arranged mortgage. Ideally the property will not be overlooked and will be difficult to observe on a long-term basis without arousing suspicion. It will be secured against conventional burglary, but not ridiculously so. The Krogers' bungalow at 45 Cranley Drive, Ruislip, in West London, came under increased suspicion when it was noticed that it was secured by an unusual number of new Chubb locks. If the property is to be used for the transmission of messages, steps will be taken to camouflage the aerials and mask the transmissions. The Krogers deliberately chose Cranley Drive because of the proximity of three airfields and the resultant intensity of military and civil radio traffic.

SAFE HOUSES

An agent will occasionally be brought into an area to perform a specific mission. He will then require a safe house in which to stay unnoticed. Unlike an operational house, a safe house will not be used for overtly illegal purposes. It will be staffed by one or more support agents, sympathisers to the cause who will in all other respects be living perfectly normal lives. The presence of the agent will be easily explained. He will be described as a friend or relative staying for a few days and will do nothing to draw attention to himself.

The recent increase in terrorist activities throughout Western Europe has made the task of setting up an espionage safe house more difficult. Terrorist active service units (ASUs) are broadly similar in their organisation to espionage cells and can be easily confused. Neighbours who would once have shown little interest in those living next door are becoming increasingly willing to report the unusual to the authorities, particularly in the wake of a terrorist atrocity.

Safe houses are also used by domestic surveillance units to help preserve their anonymity. If watchers were to operate from known counter-intelligence headquarters their identities could easily be established and their movements monitored by counter-counter-surveillance teams. Watcher organisations such as MI5's A4 tend therefore to base themselves in privately run offices and safe houses well away from the orthodox espionage network.

COURIERS

Couriers are often employed to carry information for assessment and transmission from high-risk to low-security areas. In so doing they run the very real risk of not only compromising themselves but also their contacts. Gordon Lonsdale did not come under major suspicion until he was seen meeting Harry Houghton. Thereafter he was followed by teams of MI5 watchers until, after two weeks, he was tracked to 45 Cranley Drive, Ruislip, the home of the Krogers.

COMMUNICATIONS

Many agents, particularly sleepers, receive instructions direct by radio. The system of sending seemingly meaningless messages over the open radio was first used to communicate with the Resistance during World War II and has been discussed in detail in the previous chapter. Despite the end of the Cold War, coded messages still form an important method of espionage communications. Prior to the unification of the two Germanys 'Magdeburg Annie' regularly transmitted coded messages to agents in the West. Although she is no longer operational, many stations are, and messages are still being beamed, particularly between the former Soviet Union, China and Iran and between North and South Korea.

Western Europe remains the biggest target for unknown messages. Call-sign Papa November, the busiest station, transmits on 2.707, 5.015, 7.404 and 11.108 MHz. Transmissions begin at midnight GMT and continue six hourly on the half hour. Another station, allegedly operating on behalf of Mossad and using a few bars of the Lincolnshire Poacher as a netting-in signal (NIS), transmits on 4.665 and 7.605 MHz at 45 minutes past the hour. A third station, using as its NIS the tune Swedish Rhapsody played on a music box, transmits on Saturdays at 8pm and 9pm GMT.

Information will occasionally be sent, as well as instructions received, by radio; at least three transmitters were found hidden in the Krogers' property. Some ten years later an old Soviet-manufactured transmitter was discovered buried, possibly abandoned, in the Welsh mountains. Transmitting messages in the crowded and relatively sophisticated countries of Western Europe is difficult. Even the fastest of burst-transmissions will almost certainly be intercepted by government listening posts such as Britain's GCHQ. It also requires the agent to keep his codes and ciphers uncompromised.

When Gordon Lonsdale fell under MI5 suspicion he was followed on several occasions from his flat near the American Embassy to a branch of the Midland Bank in Great Portland Street. On one occasion he was seen to deposit a suitcase and a brown paper parcel. When he subsequently disappeared, the Director-General of MI5 approached the Chairman of the Midland Bank and obtained permission to open Lonsdale's safety deposit box. The Aladdin's cave of espionage minutiae found inside included two miniature one-time code pads (one clearly in current use) secreted in the hollowed-out base of a cigarette lighter. The pads were copied and returned.

When Lonsdale returned to Britain and took up residence in his London flat, Arthur Spencer, a GCHQ technician, was moved into an adjacent property. Whenever Lonsdale received a message Spencer established the frequency and alerted a GCHQ office in nearby Palmer Street. Palmer Street then relayed the signal down to GCHQ in Cheltenham where Bill

A talcum tin with false compartments hiding a microdot reader and messages on film
Popperfoto

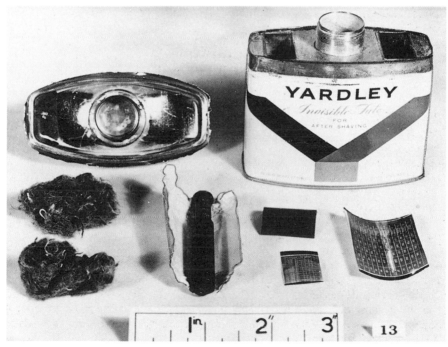

Collins, a senior cryptanalyst, decoded it using the copied one-time pad. The message was then relayed via enciphered telex link to the MI5 offices in Leconfield House in central London. Allowing for the calibre of officer used in this top-secret operation it seems likely that British counter-intelligence knew of Lonsdale's orders before the agent himself.

THE ONE-TIME CODE PAD

The one-time code pad has changed little since its adoption by the SOE in September 1943. Used properly it represents the pinnacle of development in the field of cryptography and is mathematically unbreakable. It is extremely quick and easy to use, is the embodiment of simplicity and generates few errors (*see diagram on page 56*).

There are many variations on the theme of the one-time pad. All require a cipher pad or book and a series of numbered incoming and outgoing code pages. During the final stages of World War II, uniformed teams of SAS and OSS personnel were dropped behind the retreating enemy's lines. Each team member was issued with a large silk handkerchief (approximately 50 cm [20 in] square) on which were printed some 600 code groups, each representing a standard phrase. The code groups and phrases were printed in alphabetical order to enable a single handkerchief to be used both for enciphering and deciphering. The phrases employed were tailored to the mission but, typically, might have included:

> **Containers received safely BOBO**
> **Enemy engaged at LILI**
> **Railway destroyed at NONO**
> **Resupply urgently required TUTU**

The two-letter code group was deliberately repeated within each code group to reduce coding errors and to facilitate deciphering should the message be 'broken up' on transmission. Most messages required no more than five or six groups and could be sent in less than 20 seconds.

Most modern ciphers rely upon numbers, rather than letters, to formulate their code. They contain a vocabulary of 300 to 400 words each with a corresponding three-digit number. The message to be encrypted is first translated into its numerical code and the code carried across to the one-time pad. The pad itself comprises a series of numbered 'message in' and 'message out' sheets each containing a series of four- or five-figure blocks printed in numbered, vertical columns across the page. The transmitting agent designates the area of the pad to be used by reference to the page and line number which form the first block of the message. Thus, in a five-figure code, the message block 06016 would tell the receiver to begin deciphering on line 16 of page 6 of the 'message in' sheet.

By way of example, if an agent wished to send the message, 'Information available for collection tomorrow', he would first find the four key words information—available—collection—tomorrow in his cipher pad. If the relevant numerical codes were to be:

available	132
collection	372
information	873
tomorrow	932

The encryption would read:

873   132   372   932

If he were using a five-figure block system the agent would then divide the encripted figures into blocks of five. If the final block were to add up to less than five, zeros would be used to make up the missing numbers. Thus the message (to be carried across to the one-time pad) would now read:

87313   23729   32000

The agent would now turn at random to any one of the unused lines in the 'message out' pages, for example the fifth line of the second page:

```
                                                    02
01   23785   34965   98753   96481   34684   12756
02   67804   06824   87646   92305   12505   34805
03   12458   06734   23864   05684   23579   12953
04   08749   49723   45862   06953   25792   12965
05   59481   38540   16493   84921   74329   18492
06   04372   74954   06543   05842   17463   59361
```

He would now transpose the numbers of his coded message beneath the numbers of the designated line, and would then subtract the lower number from the higher number without carrying across:

59481   38540   16493
87313   23729   32000
72178   15821   84493

The message 72178 15821 84493 would then be transmitted preceded by the block 02005 to show the page and line chosen. Once received the message would be deciphered by reversing the process. The decoder would turn to the fifth line of the second page of the 'incoming message' section, where he would find the figures:

59481   38540   16493

From which he would subtract the code:

59481   38540   16493
72178   15821   84493
87313   23729   32000

The resultant message would decipher to, 'information available (for) collection tomorrow'.

COUNTER-SURVEILLANCE

Conventional counter-surveillance is usually undertaken by teams of highly trained watchers. Watching is never an easy task. It requires immense patience, tact and diplomacy. Initially MI5 employed only male watchers. However, in the mid-1950s it begrudgingly accepted women when it became obvious that couples could far more easily blend into the background in a pub, club or restaurant.

Typically, counter-surveillance will be undertaken by teams of four, at least one a woman, supported by one or more cars. The cars will be standard saloons but with interchangeable number plates (registered in the name of a bona fide company) and highly tuned engines. Teams will change regularly, at least every eight hours, so as not to attract suspicion and will not follow the same subject on consecutive shifts unless absolutely necessary. Many surveillance successes rely on luck or on a momentary lapse in concentration on the part of the subject. Penkovsky first came under KGB suspicion when he was spotted meeting the compromised MI6 agent Chisholm, who was by then under routine Soviet surveillance.

Surveillance of a well-established operational or safe house is never easy, particularly where the occupants have succeeded in blending into the local society. When Gordon Lonsdale was tracked to Cranley Drive, Ruislip, a watch was put on the Krogers' bungalow and an observation post established some 75 m (210 ft) away in the back bedroom of a neighbour's house. The neighbour had served in the RAF and was at that time employed in Birmingham as an engineer officer on a classified gas turbine engine project. He had signed the Official Secrets Act and both he and his wife were regarded as totally patriotic and trustworthy. None the less, as the weeks progressed Jim Skardon of MI5 had great difficulty in convincing the wife that a great injustice against a charming and wholly innocent family was not being perpetrated. Even after the Krogers' property was raided, and a veritable treasure trove of Soviet espionage equipment discovered, the loyal neighbour remained sceptical.

No security service in the world monitored its people more closely than the former East German Ministerium für Staatssicherheit, or Stasi. In total, the Stasi employed more than 85 000 people full time, with a network of payrolled and volunteer secret informers

The house on the corner of Courtfield Gardens, from which the Krogers' bungalow was kept under constant surveillance. Mark Lloyd

penetrating every corner of domestic society. Not only did it keep painstakingly full records on foreigners and dissidents, but on the police, the Army and the border guards. All but the most innocuous had their activities reported on by someone, often a friend or relative. Literally hundreds of thousands of personnel files were opened in an orgy of State-sponsored paranoia. Many were probably never read, few were properly cross-referenced and hardly any seem to have been actioned.

Since reunification the new German Government has allowed former subjects access to their files. Most have declined to look, either preferring to put the past behind them or fearful of what they might find. Those who have ventured into the ex-Stasi vaults have tended to return chastened and shocked by the sheer immensity of patently useless information held by the former surveillance network.

KIM PHILBY: STALIN'S ENGLISHMAN

Harold Adrian Russell Philby was the most infamous, successful and cold-blooded of the Cambridge spies. Yet he might never have attained the heights that he did within MI6 had his iron nerve and almost total amorality not been shrouded in an outward façade of absolute charm and good humour.

Born in India in 1912, the son of the eccentric and cantankerous adventurer Harry St John Philby, he spent his formative years in Arabia. Despite a privileged education spent at Westminster School and Trinity College, Cambridge, the youthful Philby never felt a part of the English establishment. Nicknamed 'Kim' after Kipling's Indian boy-spy, he was inclined to the political left well before entering university in 1929. In 1931, he supported the Cambridge Labour Party in the elections, but resigned soon thereafter in protest at what he saw as Ramsay Macdonald's betrayal of the Party's ideals. During his time at Cambridge he came heavily under the influence of a group of pro-Soviet academics, meeting Guy Burgess and Donald Maclean in the process. As so often happens opposites attracted and Philby became close friends with Maclean, despite the latter's patent homosexuality and his own by then healthy appetite for the opposite sex.

Inevitably the trio were soon trawled for political work of a more serious and covert nature. In 1933, Philby was recruited by Samuel Cahan, the KGB Resident in London, and tasked with the infiltration of British intelligence 'in his own time'. He was introduced to Arnold Deutsch, a researcher at London University and his 'illegal' controller, by Edith Tudor-Hart, a Viennese Communist who came to the United Kingdom in 1935 and who worked ostensibly as a photographer for *Picture Post* (she was betrayed to MI5 by Blunt in 1964). While touring in Europe in February of the following year, Philby met and married Alice Friedmann, the daughter of an Austrian Jew and herself a keen Communist.

The couple quickly quit Austria to escape the attentions of the increasingly right wing and anti-Semitic authorities. Back in London Philby demonstrated no immediate interest in politics, but instead went quietly to work for the liberal magazine *Review of Reviews*. As circumstances permitted he began to disguise his true Marxist feelings, joining an Anglo-German friendship group and travelling to Spain in 1936 to cover the Civil War from a pro-Franco perspective.

Upon his return to England in 1939 Philby was appointed senior correspondent by *The Times* and dispatched to France with the British Expeditionary Force. Returning in 1940 he was trawled by British intelligence, joining SIS, Department D, responsible for sabotage, subversion and propaganda. When the Department merged with SOE in 1941 Philby was given the opportunity to train as an agent. Indeed he might well have parachuted into occupied Europe had it not been for a severe stammer which he was totally unable to control when under stress. Instead he was moved to Department S, in ultimate control of espionage, and given command of the Iberian section. In 1946, to the unbridled delight of his KGB controllers, Philby was promoted to the newly formed Soviet desk, from which he was able to supply not only information on British and American operations but suppress information damaging to the Russians.

In the summer of 1946, by now divorced and remarried, Philby was sent into the field for the first time when he was assigned the passport control office in Istanbul. Three years later he was posted to Washington as SIS liaison officer to the CIA, which was by then belatedly setting up its own Soviet counter-espionage section. A hard drinker and amusing talker he mixed well with his American colleagues, who trustingly supplied him with a seemingly limitless quantity of information, all of which found its way to the KGB archives.

Kim Philby, having adapted to everyday life in Moscow.   Popperfoto

Philby might have continued to undermine the Anglo-American intelligence community for years had it not been for a peculiar piece of bad luck involving his colleagues Burgess and Maclean. For some time James Angleton, a veteran OSS operator and head of CIA counter-intelligence, had suspected the loyalty of Donald Maclean and had passed on his suspicions to his British counterparts. On 23 May 1951, MI5 ordered Maclean's interrogation, informing the CIA of their intentions through Philby as SIS liaison officer. Impetuously Philby dispatched the less than reliable Burgess to London to warn Maclean of his predicament. The thoroughly frightened Burgess not only warned Maclean but fled with him, throwing immediate suspicion on Philby, with whom he had been staying in Washington.

Philby was recalled and returned to field work in Cyprus. In 1955, under cover of Parliamentary immunity, Colonel (Retired) Marcus Lipton, MP, named Kim Philby as the third man in the Burgess/Maclean affair. The establishment, which Philby so despised, immediately closed ranks in his defence. A few days later Foreign Secretary Harold Macmillan, one of the most honourable men of recent parliamentary history, actually advised the House of Commons that nothing could be proved against Philby.

Incredibly, despite his enforced resignation and the suspicion which by now surrounded

One of Blake's probable betrayals. A secret tunnel dug under Soviet Berlin by Western intelligence services. Popperfoto

him, Philby continued as an MI6 freelance in Beirut under cover of press credentials provided jointly by *The Observer* and *Economist*. Luckless if not loveless—he chose this moment to elope with Eleanor Brewer, the wife of the *New York Times* correspondent—he became the subject of considerable sympathy. Many of his acquaintances considered that he had been driven from his post by McCarthyist tactics.

Kim Philby's luck finally ran out in 1961, when George Blake was arrested and named him as a fellow agent. Nothing was done for several months, possibly to give Philby the chance to escape, thus obviating the need for an embarrassing trial. When this rather dubious tactic failed, Nicholas Elliott of MI6 volunteered to fly to Beirut to confront his old friend with the hard evidence now gathered against him. It was hoped that Philby might be persuaded to return to Britain for further interrogation. Instead he fled by way of the Soviet trade mission to Moscow.

When his wife visited him in Moscow she found him cohabiting with Malinda Maclean, the estranged wife of his former friend. In true form Philby later deserted Malinda to marry a local woman with whom he lived until his death in May 1988.

Kim Philby, who continued to work energetically for the KGB after his flight, was buried in Moscow with full military honours. Some 200 people, including four relatives, came to the graveyard at Kunstyevo. A contingent of 13 uniformed border guards, part of the KGB for which Philby had worked since the 1930s, lined the path as the cortège went by, firing a volley of three shots as the body was laid to rest.

F O U R

SPY IN THE SKY; AERIAL ESPIONAGE

A HISTORY OF AERIAL ESPIONAGE

THE BEGINNINGS

The history of aerial espionage is inextricably interwoven with the development of military aviation. In 1858, Felix Tournachon made aeronautical history when he photographed Paris from the basket of a captive balloon. Two years later the American J.W. Black took an aerial view of Boston in similar fashion. In 1862, during the American Civil War, General McLellan's Union Army used balloonists to spy on the Confederate positions during the siege of Richmond.

The first British foray into military aviation took place in 1863, when Captain F. Beaumont (who had witnessed McLellan's balloons in America) and Lieutenant G.E. Grover, both of the Royal Engineers, made a series of trial flights in a borrowed balloon. Notwithstanding initial War Office scepticism, balloon trials continued for the next decade with the support of a small Government grant. In 1877, a breakthrough seemed possible when Walter Woodbury patented a futuristic balloon-mounted camera operated from the ground by means of cable-borne electrical impulses. However, his gadget proved more fanciful than practical and failed to attract the support of the military.

In 1883, while serving in Nova Scotia, Major H. Elsdale of the Royal Engineers made considerable advances in the field of aerial photography when he successfully attached two cameras with mechanical shutters to tethered balloons and took a series of photographs of the Halifax Citadel. In 1885, military balloons were used operationally for the first time in minor actions in Bechuanaland and the eastern Sudan and later proved most effective during the Second Boer War.

In May 1908, Lieutenant F. Vyvyan Thomson, Royal Engineers, became the first to introduce the concept of stereoscopy to aerial photography, but with little initial success due to the sheer complexity of the equipment required. In 1909, aerial espionage was revolutionised when M. Meurisse took the first photographs from an aeroplane in flight. Three years later the French Army pioneered the use of cameras in aircraft during operations against dissident tribesmen in Morocco.

Britain formed an Air Battalion in February 1911, renaming it the Royal Flying Corps on 13 May 1912. No. 3 Squadron, Royal Flying Corps, became the first unit to practise aerial

127

photography when a number of enthusiasts purchased and adapted their own cameras. The squadron quickly became adept at developing its photographs while still in the air, thus introducing timeliness—one of the principles of good intelligence—to the equation. Unfortunately the War Office failed totally to appreciate the potential of area photography when excellent maps already existed. However, World War I was destined to change even their blinkered outlook.

WORLD WAR I

With the outbreak of war in August 1914 The Royal Flying Corps was quickly committed to aerial reconnaissance. No. 3 Squadron continued to provide informal photographic coverage of the battlefield (Lieutenant G.F. Petyman took the first series of five aerial photographs on 15 September), but it was not until January 1915 that an official experimental photographic section was set up. Within weeks the section proved its worth. A planned Anglo-French assault on the La Bassée Canal was cancelled in February 1915, when a hidden German trench system was discovered. A month later aerial photography was used for the first time to plan a successful attack during the Battle of Neuve Chapelle.

A further dimension was added to the value of aerial reconnaissance in the summer of 1915, when Thornton-Pickard introduced the first virtually vibration-free camera. At about the same time No. 11 Squadron, Royal Flying Corps, produced the first readable examples of vertical stereoscopic aerial photography. In April 1916, dedicated imagery analysts, responsible for processing, printing and examining the photographs, were posted to each Army Corps, and a School of Photography opened at Farnborough, Hampshire.

During the Battle of the Somme, fought between 1 July and 17 November 1916, the Royal Flying Corps took over 19 000 photographs, and made some 430 000 prints. By early 1917 specialist officers from the newly formed Intelligence Corps were assigned to each reconnaissance squadron, and cameras were fitted to most of the reconnaissance aircraft.

As the war progressed, photographic interpretation became an established intelligence asset. Analysts' reports were sent on a regular basis to Army headquarters, where they were merged with prisoner of war debriefings, captured documents, artillery sightings and patrol reports to give the first detailed impression of the enemy's intentions. Although the advent of improved German fighters temporarily swung air superiority in favour of the Germans, by mid-1917 the Royal Flying Corps was able to produce almost daily maps of the enemy front line and artillery positions.

In February 1918, the photographic interpreters in France discovered evidence of a build-up of men and materials behind the German front line. Reconnaissance was increased in anticipation of a large push. In the first week of March alone 10 440 photographs were examined and a wealth of intelligence produced. During the anticipated German offensive of April 1918, the photographic interpreters were employed mainly in directing artillery fire on enemy batteries located by aerial photography. Aerial reconnaissance of the battlefield was intensified and in one day, 12 April, 3358 photographs were taken from the air.

In the Middle East, aerial photography was also in constant use. By 27 October 1917, 131 Turkish artillery batteries had been photographed in the Beersheba area alone. Under the

(Opposite, top) Enemy airfields have been a prime target for aerial reconnaissance from the earliest days of military aviation. (Bottom) Aerial photography was virtually the only way of maintaining up-to-date intelligence the Western Front.

Guy Taylor

command of Lieutenant Hamshaw Thomas, Royal Artillery, the interpretation section attached to 5 Corps were able to receive a film, develop and analyse it, annotate it against the map and deliver the resultant prints by air to the front line within five hours. In January 1918, 1616 km² (624 miles²) of Turkish occupied territory were photographed for mapping purposes and, in the following May, a systematic programme of aerial photographic surveillance commenced over Mesopotamia.

By the time of the Armistice on 11 November 1918, the newly independent Royal Air Force had become highly skilled in the techniques of aerial reconnaissance. Although the RAF provided the photography, responsibility for its exploitation, whether for mapping or intelligence purposes, remained with the Army.

THE INTER-WAR YEARS

Inevitably the military's interest in imagery analysis waned with the coming of peace. The Royal Air Force School of Photography at Farnborough was expanded to include Army involvement, and an interpretation course added in April 1925, but few new photographs were made available. In 1935, the Air Ministry was forced to concede the long-term value of intelligence-gathering when hostilities in the Abyssinian conflict threatened to spread into other areas of the Mediterranean. Primitive sideways-looking cameras were fitted to a number of reconnaissance aircraft to obtain oblique photographs of the area. However, the prevailing reluctance of all the major powers to violate each other's air space prevented the formal overflying of territory actually in dispute.

By the late 1930s it had become evident that another Continental war was imminent. Imperatives replaced ethics and espionage overflights were at last sanctioned. In 1938, Major F.W. Winterbotham of MI6 obtained a series of aerial photographs of the German border from the French Deuxième Bureau. However, these concentrated on the area immediately abutting the Maginot Line and were of little interest to the British. The services of Sidney Cotton, the high-altitude aerial photographer, were therefore obtained and a series of top-secret photographs over Germany commissioned. In early 1939 a number of retired army officers were recruited as Station Intelligence Officers and seconded to Bomber Command to assess the damage caused by future bombing raids.

WORLD WAR II

With the exception of the irrepressible Cotton, by then serving in the RAF, few took aerial photography seriously during the early months of the Phoney War. Cotton himself took a series of excellent photographs of the German front line from an altitude of over 6000 m (20 000 ft), but even he failed to spot the build-up of enemy armour immediately prior to the assault on the Low Countries.

The few interpreters in France managed to escape via Dunkirk to act as a nucleus for the Army Photographic Interpretation Centre (APIC) formed in September 1940. For the next year imagery analysis remained largely defensive, tasking regular sorties over the Channel ports to monitor German invasion activity. However, as the tide of war slowly turned, so APIC became more offensive. 'R' Section was formed in March 1942 to give photographic intelligence support to the newly raised Combined Operations forces. In total secrecy it reconnoitred the St Nazaire basin prior to the Commando raid, identified the radar installation at Bruneval, discovered the Nazi rocket research facility at Peenemünde and, less successfully, analysed the beaches before the fateful assault on Dieppe.

(Top) German Air Force photo-interpreters in North Africa. (Bottom) Allied photo-interpreters analysing stereo pair photographs. AKG, Berlin

For the remaining three years of the war photographic interpreters (by now known as PIs) supported every campaign of the war. They pinpointed German artillery positions prior to D-Day and successfully reported the presence of massed enemy armour prior to 1st Airborne Division's assault on Arnhem (although, for various reasons wholly beyond their control, their information was ignored). As the Allies fought their way into Occupied Europe specialist sections were formed to deal specifically with enemy industry and communications, designating targets of particular value for Bomber Command.

Between its formation in 1941 and 'VE' Day (8 May 1945), APIC produced 3810 detailed reports and undertook a number of specialist missions, many of them top-secret. Photographic interpretation was one of the keys to the Allied success, proving a vital source of intelligence, both tactical and strategic. However, during the latter part of 1945 it lost many of its finest exponents as many of the most experienced operators were demobilised to return to civilian employment.

POST-WAR EXPERIENCES

After the war major efforts were made to husband the remaining photographic reconnaissance units to ensure that the lessons learned in six years of warfare were not lost. New PI units were established in Singapore, in Egypt and with the 21st Army Group in Germany. In July 1948 an independent APIC was formed in the Far East to help the fight against the Chinese Communists in Malaya. Although PIs had studied photography in Burma during the war, the task of the PI in Malaya was mainly that of examining photographic cover of dense tropical forest in an endeavour to find tiny clues which might indicate the presence of a terrorist encampment. Patrols quickly began to rely on air photographs rather than local maps, which were both old and inaccurate.

The campaign against the terrorists in Malaya emphasised the growing threat to the free world posed by the Communist powers. Towards the end of 1951, 104 APIS (Army Photographic Interpretation Section) was formed and sent to Korea as part of the United Nations response to the Communist invasion of the South. Korea was very much a conventional war. Daily missions were flown over the front line, and unusual enemy movement reported to divisional headquarters in the morning briefings. Troop concentrations and camouflaged gun positions were reported to the artillery, their precise locations established by means of reconnaissance or photo map comparison and counter-battery fire brought to bear.

COLD WAR BEGINNINGS

The birth of NATO resulted in a reappraisal of the defence policies of the Western nations. Soviet maps were found to have deliberately introduced errors to deter their usefulness to an enemy. Towns, cities and physical obstacles, where they appeared at all, were found to be several kilometres from their true positions. B-17 Flying Fortresses and B-29 Superfortresses were fitted with banks of cameras and sent high into Soviet air space to map the precise location of the main conurbations. Simultaneously, RAF Canberras and USAF RB-45 Tornados, RB-36 Convair Peacemakers and Boeing RB-47 Stratojets flew seemingly unopposed over the skies of East Germany, Poland, Hungary and Czechoslovakia. In their turn the remaining PI units in Europe were given an added impetus in their training and tasked with establishing a series of potential nuclear and conventional targets.

OPERATION FICON

In 1952, the gigantic ten-engined Convair RB-36 Peacemaker became party to one of the most grotesque (yet successful) improvisations of the early Cold War. Trapezes were fitted into the bomb-bays of a number of converted bombers (redesignated GRB-36 FICONs—FIghter CONveyers). A Republic F-84 fighter equipped with a hook was then coupled onto the trapeze and withdrawn into the bomb-bay, leaving its wings and anhedral tailplanes projecting beneath the fuselage.

Once airborne the pilot of the F-84 'parasite' transferred into the bomber's pressurised cabin to rest during the many hours of high-altitude flying that it often took to reach the designated objective. As the mother-ship approached its target the pilot returned to his fighter, awaited release from the trapeze and flew off independently to reconnoitre his objective. His mission completed, he returned to the bomber, connected to the trapeze and hitched a ride home. During the year 1955–56 the unlikely FICON flew several classified missions from Fairchild and Larson airbases in Washington State. The arrival of more sophisticated aircraft such as the U-2 and the RB-57D, compounded by the difficulties experienced in launching and recovering the parasite, brought the FICON project to a sudden end in 1959.

Less successful was a concurrent CIA attempt to float photographic balloons over the Soviet Union. Converted weather observation balloons—sometimes as large as 15 m in diameter—were released from Giebelstadt AB in Germany, and from bases in Turkey and Alaska and allowed to drift freely through Soviet air apace. Each contained either a radio monitoring device or an automatic camera programmed to take a photograph every 6 minutes.

Theoretically each camera was equipped with sufficient film to cover a strip 65 km (40 miles) wide by 5000 km (3100 miles) long. In reality, however, many balloons were either shot down or landed on Communist soil. The cameras that were recovered often revealed nothing more interesting than thousands of miles of intermittent darkness and cloud cover.

EARLY COMINT

As surveillance replaced reconnaissance as the number one priority, COMINT (communications intelligence) came to the fore. Specially converted RC-130 Hercules aircraft were commissioned by the United States National Security Agency (NSA) to fly eavesdropping missions along the Warsaw Pact borders. Early COMINT aircraft had no discernible markings and were therefore relatively easy to disguise as conventional freighters. As such they frequently flew into Berlin along one of the three permitted corridors and through the air space of potentially hostile Middle Eastern countries.

Not unnaturally the Soviet Union and its allies reacted vigorously to the intrusion of such aircraft. When in 1958 an RC-130 flying from the US airbase at Incirlik lost its bearings while patrolling the Turkish–Soviet border and strayed into Armenian air space it was intercepted and shot down by five Soviet MiG-15s. Initially both Washington and Moscow denied that the incident had ever taken place. However, when the Pentagon received information that 11 of the 17 crew had survived the crash the United States immediately demanded their return.

When the Soviets prevaricated, Washington took the unprecedented step of releasing intercepts, monitored by a listening post in Turkey, of the transmissions between the MiG pilots and Soviet ground control. The Kremlin responded by accusing the United States of falsifying both the sound tape and the transcription. None of the 11 survivors was ever released.

Fifteen years later, on 21 March 1973, a second RC-130, from the 7406th CSS at Rhein-Main, narrowly avoided catastrophe. While operating from Hellinikon airfield near Athens it was intercepted and attacked by Libyan jet fighters in disputed waters some 128 km (80 miles) from the Libyan coast. Fortunately the pilot received prior warning and was able to evade the enemy guns by flying into cloud.

PRIMITIVE ELINT

ELINT (electronic intelligence) flights began in earnest in the early 1950s with the introduction of the RB-29 and RB-50 photographic and electronic surveillance aircaft. The crews were trained to fly along the very edge of enemy coastal waters monitoring radio and radar transmissions. If the enemy failed to respond, the bombers would probe his air space until a reaction was provoked. Russian- or Chinese-speaking radio operators would then intercept the conversations between the pilots and their controllers, pinpointing previously secret radio frequencies or unknown radar stations.

Naturally the Soviets and Chinese did all in their power to retaliate. In April 1950, a United States Privateer with a crew of ten was shot down over the Baltic. In 1951, a Neptune was intercepted near Vladivostok and a year later a Swedish DC-3 Dakota downed in the Baltic.

On 12 March 1953 an RAF Avro Lincoln bomber was shot down with the loss of six lives while reportedly flying within the bounds of the Hamburg–Berlin air corridor. Britain claimed that the aircraft had been based at the Central Gunnery School at Leconfield, Yorkshire and had been unarmed and on a routine training flight at the time of the incident. However, it subsequently transpired that the Lincoln had belonged to No. 192 Squadron based at RAF Watton in Norfolk and tasked with the gathering of electronic information. In all probability the Lincoln had been provoking an incident to establish Soviet radar states in the area. On the same day a BEA Viking civil airliner was fired at when it 'strayed off course' in the southern Frankfurt-Berlin air corridor, and a second Lincoln subjected to a mock MiG-15 attack near Kassel in the American zone.

By the mid-1950s Soviet SAM systems and associated radar had improved considerably. The presence of MiG-17 and MiG-19 fighters in increased numbers, particularly along the border, meant that Allied espionage flights into Soviet air space were no longer safe. However, the introduction of the English Electric Canberra and high-flying United States variants, the Martin RB-57D and 57F, ensured that the initiative remained with the NATO powers for a further decade.

THE ENGLISH ELECTRIC CANBERRA

The Canberra bomber made its inaugural flight on 13 May 1949. It continued in service with the Royal Air Force for over 40 years and remains operational with a number of countries today. The prototype photo-reconnaissance variant, the Canberra PR3, first flew on 19 March 1950, to be followed a month later by the conventional bomber, the Canberra B2. Capable of flying at speeds in excess of 870 km/h (540 mph) at an operational ceiling of 14 630 m (48 000 ft), the Canberra was an ideal platform for clandestine reconnaissance.

The 'legal' PR (photo-reconnaissance) versions were the PR.3, 7 and 9. The Mk 3 was similar to the original bomber, with increased fuel capacity and provision for up to seven cameras instead of bombs. The Mk 7 had slightly more powerful versions of the same engine and a very large further increase in fuel capacity. In 1956 PR.7s flew many secret missions over Egypt before and during the Anglo-French Suez campaign, losing an aircraft over Syria in October. Later they monitored the build-up of the Soviet fleet in the Mediterranean, and in 1976 were the first to spot the formidable cruiser/carrier *Kiev*. The final variant was the PR.9, built by Short & Harland in Belfast from 1958. This had much more powerful engines, a larger wing and many other new features, and could fly at slightly above 18 290 m (60 000 ft). This made interception very difficult, but offered no protection against missiles.

The 'illegal' versions, in that they were never announced and still remain cloaked in secrecy, were original PR.3 and PR.7 aircraft fitted with a Napier Double Scorpion rocket engine in the rear of the bomb bay. In August 1957 the twin-barrel auxiliary engine thrust one of the first conversions to a world-record height of 21 430 m (70 310 ft). All that was announced was that

The Canberra PR9 was developed with larger wings, enabling it to carry out sorties at extreme altitudes.   Popperfoto

Canberras thus equipped had sampled the clouds from nuclear tests over the Pacific, and that in 1958 two RAF flight lieutenants had set a world record for emergency escape when they parachuted from such an aircraft at 'well in excess of 56 000 ft'. What was not disclosed was that such aircraft repeatedly flew spy missions over the Soviet Union.

From 1982, all remaining photo-reconnaissance Canberras were based at RAF Wyton, where they formed part of No. 1 Photographic Reconnaissance Unit (PRU), overtly responsible for 'aerial cartography'. However, it is very convenient that the Joint Air Reconnaissance Intelligence Centre (JARIC), responsible for tasking all air imagery, is based at RAF Brampton, less than 16 km (10 miles) away. Until comparatively recently, specially modified Canberra B6 ELINT aircraft flew as part of No. 192 Squadron from RAF Wyton. The squadron was renumbered No. 51 Squadron in 1974, when the Canberras and their accompanying Comets were replaced by Nimrod R Mk 1 aircraft. The existence of these aircraft was never formally conceded by the Ministry of Defence when operational. However, two Canberra B6s now form part of the extensive gate-guard outside RAF Wyton.

THE MARTIN RB-57

The Martin B-57 was effectively the Canberra bomber built under licence for the US Air Force. The aircraft was developed into a high-altitude reconnaissance aircraft, the RB-57D amid the greatest secrecy under the code-name Project Black Knight. Four versions of the RB-57D were introduced. Series A and B, comprising six and seven models respectively, were designed for high-altitude photo-reconnaissance operations. Each aircraft was fitted with a minimum of two nose-mounted vertical K-38 cameras and two sideways-looking telescopic KC-1 cameras which were suitable for high-resolution photography at higher altitudes, in excess of 18 290 m (60 000 ft).

The six Series C aircraft were introduced for electronic espionage purposes and could be easily identified by radomes installed at the wingtips. The single Series D version, designated the RB-57D-1, was fitted with an AN/ANP-107 radar installation within its large black nose-radome and an APQ-56 high-resolution sideways-looking airborne radar (SLAR) in a sausage-shaped antenna under the fuselage. The most secret of all the RB-57Ds, it was designed to undertake covert night-time or bad weather radar reconnaissance missions behind the Iron Curtain.

Inevitably, an aircraft of so radical a design suffered from a number of weaknesses. The abnormally long wingspan of 32.31 m (106 ft)–32.77 m (107 ft 6 in)—for the ELINT series—led to structural problems and premature metal fatigue. At least one aircraft broke up in flight, while two others shed a wing on landing. With the exception of the first batch of six aircraft, all RB-57Ds were capable of aerial refuelling and were therefore theoretically capable of flying immense distances. However, cramped cockpit conditions, boredom (only the RB-57D-2 ELINT aircraft carried a second crewman) and the sheer discomfort of the pressure suits tended to reduce flights to less than 10 hours' duration.

In the late 1950s and early 1960s, as part of the 4025th Strategic Reconnaissance Squadron, and later as part of the 7407th Support Squadron USAF, B-57s flew a series of clandestine photographic and electronic espionage missions deep inside Warsaw Pact air space. During the second half of the 1960s the aircraft flew in excess of 1000 high-altitude surveillance sorties over Vietnam.

The RB-57D was a regular target for interceptions when on espionage missions over enemy territory. On 7 October 1959, an aircraft flying in Nationalist Chinese colours was intercepted over the coast of Communist China and shot down. A year later a second aircraft was also shot down over the Soviet Union, under circumstances which still remain shrouded in secrecy.

In March 1962, the Fort Worth Division of General Dynamics developed a radically new variant of the RB-57D. Designated the RB-57F, it was capable of flying at altitudes in excess of 24 385 m (80 000 ft) with a 2000 kg (4400 lb) payload. As such it was ideally suited to accept the latest generation of high-altitude, oblique cameras capable of taking recognisable photographs at a distance of some 97 km (60 miles).

For normal flight the RB-57F was powered by two wing-mounted Pratt & Whitney TF33-P11 engines. However, these were supplemented by two additional Pratt & Whitney J60-P9 engines mounted under the wing to give an additional 3000 kg (6615 lb) of thrust when needed. The aircraft's huge cantilever wings spanned 37.32 m (122 ft 5 in), almost twice the length of the fuselage which was 21.03 m (69 ft).

Under conditions of extreme secrecy two RB-57Fs were lent to the Pakistani Government for use against India. Using American ELINT installations, these aircraft were able to produce electronic maps of Indian radar installations during the build-up to the 1964–65 border war. One of the aircraft was nearly lost in September 1965, when it was attacked and badly damaged by two V750 (designated 'SA-2' by NATO) SAMs.

A second RB-57F fell victim to a Soviet V750 in December of the same year while photographing hostile coastal installations from the supposed safety of international air space over the Black Sea.

THE MODERN SPYPLANE

THE U-2 PHENOMENON

The Lockheed U-2 first flew operationally in 1955. It was designed to have a limited lifespan, yet it so effectively bridged the gap between tactical and strategic intelligence that it remained in service for over 35 years. The earliest batch of U-2s was delivered direct to the CIA, who in turn hired pilots from the cream of the US Air Force to provide them with at least a notional civilian status. Every effort was made to disguise the true purpose of the U-2. The first aircraft to arrive at the US Air Force base at Lakenheath in England flew under cover of the National Advisory Committee for Aeronautics (NACA) as part of the 1st Weather Reconnaissance Squadron (Provisional). NACA insisted that the U-2 was nothing more than an ultra-high-altitude scientific meteorological test bed, a fiction happily supported by the United States and British governments. The reality could not have been more different.

The U-2 was in fact a spy plane without peer. Its huge wing area (52.5 m²/565 ft²), coupled with its extreme lightness (7190kg/15 850 lb loaded) enabled it to soar to heights in excess of 27 432 m (90 000 ft), far in excess of any Warsaw Pact interceptor. Although superficially resembling a glider, the U-2 was in fact powered by a single Pratt & Whitney J57-P-37A jet engine with 4760 kg (10 495 lb) thrust. It could glide in an emergency, but did not do so otherwise, particularly not over hostile territory, as the pilot would have had to descend to 12 190 m (40 000 ft) to restart his engine, bringing it well within the range of hostile interceptors.

The first U-2 mission over Soviet territory was flown on 4 July 1956. The aircraft flew into friendly West German air space, ascending to over 21 335 m (70 000 ft) before turning east. The pilot entered Warsaw Pact air space over Czechoslovakia, continued east to Moscow, plotted a course north to Leningrad and thence west across the Baltic to Lakenheath. The flight,

A U-2 of the USAF, then operating from Upper Heyford, Oxfordshire.   Popperfoto

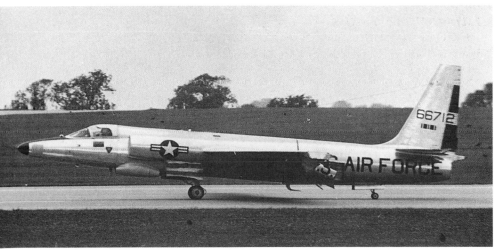

which had been personally authorised by President Eisenhower, was a great success, producing thousands of needle-sharp photographs of Soviet military installations and production centres.

A second Weather Reconnaissance Squadron (Provisional) was formed at Incirlik Airfield near Adana in Turkey and a third at Atsugi in Japan. To frustrate Soviet counter-intelligence, aircraft destined for penetrative espionage missions first flew to one of a number of closely guarded Operating Locations (OLs), such as Wiesbaden and Giebelstadt in Germany, Peshawar and Lahore in Pakistan and Bodø in Norway.

Operation Overflight

Between 1956 and 1960 CIA U-2s flew with impunity over the Soviet Union. The Kremlin protested, but always in secret lest the unpreparedness of its aerial defences became public. In its turn Washington simply denied the very existence of such an aircraft. 'Operation Overflight', the collective code-name given to the hundreds of U-2 border incursions into Warsaw Pact air space and the estimated 30 long-range flights over the Soviet Union itself, furnished the United States with a wealth of invaluable intelligence.

The Soviet strategic bomber fleet was found to be far less powerful than originally feared, reducing to some degree its perceived ability to deliver its recently acquired nuclear weapons. U-2s from Detachment 10-10 based at Incirlik discovered the existence of 8K38 ('SS-3') and 8K63 ('SS-4') medium-range surface-to-surface missile batteries at Kapustin Yar, north of the Caspian Sea. Subsequently an aircraft from the same detachment discovered an 8K78 ('SS-6') test site at Tyuratam, east of the Aral Sea.

Wreckage of four Taiwanese U-2, on public display in China.   Popperfoto

By no means all U-2 flights were confined to anti-Warsaw Pact espionage. Frequent missions were flown over the Mediterranean, Gulf and Middle East. The Arab–Israeli War and the Franco–British build-up to the Suez invasion in 1956 were closely monitored by a far-from-supportive CIA and the first hostilities were actually witnessed by an overflying U-2.

CIA U-2s were not only employed in photographic-espionage duties. Aircraft from the 3rd WRS(P) base at Atsugi in Japan, and from OLs in Bodø in Norway, Okinawa in the Pacific and Eielson in Alaska, were also deployed into the upper atmosphere to 'sniff' for fall-out from Soviet, French and British nuclear tests.

ELINT flights, equipped with extremely sensitive radio and radar receivers, flew a large number of missions along potentially hostile borders in the hope of provoking a reaction from the radar and SAM sites. The US Air Force flew a number of (for once) highly publicised flights as part of its High Altitude Sampling Program (HASP) to monitor worldwide nuclear fall-out.

Francis Gary Powers

On 1 May 1960, a U-2 aircraft flown by CIA pilot Francis Gary Powers was shot down near Sverdlovsk. Powers took off from Peshawar in Pakistan for a flight of 5955 km (3700 miles) across the Soviet Union to the OL at Bodø in Norway. His route was to take him via the missile test centre at Tyuratam; the industrial complexes at Sverdlovsk and Kirov and the naval and defensive installations at Archangel, Severodvinsk, Kandalaska and Murmansk.

Powers flew a structurally strengthened and up-engined U-2B powered by a Pratt & Whitney J75-P-13 jet engine, generating 7160 kg (15 785 lb) thrust. Empty, the U-2B could exceed heights of 27 432 m (90 000 ft). However, with its extra fuel load and bulky camera equipment, it was limited to an altitude of 22 860 m (75 000 ft). As he took off from Peshawar a second U-2 from Incirlik flew a diversionary flight along the Soviet border.

As the fragile U-2 reached Sverdlovsk it was shaken by a violent blast and went into a spin from which Powers could not recover. He ejected but was unable to destroy his aircraft (to the annoyance of many in the CIA), landing safely on Soviet soil. The Soviets' first widely deployed surface-to-air missile, the V-750 ('SA-2'), had claimed its first victim.

The repercussions were as drastic as they were immediate. Not knowing that Powers had survived, Washington embarked upon a desperate damage-limitation exercise. It was claimed that an unarmed and wholly innocent U-2 reconnaissance aircraft working for NASA had inadvertently strayed across the Turkish border into Soviet air space.

However, when it was announced that Powers had survived and had admitted his espionage mission, and when photographs of the aircraft wreckage were released, clearly demonstrating the remains of a Hycon Model 73B camera with its 900 mm lens, Washington was forced to concede at least part of the truth. Krushchev walked out of the Paris International Summit in disgust and Eisenhower was forced to undertake publicly not to fly further espionage missions over the Soviet Union. With the advent of defensive missiles the viability of future missions was in any case problematical. Powers was tried for espionage and imprisoned by the Soviets, but released two years later.

The U-2s were almost immediately withdrawn to the United States and the CIA OL bases surrounding the Soviet Union closed down. However, within two months the aircraft were once again operational. Two aircraft were secretly transferred to Taiwan and six Nationalist Chinese pilots trained in their use. For the next few years these aircraft regularly overflew the Communist Chinese mainland, providing the CIA with a wealth of intelligence on Chinese missile development.

A Cuban airfield showing Il-28 Beagle bombers and SA-2 SAM site, photographed by U-2s in 1962. (Right) Oblique photograph of a medium-range missile site in Cuba 1962.

Popperfoto

The operation was jeopardised in September 1962 when one of the U-2s disappeared under mysterious circumstances. Washington was forced to concede her involvement in the initial provision of the aircraft, but refused to intervene in domestic Taiwanese matters by attempting to stop the espionage flights. In reality United States involvement increased. On 1 November 1963, a second Taiwanese U-2 crashed near Shanghai. A third aircraft was destroyed on 7 July 1964, a fourth on 10 January 1965 and a fifth on 8 September 1967. How many U-2 espionage aircraft were ultimately delivered to Taiwan remains a closely guarded secret, although it has been suggested that the number probably totalled nine.

The Cuban Missile Crisis
United States paranoia about all matters Cuban was never stronger than in the 1960s. It reached a peak in August 1962 when a routine U-2 overflight of the island brought back photographs of two previously unknown 'SA-2' missile sites. Thoroughly alarmed, President Kennedy called for increased U-2 surveillance. However, he was almost immediately frustrated by a Congressional demand for a moratorium in response to highly embarrassing, if wholly unrelated, U-2 incidents in Europe and the Far East.

When the flights recommenced in early October they produced evidence of frantic construction work throughout the island. US Air Force U-2s from the 4028th Strategic Reconnaissance Squadron based at Laughlin AFB, Texas, were ordered to augment the CIA U-2s to maintain round-the-clock surveillance. On 14 October 1962, a U-2E flown by Major Steve Heyser, USAF, photographed an 8K63 ('SS-4 Sandal') surface-to-surface missile site near San Cristobal, west of Havana. Within a few days a total of nine SS-4 missile sites, and about 40 Il-28 bombers, old but none the less capable of nuclear delivery, were discovered on the island.

On 22 October, Kennedy announced a maritime blockade of Cuba which would last until all Soviet offensive missiles and bombers had left the island. The world held its breath. Would Krushchev risk war rather than face a climbdown? Only a very few in the highest echelons of Government knew that Oleg Penkovsky had already intimated that the Soviet Union was in no position to fight a nuclear war. On 29 October, Krushchev relented and ordered the dismantling of the missile sites.

The Lockheed U-2R
The U-2R entered service in 1968, but remained a closely guarded secret for several years thereafter. With its extended-span wing, longer fuselage and underwing equipment pods it was effectively a new aircraft.

Unsolicited U-2 flights over hostile territory diminished in the 1970s as surface-to-air missile technology improved. Cyprus-based U-2Rs monitored the Suez Canal zone in 1970 and the Sinai demilitarised zone in 1973, but were withdrawn when Egypt threatened to treat the aircraft as hostile and therefore legitimate targets for its SAMs.

The final version of the U-2 family to enter service, the TR-1, first flew in September 1981 and, with completely new General Electric engines, remains in current service. A flight of TR-1As continues to fly non-attributable sorties from RAF Alconbury, in Cambridgeshire, but are likely soon to be withdrawn to the United States. Heavier than the U-2R, the single-seater TR-1 features an interchangeable nose and a different-pattern dorsal UHF antenna. It carries an improved ECM (Electronic Counter Measures) system and an advanced synthetic-aperture radar system (ASARS) based on the UPD-X sideways-looking airborne radar (SLAR).

The latest TR-1A carries extensive new avionics in its pods, together with more comprehensive ECM. Additional equipment is carried in the nose, in the Q-bay behind the cockpit and between the inlet ducts. To facilitate maximum-endurance flights the pilot is provided with special facilities for his personal comfort and the intake of warm food. Even so, he can expect to lose 1 kg (2.2 lb) per mission.

LOCKHEED SR-71 'BLACKBIRD'

Until the recent advent of radar absorbing stealth technology the Lockheed SR-71 Blackbird was without doubt the most unusual, and in most respects advanced, aircraft in the world. Developed by C.L. 'Kelly' Johnson and his Lockheed Advanced Projects team at its famous 'Skunk Works' as a replacement for the U-2 a total of 32 models were built, of which all but two were two-seaters. Lockheed flew the first prototype, designated the A-12, in complete secrecy on 26 April 1962. Deliveries of the A-12 began later that year with a total of 15 models being built. The improved SR-71 flew on 22 December 1964, entering service with Strategic Air Command on 7 January 1966.

An experimental YF-12A interceptor variant was flown in August 1963 but never adopted for service. When the existence of the YF-12A became public knowledge in February 1964 the press were granted limited access to the aircraft. Photographs were released of the doomed interceptor in the hopes that they would divert press attention away from the still top secret A-12. However, the lack of an obvious test programme, coupled with the cloak of secrecy surrounding the project's funding, left the media experts sceptical.

Resultant publicity surrounding the new Lockheed aircraft caused President Johnson to

The SR-71 Blackbird, on public display at Farnborough after crossing the Atlantic in 1 hr 55 min 4 s. Popperfoto

make a statement on 25 July 1964, formally conceding the aircraft's existence. He told the world that the United States had a new strategic reconnaissance aircraft capable of speeds in excess of 3219 km/h (2000 mph) at 27 432 m (90 000 ft). However, he admitted none of its production history nor its true purpose.

The original A-12 was a single-seater aircraft of titanium construction. It had a small delta wing and two very powerful Pratt & Whitney JT11D-20 jet engines. When flying at its maximum speed of Mach 3+ (much faster than a bullet) the temperature of its fuselage rose to 650°C (1202°F) causing it to expand almost 80 mm (3 in) in length. The resultant fuel spillage when parked and taxiing was alarming, but not dangerous, as the Shell JP-7 kerosene specially formulated for the engines had an extremely high flash-point.

The CIA have never admitted that the A-12 was built for other than test purposes. However, it seems extremely unlikely that Lockheed should have been asked to build 15 identical prototypes. It is known that at least six A-12 'Blackbirds' crashed between 1963 and 1968, an undisclosed number of them abroad, and it therefore seems almost impossible that the aircraft was not involved in clandestine operations. A-12s were certainly operational from an OL at Kadena airbase, Okinawa, from August 1967. Given that Eisenhower kept his promise, made after the Powers incident in 1960, not to overfly Soviet air space, these A-12s can only have been targeted at China or North Korea.

The last CIA A-12 flight took place on 5 June 1968. The Lockheed SR-71 was first flown overtly by USAF pilots from 4200 Strategic Reconnaissance Wing, subsequently renamed the 9th Strategic Reconnaissance Wing, in early 1967. It is highly likely that the CIA flew the aircraft on top-secret missions before then, but this has never been firmly established.

At 32.74 m (107 ft) the SR-71 is longer than the A-12, allowing more space for fuel and additional reconnaissance systems. It has a stated top speed of 3380 km/h (2100 mph) and altitude ceiling of 24 384 m (80 000 ft), although many regard these figures as conservative. The 55 000 litres (12 100 gallons) of fuel carried offers an estimated range, flying at maximum speed, of 5000 km (3100 miles) although, in practice, the aircraft is refuelled from a KC-135Q aerial tanker every two to three hours. An SR-71 set a world record in September 1974 when it flew from New York to London in 1 hour 55 minutes and 42 seconds, and non-stop from London to Los Angeles in 3 hours 47 minutes and 39 seconds.

A series of cameras, sideways-looking radars and ELINT systems are carried by the SR-71 in its five equipment bays in the fuselage chines and nose. A combination of oblique long-focal-length cameras, a nose-mounted panoramic camera and 1524 mm (60-in) focal-length LOROP cameras allow the aircraft to photograph 258 980 km² (100 000 miles²) at 24 384 m (80 000 ft). However, the standard of imagery of much of this outer coverage is of limited application.

Early Espionage Flights

Throughout the late 1960s and 1970s two or three SR-71 aircraft based at Kadena AFB, Okinawa kept a constant surveillance of China and North Korea, invoking in excess of 500 formal objections from the Chinese. Keen not to fall foul of the Korean Military Armistice Commission, the aircraft did not actually overfly North Korea. Instead they kept a constant check on the 4 km (2½ mile) demilitarised zone, using their ultra-sensitive infra-red cameras to search for newly dug infiltration tunnels. Other aircraft flying from Kadena in Thailand overflew North Vietnam and southern China in a vain attempt to monitor North Vietnamese Army (NVA) build ups and provide targets for the conventional B-52 bombers.

During the 1973 Arab–Israeli conflict, intelligence gained by SR-71 reconnaissance placed the CIA on the horns of a dilemma. During a high-altitude pass over the Negev Desert, an aircraft flying from Beale AFB gathered irrefutable evidence that Israel was about to arm its Jericho missiles with nuclear warheads. Two Israeli F-4 Phantoms were scrambled and attempted unsuccessfully to intercept the SR-71, which returned safely to the United States.

President Nixon was forced to inform 1st Secretary Brezhnev of his discovery, and advise him to sanction the movement of Soviet nuclear warheads to the SS-1 Scud-B sites ringing Cairo and the Aswan Dam. With both sides similarly equipped the principle of mutually assured destruction (MAD) would have been invoked, avoiding superpower intervention. Before Brezhnev could react the Israelis scored a series of resounding victories, obviating the necessity for escalation.

SR-71 overflights of Cuba were curtailed by President Carter as an act of good faith in January 1977. However, two years later they were reintroduced by President Reagan, when it was discovered that the Soviets had supplied Castro with a squadron of MiG-23 'Flogger' aircraft. Although MiG-23s were deployed conventionally in the fighter-ground attack and interceptor roles, certain variants could be used in a limited nuclear role and it was felt imperative to ensure that the aircraft in Castro's possession were not of this type.

Reagan attempted to gain public support for his actions by televising photographs taken by an SR-71 of the MiG-23s on the ground and of a large Soviet eavesdropping facility near Lourdes in western Cuba. However, the imagery which the Pentagon would agree to release was so old and of such poor quality that Reagan failed to stir the national paranoia. The anticipated outcry did not follow and, when it was discovered that the MiG-23s were purely conventional, the surveillance was dropped.

During the 1980s, a detachment of SR-71s was based at RAF Mildenhall in East Anglia, from where it regularly flew reconnaissance missions into the Baltic or along the Inner German Border. However, keeping this elderly aircraft operational was by then proving increasingly demanding. When it was announced that the cost of maintaining the surviving fleet of 12 aircraft equated to the cost of maintaining two entire wings of conventional fighters, pressure was put on the Pentagon to reassess the SR-71's future. The numbers maintained in operational state were reduced from 12 to 6 and, in 1989, plans to retire the remaining aircraft were announced. The SR-71 was finally phased out in the spring of 1990. Three aircraft were passed to NASA's Dryden Flight Research facility and a further 6 mothballed.

THE RC-135

Superficially the Boeing RC-135 electronic reconnaissance aircraft is completely innocuous. Although numerous versions of it have been flying in USAF Strategic Air Command service since 1964 it has attracted none of the notoriety of the far more outwardly sinister U-2 or the SR- 71.

The Kamchatka Incident

Had it not been for the highly regrettable destruction of a Korean Air Lines Boeing 747 over the Kamchatka Peninsula, with the resultant loss of 269 lives, it is highly unlikely that many non-experts would know of the existence of this veritable wolf in sheep's clothing, the RC-135, today.

After the incident the Soviets argued that the pilot of the Sukhoi Su-15 which had shot down the civilian aircraft had mistaken it for a military RC-135. Chief of the General Staff Marshal Nikolai Ogarkov produced a large radar trace showing the course of both aircraft. He

A USAF RC-135 ELINT aircraft at Mildenhall, England.   Guy Taylor

showed that at one point their radar images had merged, and that Chief of Staff of Soviet Air Defence Colonel-General Romanov had therefore been correct in ordering the interception and shooting down of the 'spy' aircraft. Ogarkov made no attempt to say why the highly experienced Sukhoi pilot had failed to differentiate between a Boeing 747 and the significantly different, smaller military Boeing RC-135 on a clear night and at a relatively close range, nor why he had not attempted to order the interloper to land.

The United States conceded that an RC-135 had carried out a reconnaissance mission east of Kamchatka earlier, and had indeed crossed the KAL 747's flight-path at a distance of 120 km (75 miles). The RC-135 had, however, returned to its base in Alaska and been on the ground for an hour at the time of the incident. Even with the advent of Glasnost and the demise of the Soviet Union the full truth behind the tragedy is never likely to be made public. It is probable, however, that the death of so many innocent people was caused by a fundamental miscalculation on the part of an unusually edgy Soviet pilot and ground control (Romanov was subsequently dismissed).

There is little doubt that so experienced a crew as the 747s could never unknowingly have strayed so far from track, especially in such a sensitive area. The RC-135 has neither the speed nor the altitude to violate the air space of a sophisticated adversary. It tends therefore to fly along established flight paths. Crews might occasionally deviate from an established course to monitor their target's electronic response, but will take immediate evasive action when challenged.

The RC-135 is superficially similar to the Boeing 707 civil airliner. However, a close inspection will clearly identify it as a military aircraft. Most of the numerous variants have a thimble-shaped nose radome, narrow fairings for SLAR on the forward fuselage and dipole antennae arranged around the front fuselage.

Three RC-135Cs, converted and redesignated RC-135Us in 1971, have also been fitted with a distinctive chin-mounted radome, a small ventral radome, reworked wingtips housing antennae, an ovoid fairing at the top of the rudder and an extended tailcone. Seven RC-135Cs were rebuilt between 1973 and 1977 to create the -135V with a standard 'thimble' nose and a series of large ventrally mounted blade antennae. All models carry a crew of between 20 and

30 COMINT and SIGINT specialists and are fitted with in-flight refuelling probes to facilitate extended flights when necessary.

The United States has always admitted the existence of the RC-135, but has never released details about its operational missions. Notwithstanding this, it is known that during the 1980s, RC-135s attached to the 24th Strategic Reconnaissance Squadron, a part of the 6th Strategic Wing based at Eielson, Alaska, undertook highly specialised Telemetry Intelligence (TELINT) duties. Soviet missiles fired from the test beds at Tyuratam and Plesetsk were monitored en route to their target areas in the Sea of Okhotsk. Telemetry information relating to the missile's performance and precision transmitted to Soviet ground stations was intercepted for subsequent decoding and analysis by the National Security Agency at Fort Meade, Maryland.

More conventional communications and signals intelligence gathering flights were undertaken until recently from Mildenhall in Suffolk. Aircraft attached to the 922nd Support Squadron at Hellenikon near Athens still monitor Middle East and North African activity, while RC-135s from the 82nd Strategic Reconnaissance Squadron at Kadena Airbase on Okinawa continue to fly eavesdropping missions along the coasts of China, the former Soviet Union, North Korea and Vietnam.

THE RUSSIAN RESPONSE

It would be wholly wrong, and dangerous in the extreme, to think that Russian aerial espionage died with the Cold War. The former Soviet Union regarded itself as encircled by enemies jointly plotting its ultimate downfall. It was conscious of the fact that it was surrounded by powerful listening stations and that its airspace, and more particularly that of its satellites, was constantly being overflown. Not unnaturally it retaliated.

The Baltic Experience

Throughout the 1970s and 1980s, the Baltic became a focal point for aerial espionage. In 1974, the RAF introduced the Nimrod R1 into the Baltic as a replacement for the elderly Comet R2. Flying from RAF Wyton, near Huntingdon, the Nimrods officially undertook 'radar and radar calibration' duties, but in fact flew ELINT missions along the western and southern borders of the Warsaw Pact countries.

To the annoyance of the Swedes, flights were undertaken deep into the Baltic, occasionally violating the neutral's air space (there were no fewer than 48 recorded violations in the third quarter of 1979 alone—45 of them by NATO aircraft!). USAF SR-71s and Boeing RC-135s, West German Marineflieger (Naval Air Service) Atlantics and at least one French Air Force DC-8 also operated in the same area, presumably without recourse to each other and certainly with scant regard to civil airline routes. Near misses were common, occasionally involving Aeroflot civil aircraft flying lawfully within international air corridors.

The Soviet Union regarded the Baltic as a closed lake. It could not prevent NATO espionage incursions into the area, but none the less ensured that its own presence remained constantly high. The recently acquired independent status of Latvia, Lithuania and Estonia has reduced to a degree modern Russia's pre-eminence in the area, but has far from removed it completely.

Prior to the disintegration of the Warsaw Pact, squadrons of bombers would carry out simulated missions over the Baltic to within a few minutes' flying distance of Danish territorial waters. Simultaneously, Tu-16 'Badger-E' and Tu-22 'Blinder-C' photo-reconnaissance aircraft from Aviatsiya Voenno Morskovo Flota (AVMF), the Soviet naval aviation arm, supported by 'Badger-D, -F and -K' ELINT aircraft, would monitor the sortie, testing the NATO radar reaction.

Up to 66 AVMF electronic and photo-reconnaissance aircraft were based in the Baltic, constantly probing both Swedish and NATO defences, particularly the advanced NATO monitoring post on Bornholm.

More routine electronic reconnaissance was undertaken by a fleet of approximately 20 four-engined Antonov An-12 'Cub-B' and Ilyushin Il-20 'Coot-A' aircraft. The 'Coot-A', which was first sighted in 1978, was a Soviet equivalent of the Boeing RC-135. It was adapted from obsolescent civil and military transport airframes and has undergone few changes since its introduction. Despite its age, noise and superficial lack of sophistication it remains a potent ELINT espionage asset.

A large cylindrical container beneath the forward fuselage of the 'Coot-A' houses a J-band SLAR antenna. Smaller canoe-shaped fairings on either side of the forward fuselage just aft of the flight deck may house secondary SLAR antennae or electro-optical sensors. Several light-coloured rectangular fibreglass panels, three on either side of the aft fuselage and a seventh mounted in the starboard rear door of the cargo hold, act as radio transparencies for wide-angle microwave antennae used to monitor radar and radio radar transmissions in the flightpath.

Air Early Warning

The Tupolev Tu-126 'Moss', a military variant of the now redundant Tu-114 civil airliner, was operated in the Baltic as a flying radar station. Easily identifiable by its large flat radome (NATO code-name 'Flat Jack'), the Tu-126 fulfilled the same functions as the NATO E-3 Sentry AWACS aircraft but with a much lesser capability. The Tu-126, of which only 12 were built, served with the Russian air-defence command, by whom it was used as an airborne radar co-ordination station.

The Beriev A-50 began to replace the elderly Tu-126 in the Baltic in 1984. Production problems with its radar caused delays with the aircraft's introduction, although there are now

A Nimrod MR1 maritime reconnaissance aircraft.   Topham

some 50 models operational. The 'Mainstay' is based on the highly successful Il-76 transport aircraft. The rotodome is located much further forward than on the Tu-126 or E-3, and a radome replaces the traditional glazed nose fitting of the Il-76, while a refuelling probe has been added to the upper surface of the nose.

Unlike most Russian transports, 'Mainstay' has no tail gun position. Its tail cone terminates in a small radome, probably designed to accept an EW system. A new IFF (identification friend or foe) system has been fitted, and the aircraft is extensively fitted with EW equipment, most of it ESM gear intended to detect targets beyond radar range, or to allow the aircraft to operate in passive mode. Unlike the Tu-126, 'Mainstay' is able to detect low-flying targets the size of cruise missiles over any terrain.

CIVIL ESPIONAGE

AEROFLOT

Until the disintegration of the Soviet Union, Aeroflot, the Soviet national airline, was the biggest airline in the world. It was founded as Dobrolet in March 1923, commencing its first internal flight, between Moscow and Nizhniy Novgorod, in July of the same year. It was renamed Aeroflot in 1932. Despite acute fuel shortages and inherent financial problems parts of it continue to operate under the auspices of the new Russian Republic. Smaller republics have formed their own airlines.

The company undertook far more than conventional national and international flights. It was responsible for fire-fighting patrols, air mapping, medical transport, fishing and ice patrols. In practice, the dividing line between Russian civil and military aviation is blurred. Aeroflot helicopters are painted in grey camouflage and many of its transports are identical to aircraft in military service, which they supplement as necessary. Many pilots hold commissions in the Air Force reserve. In short, Aeroflot was ideally suited to large-scale espionage.

For many years Aeroflot took blatant advantage of NATO's unwillingness to intercept civil airliners clearly deviating from their flight path. Even when cameras were spotted in the fuselage of such aircraft seen 'accidentally' overflying defence installations, the Soviets knew that no action would be taken.

On 8 November 1981, Aeroflot Flight 315, en route from Moscow to Washington via New York, blatantly wandered from its usual flight path. Instead of flying along the east coast of America it flew inland, passing over a squadron of Strategic Air Command FB-111 bombers and several defence installations at Pease Air Force Base. Despite warnings to return to its course it continued its espionage activities, overflying the naval ship building yard at Groton, Connecticut, at the very time that work was being carried out on the US Navy's first Ohio-class Trident submarine.

To add insult to injury the Aeroflot Il-62 'accidentally' followed an identical route during the homeward flight. When questioned, the Soviets blamed Canadian Air Traffic Control for the problems encountered on the inward flight, and unspecified air traffic difficulties for the 'confusion' which had occurred en route home to Moscow. In retaliation, the State Department ordered a ban on all Aeroflot aircraft from flying over United States territory for one week! When martial law was subsequently proclaimed in Poland, the State Department at last felt sufficiently confident to act realistically and banned Aeroflot flights completely.

The Soviet Union regularly used military transport aircraft flown by crews from the Military Transport Aviation, or VTA (Voeyenno Transportnaya Aviatsya), to carry international relief supplies. Adorned as they were with civilian registration numbers and the Aeroflot emblem, these aircraft were given virtual *carte blanche* to fly (and spy) almost anywhere.

During a humanitarian airlift to Peru giant Aeroflot An-22 freighters undertook detailed espionage operations over Sweden, Iceland and Greenland. During the months of July, August and September 1970 the Soviets made 53 relief-supply flights to Peru, refuelling at the Icelandic base of Keflavik en route. When it was noticed that the Aeroflot pilots were flying in unusually wide circles before landing at Keflavik, 'coincidentally' taking them over a number of US Air Force facilities, fighters were scrambled to investigate.

It was discovered that every third group of civilian freighters was accompanied by a Tupolev Tu-95 'Bear' bomber. As the freighters veered off for Keflavik, the bomber continued on its flight path, photographing targets of opportunity before turning and heading for home. Only after the Americans began to meet, and monitor, every incoming group of Soviet relief aircraft over international waters did this practice cease. Subsequently it was reported by the Swedish authorities that 21 of the 53 flights had deviated from the normal course over Swedish territory, and in ten cases had overflown radar and other military installations.

Civil aerial espionage was occasionally undertaken by proxy. In February 1983, the Italians intercepted Libyan aircraft flying outside the normal air routes. In September of that year a Bulgarian Tu-134 was intercepted over Swiss airspace.

THE WESTERN RESPONSE

In fairness to the Russians, and before them the Soviets, it should not be assumed that they held a monopoly of civil airline espionage. In the 1970s, it is alleged that Air France Caravelle jet airliners, crewed by highly experienced pilots in the employ of Service 7, frequently got lost en route to Moscow. In more than 100 instances they were able to take extremely useful photographs from the cockpit window, discovering five new missile bases in the process. This activity has always been denied by both France and Russia. However, Service 7 was set up within SDECE specifically to obtain accurate intelligence on foreign countries from domestic sources. The taking of clandestine photographs by Frenchmen abroad would therefore appear to fall neatly within its remit.

In 1992, France was accused of targeting a number of her allies in her on-going search for commercial and industrial intelligence. It is known that Service 7 was, at one time, ordered by General de Gaulle to intercept United States diplomatic intelligence. It is quite possible therefore that this most secretive of clandestine organisations is continuing to use all means possible, including civil airlines, to further its aims.

REMOTELY PILOTED VEHICLES

Remotely Piloted Vehicles (RPVs), or drones, are highly cost-effective. Relatively cheap to manufacture and easy to maintain they make ideal spotters for long-range artillery or fighter ground attack aircraft. They can also be used as aerial targets and, in extreme cases, flying bombs. In these days of increasing battlefield fluidity, their ability to produce intelligence quickly makes them a paramount source of short-range information.

There is no simple definition of an RPV or drone. They are basically unmanned aircraft with a configuration similar to an aeroplane, and whose flight path can be controlled. The category does not include ballistic or guided missiles. However, cruise missiles, from which many drones have been evolved, are a borderline case.

THE EARLY DRONE

The Royal Navy introduced its first operational drone, the radio-controlled 'Queen Bee', in 1934. The first reconnaissance drone followed in 1939. The Soviet Lavochkin design bureau developed a remote-controlled variant of the Yak-25RD 'Mandrake' high-altitude reconnaissance aircraft in the mid-1960s. This was quickly followed by the 'Yastreb' (Eagle) reconnaissance-ELINT RPV. The Yastreb was launched from a mobile rocket launcher and could be radio-controlled or set to follow a pre-programmed course. Powered by a single Tumansky R-31 engine it had an operational ceiling of between 27 430 and 30 500 m (90 000 and 100 000 ft), a range of 1000 km (620 miles) and a top speed exceeding 3500 km/h (2175 mph).

The Yastreb provided the Soviets with their main European reconnaissance system until the mid-1970s. However, the advent of satellite reconnaissance coupled with the fear of compromise limited its deployment to national emergencies.

Drone development in the West, accelerated with the worsening situation in Cuba and the escalation of the war in Vietnam. The United States produced the Ryan AQM-34 (Model 147) in over 20 versions, including one with a droppable payload. It was used extensively over China, North Vietnam, Laos and North Korea, flying some 3000 missions and taking an estimated 127 million photographs. Scores were shot down over China and North Vietnam, but because Peking and Hanoi could exhibit only dismembered and highly anonymous wreckage, and because no pilots could be produced—dead or alive—the United States was able to continue to deny all accusations of espionage.

Attempts were made in 1962 to convert a number of old post-World War II Ryan Firebee 1 target drones to aerial espionage use. In the greatest secrecy, four Model 147A RPV conversions were tested with 4080th Strategic Reconnaissance Wing, but with limited success. Their use at the time of the Cuban missile crisis was contemplated but ultimately abandoned.

The shooting down of a manned U-2 over Cuba on 27 October 1962 provided the impetus for the construction of a radically new RPV. The Ryan Model 147B, code-named the Lightning Bug, had an extended wingspan of 9.14 m (30 ft) (as opposed to 3.96 m [13 ft] in earlier models). Its greater speed and improved ceiling of 18 900 m (62 000 ft) gave it a far greater chance of survivability against SAMs and intercepting aircraft yet in no way diminished the resolution of the photographs taken.

The Model 147B flew its first espionage mission, over southern China, on 20 August 1964. It was launched from a DC-130 Hercules 'mother aircraft' near the Chinese island of Hainan and was recovered by parachute over the Taiwanese airbase at Toayuan. In October 1964, the 4080th Strategic Reconnaissance Wing RPV unit moved to Bien Hoa in Vietnam, from where it operated in close cooperation with a flight of U-2 manned aircraft from the same wing.

THE VIETNAM EXPERIENCE

The majority of Lightning Bug flights over Vietnam took place between November 1964 and April 1975. High-altitude flights were undertaken by the AQM-34N (Ryan 147H). Powered by a boosted Teledyne CAE J69 jet engine, the AQM-34N was capable of flying at an altitude of nearly 21 336 m (70 000 ft). Its nose-mounted 600 mm tele-lens Hycon 233A camera could photograph an area 1400 km by 28.6 km (870 miles by 24 miles) in 885 pictures.

From January 1969, the AQM-34L (Ryan 147SC) Buffalo Hunter flew thousands of low-level missions over North Vietnam and southern China. Far more accurate than the larger RPVs, which occasionally veered too far off course to make their imagery usable, the Buffalo Hunter could be relied upon to bring back aerial photographs of the highest quality. It flew at no more than 700 km/h (435 mph), usually at altitudes as low as 245 m (800 ft), and was thus a frustrating target for Communist fighter pilots, who had great difficulty in locating its camouflaged outline.

RPVs were occasionally used as decoys to monitor North Vietnamese 'SA-2' launch sequences. Modified craft were deliberately programmed to overfly the sites in the hope that a missile would be launched to intercept them. Essential information about the missile's guidance system was then relayed back to a ground station as the warhead approached and detonated.

Other electronic reconnaissance missions were carried out between 1970 and 1975 from the South Korean airbase at Osan. Approximately 500 Communication Intelligence (COMINT) flights were undertaken by Ryan AQM-34R (Model 147TE) RPVs to intercept radio transmissions from the Chinese and North Korean military.

ISRAELI RPVS

Israel has long been interested in the RPV as a clandestine intelligence gatherer. The Mastiff 1, which entered service in 1979, was quickly replaced by the second-generation Tadiran/Israel Electronics Industries Ltd Mastiff Mk 2. Configured with a twin-boom tail, high wing and pusher engine, the Mk 2, which weighed less than 100 kg (220 lb), could carry a 25 kg (55 lb) sensor load for four hours at a height of 3000 m (9840 ft). It was catapulted into the air along an inclined ramp fitted to the back of a standard army truck; retrieval was by way of a tail hook and arrester wire arrangement.

Successful deployment of the Mastiff 2 has led Israel to expend considerable resources on the development of an updated Mastiff 3 and on the Scout RPV surveillance platform. Scout adopts the same configuration and basic design as Mastiff 3 but is larger. It has a length of 3.7 m (12 ft 2 in), a span of 3.6 m (11 ft 9 in), weighs 118 kg (260 lb) on take-off and can carry a 45 kg (90 lb) payload. The 18 hp twin-cylinder engine, driving a pusher propeller, is mounted at the rear of the square section, aluminium fuselage. It has a maximum speed of 147 km/h (92 mph), a ceiling of just over 3050 m (10 000 ft), can remain airborne for 4.5 hours and has an operational range of up to 100 km (62 miles) from base. The Scout's Taman optical payload is so well gyro-stabilised that turbulence and turns occasioned by changes in course are not noticeable.

The base comprises a truck-mounted, air-conditioned ground control station with provision for a pilot, who sets the altitude, speed and bearing by remote control. Data is fed via a roof-mounted command uplink antenna and received via a downlink antenna. If communications are lost the Scout is programmed to climb to a pre-set height and, if communication is not re-established within four minutes, sets an independent course for home. A navigator, co-located with the pilot, constantly updates the RPV's position in relation to a 1:125 scale map, while an observer controls the cameras and other equipment. A Scout unit comprises five RPVs, a ground control station, launcher, retrieval net and 12 personnel.

The Scout came into its own in the loiter-surveillance role during the 1982 operations against PLO sites in the Lebanon. It provided real-time electro-optical and digital data links between Syrian positions and Israeli battle commanders in the field, continuously observing SAM site activities and aircraft on the ground. Live TV coverage was provided for target assignment and threat identification and decoys were also flown to provoke target illumination by SAM acquisition radars.

EUROPEAN DEVELOPMENT

The Canadair CL-89 reconnaissance drone (NATO designation AN/USD-501) first flew in 1964 and was introduced into the German Army in 1970. It became the most widely used battlefield surveillance RPV in Europe. It has seen service with the armies of Canada, France, Italy, West Germany and the United Kingdom, and was battle-tested in the Gulf War (as the British 1st Armoured Division's only direct aerial reconnaissance vehicle) and is only now being replaced.

Designed for maximum survivability, the USD-501 uses a missile format rather than the more conventional aircraft configuration. Launch is by means of a Bristol Aerojet Wagtail rocket booster assembly with in-flight power being provided by a Williams WR2-6 turbojet. At launch, the USD-501/booster combination has a length of 3.73 m (12 ft 3 in), which reduces to 2.6 m (8 ft 6 in) for the basic vehicle in flight. Maximum range varies between 58 km (36 miles) and 69 km (43 miles) across the front line, depending on whether or not extra fuel tanks are fitted, at speeds of up to 740 km/h (460 mph). Normal operational height is between 305 and 1220 m (1000 and 4000 ft).

Sensor loads comprise either a Carl Zeiss KRG 8/24 tri-lens camera or a BAe Type 201 linescan unit, both carried in quick-change packs mounted centrally within the vehicle's airframe. A single strip of vertical infra-red line scan (IRLS) imagery or a reel of three overlapping negatives (giving near horizon-to-horizon coverage across the flight track) are produced. For night photography, up to 12 flares can be carried in a bay above and behind the sensor pack. A pre-programmed control system handles altitude, navigation and sensor operation. The USD-501 is recovered by beacon. A parachute deploys from the bottom of the RPV, inverting the airframe to protect the sensors, and air bags inflate before impact to cushion the landing.

The CL-289 (NATO designation AN/USD-502) entered service with Canada, France and the former West Germany as a replacement for the USD-501. Although it resembles the latter in construction and mission programme, it enjoys a number of important innovations. It has greater penetration and sufficient payload capacity for two simultaneous sensors. It is capable of more frequent course changes, is far more accurate, and is able to transmit real-time IR data.

France deployed the Apilles Mini Avion de Reconnaissance Télépilote (MART) reconnaissance drone to the Gulf. The system was built as a collaboration between the French Army Section Technique de l'Armée de Terre Capable, and Apilles (ground Station), Thomson-CSF (computer and navigation), Cofras (training and service) and Britain's Target and Surveillance Ltd (aircraft launcher and avionics). It transmitted video images to the French Daguet Division from behind enemy lines, enabling a number of Iraqi supply points to be targeted and destroyed.

Russia, which must now be regarded as a commercial competitor rather than as hostile, has recently developed the 'Sterkh'. A compact, mobile, all-weather system, 'Sterkh' comprises a 'Shmel-1' dart configuration recoverable vehicle with a pusher propeller launched from a converted SA-13 chassis. In flight, stability is provided by an autopilot incorporating a microprocessor, a vertical gyroscope, angular velocity transducers and electronic drives to the

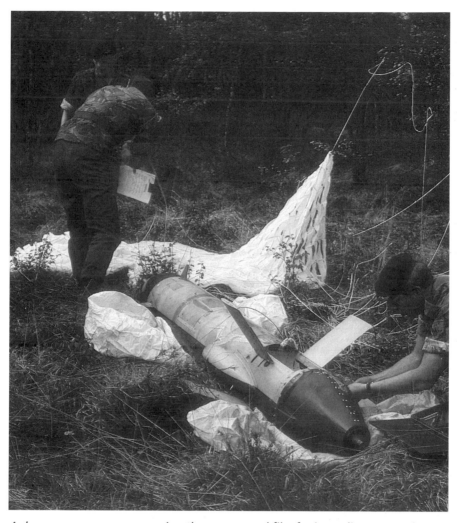

A drone recovery crew removing the camera and film for immediate processing and interpretation.

Mark Lloyd

ailerons, elevators, rudders and throttle. 'Shmel-1' has a gross weight of 130 kg (287 lb), a cruising velocity of 140 km/h (87 mph), an operational ceiling of 100–3000 km (328-9843 ft) and is recovered by parachute.

Although 'Sterkh' has clear military and espionage potential it is perhaps a sign of the times that it is being marketed with the civil sector in mind. Its sales brochure describes it as being ideally suited to ice and avalanche patrolling, to the inspection of mains and pipe lines, to the monitoring of unmanned plants in remote areas and, in the Russians' own words, to 'Atomic power stations radiation survey'!

THE UNITED STATES RESPONSE

Operation Desert Storm gave the United States military its first real opportunity to demonstrate the utility of drones and RPVs. The AAI Corporation Pioneer flew 533 sorties in the war, totalling 1688 hours. At least one Pioneer was airborne at all times during Operation Desert Storm, acquiring regular real-time battle-damage assessments, reconnaissance and threat intelligence. The Navy used Pioneers to spot targets for the 16-inch guns of the battleships *Wisconsin* and *Missouri*, while the Army used them as reconnaissance systems for their Apache helicopters. A reported 12 Pioneers were destroyed during Desert Storm, some of them intentionally, and a further 15 damaged.

The US Marine Corps employed between 55 and 60 Exdrone, equipped with daytime surveillance cameras, to observe barriers and minefields in southern Kuwait City. AeroVironment Inc Pointer mini-RPVs were also used by the Marines for real-time battle damage assessment, artillery adjustment and reconnaissance. Pointer proved unsuitable for the desert conflict due to the lack of visible landmarks, the high winds and the inability of the Marines to see across the flat desert for great distances.

However, this is not to say that Pointer is a flawed system. Extremely quiet and easy to use (familiarisation takes less than an hour), Pointer is small enough to be hand-launched and carried on the back of a single soldier. At present its performance is limited by its range (only 5 km [3.1 miles]) and by the fact that it can only take a day, black-and-white TV camera. Both problems are being addressed and are likely soon to be rectified.

The lack of a position locating system for Pointer is more fundamental. Navigation is accomplished using a combination of good map-reading skills and a magnetic compass readout on the air vehicle. Although this works satisfactorily in environments where there is variety in the landscape, it proved of little use in the desert.

AIRCRAFT

Only a small number of aircraft have been designed specifically for espionage. The sheer cost of development, the relatively few airframes required and the acceleration in counter-espionage techniques have combined to make their production financially all but impractical. Most air forces have been forced to rely upon the introduction of specialist reconnaissance variants of otherwise conventional aircraft.

GENERAL DYNAMICS/GRUMMAN EF-111A RAVEN

In January 1975, the US Air Force deemed it impractical to replace its ageing Douglas EB-66 electronic warfare fleet with a variant of the US Navy EA-6B Prowler preferred by Congress. Immediate steps were taken to convert two F-111s into prototype EW platforms. The transformation was not without its problems. The F-111 was well into its planned operational life and it was feared that there would not be enough airframes available to make a rebuild for the new role feasible. However, the tests proved so successful that in November 1979 the US Air Force ordered 42 converted aircraft.

Between 1980 and 1985, Grumman stripped the original aircraft, rebuilding them to an estimated fatigue standard of 8000 hours. The main changes lay in the introduction of fintop receivers and the installation of a Sanders ALQ-137CW deception jammer for self-protection. An improved version of the Eaton AIL ALQ-99EW suite, designed originally for the EA-6B Prowler but now modified for single-operator use, was incorporated. With its in-flight-adaptable antennae, the ALQ-99EW jamming system is capable of detecting, identifying, locating, recording and, where desired, jamming every kind of hostile emitter using computer control over direction and time at ranges of up to 233 km (145 miles).

A proposed update to the ALQ-99EW system was mooted, but cancelled in June 1988 due to financial constraints. A laser-gyro inertial navigation system and a GPS navsat receiver have, however, been retrofitted. The EF-111A is likely to remain in service into the early 21st century.

Data:

Role:	Electronic warfare aircraft
Length:	23.16 m (76 ft 0in)
Height:	6.10 m (20 ft 0 in)
Wingspan:	9.74 m (31 ft 11 in)—swept 19.2 m (63 ft 0 in)—unswept
Powerplant:	Two Pratt & Whitney TF30-P-3 turbofans
Radius:	1497 km (930 miles)
Max. speed:	2269 km/h (1410 mph)
Ceiling:	13 700 m (45 000 ft)

LOCKHEED F-117A 'SENIOR TREND'

It is highly probable that a reconnaissance version of the F-117A strike aircraft, which proved so lethal in the Gulf, has been developed. The SR-71 'Blackbird' has now been retired, and although the TR-1A remains in service, without the F-117A there is no obvious recon-naissance aircraft currently available for covert intelligence-gathering missions over foreign territory.

Development of the F-117A was ordered by the US Air Force in 1978 under the code-name 'Senior Trend'. The first flight took place in June 1981 and the aircraft entered service in October 1983 with delivery completed in 1990.

To keep the radar cross-section to a minimum the fuselage was constructed from a series of flat facets to ensure that as much radar energy as possible was deflected at harmless angles. Radar reflectivity was further reduced by covering the airframe with sheets of radar-absorbent material (RAM). Radar energy is reflected from the engine air inlets by a knife-edge grille structure, a technique used on the Firebee reconnaissance drone during the Vietnam War. The engine exhaust is deflected by wide slot-shaped outlets which force the efflux to disperse and cool quickly.

The F-117A carries no radar. However, a hemispherical housing mounted forward of the cockpit contains optics for a combined FLIR and laser-designation system, possibly with two fields of view—wide for navigation and target location, and narrow for attack. It has been suggested that on reconnaissance missions the sensor could be used to identify and record targets of interest while the weapons bay could be converted to accept cameras, IR scanners or ELINT receivers.

The F-117A is not an easy aircraft to fly. Although none were lost during the Gulf hostilities, several have crashed in training.

Data:

Role:	Reconnaissance/strike fighter
Length:	20.09 m (65 ft 11 in)
Wingspan:	13. 21 m (43 ft 3 in)
Powerplant:	Two non-afterburning General Electric F404 turbojets
Radius:	1505–2205 km (935–1370 miles)
Max. speed:	High subsonic

LOCKHEED EC-130E, G, H, Q HERCULES

The versatility of the C-130 has made the Hercules a natural choice for a number of specialist applications, several relating to ELINT and radar jamming.

The MC-130E, which currently serves with the 1st Special Operations Squadron, 3rd Tactical Fighter Wing, is one the most unusual versions of a conventional aircraft flying. Its ALQ-8 ECM pod mounted under the port wing gives it excellent low-level survivability, making it ideally suited to covert exfiltration and infiltration missions.

The EC-130G provided the US Navy with its original TACAMO (TAke Charge And Move Out) communications aircraft for the provision of survivable communications with the ballistic submarine fleet. Four were built, but were soon replaced by 16 EC-130Q follow-on TACAMO aircraft with improved equipment and crew accommodation. Communications to the submerged submarines were effected by a 100 kW Very Low Frequency (VLF) transmitter attached to a 10 km (6.2 mile) trailing wire antenna. The EC-130Q is now being replaced by the E-6A derivative of the Boeing 707 civil airliner.

The EC-130H electronic warfare version entered service with the 41st Electronic Combat Squadron and the 66th Electronic Combat Wing in 1982. A total of 16 aircraft were built to carry the classified Compass Call EW communications jammer and are likely to remain in service into the late 1990s.

Data:

Role:	Various EW roles (see text)
Length:	29.79 m (97 ft 9 in)
Height:	11.66 m (38 ft 3 in)
Wingspan:	40.41 m (132 ft 7 in)
Powerplant:	Four Allison T56-A-15 turboprops
Range:	7402 km (4600 miles)
Max. speed:	603 km/h (375 mph)
Ceiling:	10 060 m (33 000 ft)

MCDONNELL DOUGLAS RF-4C/RF-4E PHANTOM II

The F-4 Phantom was one of the most famous and distinctive aircraft of its day. Large and robust, although designed primarily as an interceptor it was ideally suited to the deep reconnaissance role. The RF-4C was acquired by the US Air Force in 1963 and immediately set new standards in multisensor reconnaissance. Two patterns of camera were fitted: the first with a flat underside to the camera fairing, the second with a rounded lower surface. The new longer and slimmer nose houses a Goodyear APG-99 'forward-looking' radar capable of allowing the aircraft to fly in terrain-following mode.

The lower nose, including the chin fairing, housed three optical cameras mounted in the oblique, vertical and lateral oblique modes. A Goodyear APG-102 SLAR backed up by an AAS-118 infra-red detecting set, both mounted in the fuselage, recorded a broad strip of terrain on either side of the flight path. AN ALR-17 Countermeasures Receiving Set allowed hostile radars to be identified and classified on the photo imagery, while an ALQ-161 system, mounted on the centreline, handled ELINT. External jamming pods enabled the aircraft to operate in the vicinity of all but the most sophisticated SAM systems.

Development of the aircraft was extremely successful. The US Air Force ordered 505 models while the US Marine Corps purchased 46 RF-4Bs with similar equipment but including cameras mounted on rotating mountings aimed by the pilot, and an inertial navigation system. The last, and best, model was the RF-4E, manufactured exclusively for export and first flown in September 1970. It was fitted with more powerful engines, an extra fuel tank in the tail, slatted stabilisors and, in the later models, automatic manoeuvring slats on the wing. However, many of the sensors fitted to the domestic aircraft were too highly classified to be exported. In all, 130 RF-4Es were manufactured, although 16, ordered by Iran, were never delivered.

The US Air Force updated the APQ-99 radars in 312 of its aircraft and installed a Litton Amecom ALQ-125 Tactical Electronic Reconnaissance (TEREC) set and a Ford Aerospace AVQ-26 Pave Track laser designator/fire-control system in selected models. Attempts to retrofit an electro-optical sensor 'tactical reconnaissance roadmap' in place of the cameras was abandoned due to cost in 1988.

Data:

Role:	Reconnaissance fighter
Length:	19.17 m (62 ft 11 in)
Height:	4.96 m (16 ft 3 in)
Wingspan:	11.70 m (38 ft 5 in)
Powerplant:	Two General Electric J79-GE-17 turbojets
Range:	3700 km (2300 miles)
Max. speed:	2304 km/h (1432 mph)
Ceiling:	17100 m (56120 ft)

DASSAULT-BREGUET MIRAGE F1CR-200

The Mirage F1CR-200 was designed to replace the delta-wing Mirage IIIR and IIIRD which had served for almost 20 years with the three squadrons of the 33e Escadre de Reconnaissance based in Strasbourg. The original prototype flew on 20 November 1981, the first production model was completed in November 1982 and the aircraft entered service in September 1983.

The F1C-200 is some 8 cm (3 in) longer than the standard F1 fighter and can be differentiated by the in-flight refuelling boom mounted slightly off-set to starboard just forward of the windscreen fitted to some fighter versions. Two optical cameras may be fitted into the nose-mounted blister fairing: an Omega 35 for high-level vertical imagery and an Omega 40 with a 75 mm lens for medium-/low-level use. A SAT SCM Super Cyclope linescan unit located in the lower edge of the starboard intake provides real-time signals which are transmitted direct via data link to the SARA (Système Aéro-Transportable de Reconnaissance Aérienne) ground station.

The F1CR-200 carries a Thomson-CSF Cyrano IVMR radar capable of ground-mapping, contour-mapping, air-to-ground ranging and blind let-down. A Sagem Uliss 47 inertial platform is linked to an ESD 182 navigation computer. The Mirage F.1 may also be used in the anti-radar role, carrying either the Thomson-CSF Astac ELINT pod to detect hostile emitters, or the Matra Armat anti-radar missile. It will also accept the Raphael TH sideways-looking radar pod. The aircraft is battle-tested, having seen action in Chad in 1987 and in support of the French Daguet Division in the Gulf.

Data:

Role:	Reconnaissance fighter
Length:	15.3 m (50 ft 3 in)
Height:	4.5 m (14 ft 9 in)
Wingspan:	8.40 m (27 ft 7 in)
Powerplant:	One SNECMA Atar 9K-50 afterburning turbojet
Range:	1000 km (620 miles)
Max. speed:	2335 km/h (1450 mph)
Ceiling:	20 000 m (65 600 ft)

NORTHROP RF-5/RF-5E TIGEREYE

Tigereye was developed by the Northrop Corporation as a private venture exclusively for the export market. The RF-5A first flew in May 1968, initial deliveries were made to Norway a month later and 89 aircraft were built in all. The much improved RF-5E was introduced in January 1979.

The elongated nose of the RF-5E, 20 cm (8 in) longer than that of the basic fighter, incorporates a series of optical windows and has a large downward hinging door for ease of access. It accommodates a single KS-87D1 camera with a 15 cm (6-in) or 30 cm (12-in) lens in the tip and will accept a series of easily interchangeable pallet-mounted sensor systems. One pallet carries a KA-95B medium-altitude panoramic camera, a KA-56E low-altitude panoramic camera and an RS-710E IRLS. A second combines a KA-56E with a KA-93B6 panoramic camera with a 145° scan for use at heights from 3 to 15 km (10 000 to 50 000 ft) and a third a 1.68 m (66-in) focal length LOROP camera for LOng-Range Oblique Photography.

The pilot is provided with an integral navigation system and a TV display for visual correction of photographic runs. The RF-5E has been test-flown by pilots from 31 different countries, including Malaysia and Saudi Arabia.

Data:

Role:	Reconnaissance fighter
Length:	14.65 m (48 ft 1 in)
Height:	4.07 m (13 ft 4 in)
Wingspan:	8.13 m (26 ft 8 in)
Powerplant:	Two General Electric J58-GE-21B turbojets
Range:	2863 km (1545 miles)—with external tanks
Max. speed:	1734 km/h (1077 mph)
Ceiling:	15 790 m (51 800 ft)

SAAB SF37/SH37 VIGGEN

Two versions of the highly successful System 37 Viggen were ordered by the Swedish Air Force, the SF37 for general reconnaissance duties and the SH37 for maritime surveillance.

The SF37, which first flew in May 1973 as a replacement for the S35E Draken, has no nose radar. A chin fairing houses four low-level vertical or oblique cameras, two long-range high-altitude vertical cameras and a VK IRLS. A camera sight, an IR sensor giving horizon-to-horizon coverage and a series of EW systems including an ELINT recorder, are carried in the fuselage. An additional FLIR pod, a night-illumination system or an IRLS may also be carried in a Red Baron pod beneath the fuselage.

The SH37, which was introduced to replace the S32C Lansen, first flew in June 1975. It retains a modified version of the nose-mounted LM Ericsson PS-37/A multimode radar, Marconi HUD (Head-Up Display) and central digital computer fitted to the standard AJ37 interceptor, supplemented by a series of underwing pods. The port fuselage pod carries a night reconnaissance fitting with IR linescan and LLTV, the starboard pod a Red Baron. The inboard wing pylons can be fitted with either active or passive ECM jammer pods or very comprehensive ELINT and EW recorders. A tape recorder and a data camera record film coordination figures, including the date-time-group, the aircraft's course, position and height and the target location. Both aircraft may be fitted with a large additional fuel tank on the centreline.

A total of 28 SF37s and 26 SH37s were built before production ceased in February 1981. Most remain operational, flying with F13 at Norrköping, F17 at Rønneby and F21 at Lulea.

Data:

Role:	Ground/Maritime Reconnaissance
Length:	16.3 m (53 ft 6 in)
Height:	5.8 m (19 ft 0 in)
Wingspan:	10.60 m (34 ft 9 in)
Powerplant:	One Volvo Flygmotor RM8A augmented turbofan
Max. speed:	2124 km/h (1320 mph)

SIKORSKY EH-60C QUICKFIX IIB BLACK HAWK

The UH-60 Black Hawk helicopter was selected by the US Army as its basic utility rotary-wing transport in 1976. Designed to carry a squad of 11 fully equipped infantrymen and a crew of three, the UH-60 can also carry four litters or an external load of 3628 kg (8000 lb). Large, robust and with an excellent range, it proved ideally suited to the ECM role when a successor was sought for the Bell EH-1 series of helicopters in the early 1980s.

The YEH-60A prototype first flew on 24 September 1981. The production model, the EH-60C, entered service at the end of that decade and remains highly classified. It is known that the prototype mounted the Quickfix II ECM system, incorporating an improved ALQ-151 EW intercept/jamming suite able to cover frequencies between 2 and 76 MHz emitting between 40 and 150 W of jamming power. An Aircraft Survivability Equipment (ASE) package, comprising an APR-39(V)2 radar-warning receiver and several M-130 chaff/flare dispensers in the tailboom, was also carried.

The EH-60C is fitted with a large antenna, on a swing-down mounting, beneath the fuselage and four small direction-finding (DF) dipoles on the tailboom. The aircraft has a crew of five: a pilot, co-pilot, crew chief and two EW operators.

A total of 66 models of the EH-60C were built before construction ceased in 1988. The aircraft is likely to remain in service until the late 1990s, when it is scheduled to be replaced by the Common Heliborne Jammer. Plans to develop an EH-60B SOTAS (Stand-Off Target Acquisition System) were abandoned in 1981.

Data:

Role:	EW Helicopter
Length:	15.26 m (50 ft 1 in) ignoring rotors
Height:	5.13 m (16 ft 10 in)
Rotor Diameter:	16.38 m (53 ft 8 in)
Powerplant:	Two General Electric T700-GE-700 turboshafts
Range:	600 km (373 miles)
Max. speed:	296 km/h (184 mph)
Ceiling:	3170 m (10 400 ft)

TUPOLEV TU-22

The Tupolev Tu-22 was designed primarily as a supersonic bomber. However, development took longer than anticipated with the result that the aircraft was already redundant when it entered service in 1959. By then the West had a number of interceptors capable of outstripping it in performance, severely limiting its usefulness as a long-range penetrating bomber.

The missile-armed Tu-22K, capable of carrying a single Kh-22 cruise missile on the centreline, quickly followed. Some 150 were built, of which some 125 entered service with the Soviet Naval Air Force. Surplus models were stripped of their missiles and nuclear delivery means and exported to Iraq (12) and Libya (24). These aircraft proved excellent against an unsophisticated enemy when Iraq used them against the Kurds and Libya against the Tanzanians. However, their vulnerability against a well-equipped, modern force became

The RAF's latest tactical reconnaissance aircraft, the Tornado GR 1A, carries a thermal imaging system in place of the 27 mm cannon.   Guy Taylor

apparent when a French Hawk battery shot down a Libyan aircraft attempting a raid on Chad.

The AVMF (Soviet naval aviation) received about 60 examples of the Tu-22R, called 'Blinder-C' by NATO. This had the bomb bay reconfigured for up to seven AFA-series cameras and, from 1975, IR linescan or a side-looking radar, all mounted on pre-loaded pallets 5.55 m (18 ft 2 in) long. Later Tu-22K missile-carriers were completely rebuilt as various sub-types of Tu-22P (NATO 'Blinder-E') for ELINT or ECM jamming. Immediately identifiable by the electronics-filled tailcone replacing the tail gun turret, they carry either of two comprehensive suites of receivers and jammers. About 30 were still operational in 1993, though they seldom fly.

Data:

Role:	Maritime Reconnaissance Aircraft
Length:	42.6 m (139 ft 9 in)
Height:	10.67 m (35 ft 0 in)
Wingspan:	23.5 m (77 ft 0 in)
Powerplant:	Dobrymin RD-7M-2 turbojets
Range:	4900 km (3050 miles)
Max. speed:	1610 km/h (1000 mph)
Ceiling:	13 300 m (43 635 ft)

TECHNIQUES

IMAGERY AND ANGLES
Imagery Quality

Imagery quality is vital if the film produced by an espionage flight is to be fully exploitable. Quality depends upon a number of factors, including the optical performance of the lens, the resolution and contrast of the film emulsion, external environmental factors such as light conditions and atmospheric haze and finally the clarity of the potential subject.

Lens requirements are broadly similar to those facing a conventional photographer. Analysts demand a distortion-free image, with evenly distributed definition and contrast from the centre of the picture to its edge. Lens 'flare', solar reflections from the various glass surfaces—all too common in amateur photography—must be kept to a minimum, even when a sortie is flown with the sun low, which emphasises the shadows.

Focal length, which dictates the magnification of the imagery, is crucial. Low-level, relatively fast moving platforms will usually carry cameras fitted with lenses of focal length of between 8.8 cm (3.5 in) and 30 cm (12 in). Shorter focal-length lenses will produce a much larger area image, which can occasionally prove advantageous. The photograph will tend to be a more 'conventional' image, which is more easily understood by untrained 'eyes', making it useful for operational briefing purposes.

Analysts are trained to look for the unusual, particularly when seeking a well-hidden target. Dead foliage caused by old camouflage or unusual track patterns are typical give-aways and are best spotted on a large-scale photograph. The German 'V-1' installation at Peenemünde was discovered only by chance when it was noticed that a well-worn track seemingly led into the side of a hill. Only then did more detailed follow-on reconnaissance establish the presence of a well-hidden bunker complex in the area.

High-altitude platforms, particularly those carried on spy planes and satellites, require ultra-telephoto lenses. Over 400 types of optical glass are available for the manufacture of such lenses from which a computer-aided mix is used to attain the best combination for the specialist task at hand. Despite the obviously clandestine nature of high-altitude military photography, many of the best lenses are obtained on the commercial market, particularly from Japan, which has consistently refused to place an embargo on such technology.

THE CHOICE OF FILM

A film's speed is inversely proportional to its resolution. A 'slow', less sensitive, film will produce a far finer (more enlargeable) image than a 'fast' film used under the same light conditions, but will require a far slower shutter speed or larger lens aperture. As a slow shutter speed may result in blurring due to the forward movement and possible jarring of the camera platform and too wide an aperture may result in loss of definition the precise film speed to use is a matter of compromise. High-resolution colour reversal stock and false-colour film, ideal for the detection of camouflage, are also available.

Camera-platform motion, the greatest enemy of the low-resolution film, can be overcome to a degree by fitting the camera with forward motion compensation (FMC), involving the movement of the film by the exact amount needed to offset the image movement caused by the platform motion. Although helpful, FMC is not however foolproof, and many analysts will argue that a grainy image produced by a fast film is far easier to read than a blurred image produced by a slower alternative.

Yellow and orange filters, similar in principle to those in domestic use, may also be fitted to the camera lens to enhance contrast. However, as filters require a slower camera shutter speed, a wider aperture or a slower film, their use again involves a carefully considered compromise.

INFRA-RED LINE SCAN

Infra-Red Line Scan (IRLS) operates a little like a TV camera, scanning a narrow transverse strip of terrain on either side and below the camera platform; the platform's forward motion gradually builds up a linear image of the terrain being overflown. A thermal sensor detects heat radiated from the target, which is converted to produce a photographic image. This thermal picture is built up from a series of dots; the hotter the object the more intense white the dots are against an otherwise black background.

IRLS is ideally suited to night operations, when it will detect the heat from a camp fire or a vehicle engine and can even tell the readiness state of certain equipment. It can show whether an aircraft has recently landed, is preparing to take off, or is just parked, from the heat image of its engines. On a hot day it will even betray the outline of a recently departed aircraft or vehicle by showing its thermal shadow, which is cooler (darker) in relation to its background.

IRLS is not perfect. It is not always able to identify vehicles by type, and rarely by model. Thus a tank will appear as a larger blob than a truck, but can easily be confused with an armoured personnel carrier (the United States Abrams series main battle tank, with its massive exhaust thermal signature, is an exception to this rule). IRLS is severely impaired by cloud and fog and is of little use in mist.

It is also liable to morning and evening 'thermal crossover'. Certain objects retain heat more effectively than others. Masonry bridges, steel girders and tarmac roads will cool down faster than the surrounding countryside during the night, but will warm faster during the day. Inevitably, twice a day, shortly after the Sun rises and sets, they will be the same temperature, and therefore emit the same thermal signature, as their surroundings. When this phenomenon (known as 'thermal crossover') occurs, and it can last for up to an hour a session depending on the climate, accurate IRLS photography is less informative.

SIDEWAYS LOOKING AIRBORNE RADAR

SLAR records a broad strip of terrain on either side of the flightpath in the form of a radar image on photographic film. SLAR can be designed to operate in several modes, the most common being a low-level mode and a high-level mode. A fixed antenna is mounted to each side of the system to give full cover on both sides of the aircraft, the extent of the cover being determined by the aircraft's height, the radar-beam depression angle and the display limits.

Systems such as the Goodyear UPD-4 synthetic-aperture SLAR are gimbal-mounted to ensure the maintenance of a constant look angle and can be set for a number of operating modes, recording fixed target imagery only or mixed and moving-target data.

The more modern Goodyear UPD-6 system, retrofitted to Luftwaffe RF-4E reconnaissance aircraft, incorporates a data link capable of transmitting real-time radar imagery to a ground station. The newer UPD-8 radar, with its wideband datalink, was fitted to the US Air Force's fleet of RF-4Cs, and the pod-mounted UPD-9 system to the F-18.

The Hughes Advanced Synthetic-Aperture Radar System (ASARS-2), fitted to the TR-1A, has an advertised maximum range in excess of 161 km (100 miles) at an aircraft height of 22 860 m (75 000 ft) and can be pintle-mounted with the addition of a Hughes VHSIC (Very High Speed Integrated Circuit). It has two electronically scanned antennae capable of detecting and locating static and moving ground targets on either side of the TR-1 on a single pass. Data are formatted and transmitted to the ASARS-2 processing segment. It has a unique ability to produce constant-scale imagery in plan view unlike conventional optical systems. Its resolving power remains classified but it was a 'vital part of the intelligence and targeting process' in Operation Desert Storm.

VERTICAL AND OBLIQUE IMAGERY

Conventional photographic imagery can be either vertical or oblique. Vertical photography is far more versatile, but is limited by its comparative lack of cross-track coverage and is thus normally incorporated into a fan. Fan photographs are taken by installing two or more cameras in the platform, the cameras being mounted so that the resultant photographs overlap on adjacent prints, thus ensuring uninterrupted lateral or 'across track' cover of the area photographed.

Vertical photographs can be scaled by a number of methods, including photo-map comparison, and as such can be used to deduce the precise size and, with the aid of a shadow, the exact height of an object. Unidentified objects can be studied in relation to their shape, size, shadow, tone and associated features to give the analyst an indication of their type and purpose.

Oblique photographs are those in which the centre of the image is other than directly beneath the camera platform. They are subdivided between high obliques, which incorporate the horizon, and low obliques, which do not. As the scale of a photograph is dependent upon

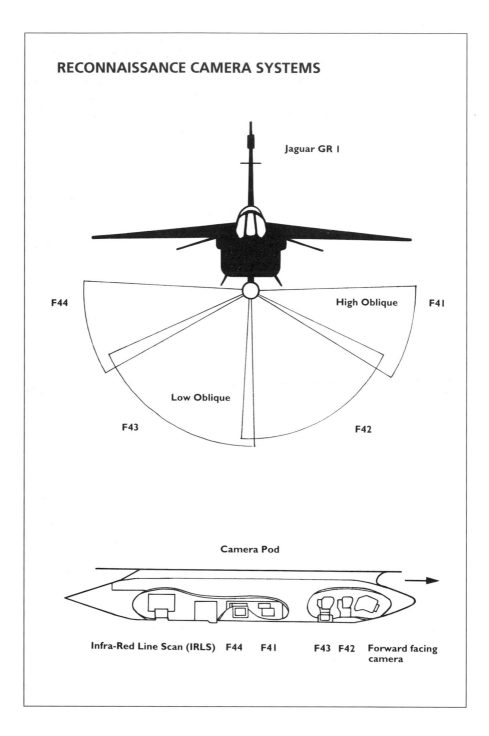

RECONNAISSANCE CAMERA SYSTEMS

Jaguar GR I

F44

High Oblique   F4I

Low Oblique

F43   F42

Camera Pod

Infra-Red Line Scan (IRLS)   F44   F4I   F43 F42   Forward facing camera

the distance of the subject from the camera it follows that the scale of an oblique photograph will vary, reducing its usefulness to an analyst. It does, however, sometimes allow the imagery analyst to see equipment or activity hidden from vertical photography by overhead cover.

Panoramic (horizon to horizon) photography can be achieved by means of special lenses or systems of rotating prisms fitted into the camera. Its main advantage is that it allows a wide area of ground to be displayed on a single print. However, the continuous change in scale from the perpendicular outwards can impart a false or confusing impression of the terrain.

INFRA-RED PHOTOGRAPHY

Infra-red photography, as opposed to IRLS discussed above, is best regarded as no more than a complementary aerial reconnaissance system to be used mainly for the detection of camouflage and for haze penetration. Exaggerated claims are often made for infra-red photography, but its penetrative power is far more limited than is generally believed. In normal infra-red photography cloud and thick fog cannot be penetrated.

Infra-red sensitive, or camouflage detection, film is sensitive to infra-red emissions. It can be fitted into an ordinary camera and used in black-and-white or colour format.

In black-and-white film all vegetation appears light in tone. However, as it starts to lose its chlorophyll content (when cut and used for camouflage) it darkens in tone, until eventually it appears as a black mass. Water appears black in tone irrespective of its depth.

With infra-red colour film, living green foliage appears rose in colour and dead foliage as black. Green camouflage netting appears as orange while water will vary from black to light blue depending upon the depth.

STEREOSCOPY

Stereoscopy is a somewhat complex science dealing with the appreciation of the third dimension when two 2D photographs of the same object, taken from different viewpoints, are observed through a stereoscope.

Any two consecutive prints from a single photographic run can be used as a 'stereo pair' provided that the object to be studied appears on both prints. On any stereo pair of prints any object having height (a bridge) will have its top radially displaced in relation to its base. The direction of displacement will differ on each print. When an object on a stereo pair is viewed under a stereoscope the two different images fuse into one picture. The eyes can focus on one point only at any given moment, so in order to look from bottom to top of the bridge the eyes must converge along the lines of the apparent displacement of the two images. The amount of convergence is converted by the brain into terms of height and the object is seen in '3D'.

Not everybody's brain will accept the 'fiction' of stereoscopy. However, those who are able to exploit the principle find it tremendously advantageous, particularly in the reading of detailed or small-scale imagery.

Used incorrectly stereoscopy can be dangerous. Prints viewed in reverse order or negatives viewed upside down will produce a reverse stereo image. The eyes will be forced to diverge when switching from the base to the top of an object, giving the impression that the top is further away from the viewer than the base. This will cause houses to appear as holes in the ground, hills as valleys and embankments as cuttings.

When stereoscopy was in its infancy stereo pairs were taken of the area designated for the glider landing sites at Arnhem. Unaware of the dangers of reverse stereoscopy the analysts

viewed a number of photographs out of sequence and reported that the potential LZs contained nothing more sinister than a series of drainage ditches. Only when the horrified glider pilots came in to land did they discover that many of these 'innocent' drainage ditches were in fact solid earthen dikes.

PLANNING A DRONE MISSION
Characteristics
The Midge Drone, in service with the locating batteries of the British Royal Artillery, is old but thoroughly reliable. It was introduced to provide counter-battery targets for the 175 mm M-107 heavy regiments attached to 1 (British) Corps in Germany. It remains in temporary service with the two MLRS regiments stationed in Dortmund and is soon to be replaced by Phoenix. It acted as the long-range reconnaissance eyes for the British 1st (Armoured) Division in the Gulf.

The Midge drone has a range of approximately 110 km (68 miles), a penetration range across the front line of 30–35 km (19–22 miles), can make a maximum of four turns of 3 km (1.86 miles) radius and fly on five straight legs. It is launched from a pallet mounted on a standard 4-ton chassis by a booster which is jettisoned between 800 and 1900 m (2625 and 6234 ft) into flight. It can operate at heights of between 300 and 1200 m (985 and 3937 ft) above the launch vehicle and has a ceiling of 3000 m (9842 ft).

The Midge drone is normally fitted with three KRB 8/24 Zeiss cameras, giving an inclusive field of view of 143°. The centre lens provides vertical photography, with a cross-track coverage nearly equal to the drone's selected altitude, the outer lenses provide low oblique views. Total cross-track coverage of all three lenses is approximately six times that of the drone's height above the ground. The cameras can be turned on and off twice to give a maximum along-track coverage of approximately 50 times the drone's height.

A typical sortie will produce cumulative coverage of 3–25 km (1.86–15.5 miles). A drone can fly a maximum of 18 to 20 sorties per day, of which some 60 per cent will be tactically successful. Response time for a trained crew is 70 minutes from reception of request to transmission of result during the day, extending to 90 minutes at night.

Overlapping prints such as these, if viewed through a stereoscope, can be seen in three dimensions.
Mark Lloyd

MISSION PLANNING

Daily intelligence-gathering priorities are listed by the divisional commander at his morning briefing. Certain of these will subsequently be allocated in the form of intelligence-gathering tasks to the Air Liaison Officer (ALO) responsible for manned aerial reconnaissance, and others to the Divisional Artillery Intelligence Officer (DAIO) responsible for the drone troop. Once tasked the DAIO will then return to his battle map, which will show among other things the latest known and estimated friendly and enemy dispositions and the latter's likely axes of advance. In planning his drone missions for the day, he will take into account the number of drones available, their disposition and enemy activity to their front. A drone troop is large and vulnerable and cannot be allowed to get too close to a potential enemy thrust.

Once the DAIO has passed his mission details to the drone troop, the troop commander (TC) will prioritise the tasks and test them for feasibility against his own larger-scale and more detailed maps. Occasionally it will be discovered that a potential mission, however crucial, will simply prove beyond the scope of the Midge with its limited number of turns and height changes. Missions which prove feasible will subsequently be planned in detail and passed in trace form to the analysts to enable them to study the terrain under the proposed flight path. In the meantime the photographers, who are co-located with the analysts in the Photographic Processing and Interpretation Vehicle (PPIV), will ensure that all is in a state of readiness to begin developing immediately the film is brought in.

Simultaneously full details of the proposed flight will be sent to the troop maintenance area located in a camouflaged hide to the rear, to enable the mission parameters to be keyed into the flight control unit. Unlike more advanced systems, once airborne an error in the Midge flight path cannot be rectified and a mistake in the original programming will, therefore, prove catastrophic. Details of the camera type and filters required will also be sent to maintenance to allow the camera to be prepared.

As soon as the camera platform has been secured inside the belly of the drone and the drone itself fully tested, the Midge will be brought forward to the launch vehicle and fitted. The launcher will move as quickly as possible to its pre-surveyed launch site and the drone released on its 20- to 30-minute flight. The launch commander will take both safety and accuracy into account when overseeing the firing. His vehicle, which must operate from the open, will be extremely vulnerable to enemy action during the run-up to the launch, yet it is imperative that he does not rush the launch as the Midge must be fired at precisely the correct angle and traverse if the mission is to be accurate. An error of even 2–3 degrees will cause the drone to fly totally off course and perhaps land in enemy territory.

During or immediately prior to the flight the Land-Rover-towed recovery vehicle will proceed to the area of the anticipated mission end. At a pre-determined time the homing beacon will be activated, the drone will turn towards the recovery crew, and the engine will cut. As the drone begins to fall, parachutes will deploy, causing it to invert, after which large air bags will be inflated, protecting the cameras from the worst of the impact.

As soon as the film is recovered from the camera platform it will be taken by the quickest possible means to the PPIV, where it will be developed in 3 to 4 minutes. The film will then be passed in negative form to the analysts for initial interpretation and the immediate findings forwarded via the TC to the DAIO. If time permits the negatives will then be printed, studied in greater detail and individual frames enlarged for more detailed analysis. Finally the drone itself will be returned to maintenance, where it will undergo a thorough 6-hour overhaul before reallocation.

A typical training flight plan for a drone mission.
Mark Lloyd

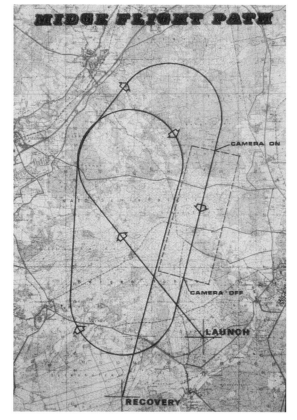

FIVE

THE SILENT WAR; ESPIONAGE AT SEA

THE BIRTH OF NAVAL INTELLIGENCE

ROOM 40

At midnight on 4 August 1914, Great Britain declared war on Imperial Germany. While the attention of the whole world concentrated on the vast and bloody struggles on land, the British Grand Fleet disappeared from Scapa Flow to involve itself in the routine of blockade and counter-blockade. The two fleets met twice, on the Dogger Bank and in the indecisive Battle of Jutland, yet without the Royal Navy Britain would have been starved into submission.

Throughout the war the Royal Navy owed a great deal to its Director of Naval Intelligence, Captain (later Admiral) Reginald 'Blinker' Hall, and to his tiny band of code-breakers occupying Room 40 of the Old Admiralty Building. The foundations of Room 40's tremendous success were laid in the first three months of the war, when a series of seemingly unimportant events took place quite unnoticed by the world at large. In 1912, the Committee of Imperial Defence decided to cut all Germany's overseas telegraph cables in the event of war. On 5 August 1914, the cable ship *Telconia* began to dredge up and sever the first of five German cables which ran from Emden, on the German–Dutch frontier, to France, Spain, the United States and the German colonies. Unable to communicate by cablegram, Germany was forced to resort to letters—slow and in constant threat of interception—or to wireless.

Wireless telegraphy was a relatively recent invention in 1914. Although it was widely used by all warships and many merchantmen, no one had fully appreciated the enormous increase in wireless traffic which wartime conditions would bring. All countries employed codes, but only two, France and Austria-Hungary, employed code-breakers. Britain was quick to learn from her omission, and within ten days of the outbreak of hostilities set up her own decrypting agency.

Luck was with the British. Germany started the war with three principal codes, and within four months the Admiralty was in physical possession of copies of all of them. One fell into British hands on 11 August, when the German–Australian steamship *Hobart*, unaware that war had been declared, was seized off the coast of Melbourne. A second was captured by the Russians when the cruiser *Magdeburg* ran hard aground off the coast of Estonia. The third was retrieved when a lead box jettisoned by the commander of the destroyer *S.119*, sunk in an engagement with the cruiser *Undaunted*, was dredged up by a British trawler. From then until the end of hostilities the Admiralty was able to decipher virtually every German transmission intercepted.

Room 40 comprised a motley staff. It was headed by the 59-year-old Sir Alfred Ewing. The son of a Church of Scotland minister, he graduated in Engineering from Edinburgh University: after a few years' practical experience with a number of cable firms, he returned to undertake engineering research. Subsequently appointed Professor of Engineering at Tokyo and Dundee Universities, he accepted the Chair of Mechanical Engineering at Cambridge in 1890. In 1902, Ewing accepted the post of Director of Naval Education, from which he was spirited to Room 40 in 1914.

Ewing was ably assisted by a number of lecturers from the Royal Naval colleges at Osborne and Dartmouth. Alastair Denniston, Ewing's second-in-command, was a man endowed with considerable sporting as well as academic prowess. After the war it was he who became head of the Government Code and Cipher School (GC&CS), and as such laid the foundations of Bletchley Park's immense successes in World War II. R.D. Norton and Lord Herschell, the son of a former Liberal Lord Chancellor, comprised the remainder of the initial permanent cadre.

At first Room 40 relied upon the Post Office, a number of Marconi wireless stations, the Admiralty listening station at Stockton and three enthusiastic amateurs for its intercepts. After a few months matters improved when the coastguard station at Hunstanton, on the Norfolk coast of the Wash, linked with Stockton to form the core of 'Y' (Interception) service. From these humble beginnings 'Y' service grew steadily, until ultimately it could intercept and record virtually every naval and diplomatic message transmitted by the German authorities.

By 1916, it had become clear that Room 40 had grown too swiftly for the Royal Navy either to handle its traffic or properly assess its importance. Equally, many officers not only had inadequate training in communications generally, but lacked the ability to check back on signals that failed to make sense. Room 40 passed signals, without comment or guidance, to the Operations division, where it might easily happen that the officer on duty at any given moment might be inexperienced. Eventually an Intelligence Advisory Centre was introduced as an intermediary to interpret the material it was getting from the decipherers.

THE CIPHER WAR

It was not until after Jutland that Germany began to realise that Britain had solved the whole of her naval code system and introduced changes accordingly. Early attempts at burst transmission proved successful in the short term. The German naval-controlled station at Nauen followed its evening broadcast with signals transmitted at such speed that they offered no clue as to whether they were actual messages or merely testing signals. It was not until a recorded sample was played on a ship's gramophone, and the gramophone was inadvertently allowed to run down, that the meaningless gibberish was translated into a series of comprehensible cipher groups.

As soon as one side discovered the ciphers of the other it began to feed the other with disinformation. It was the British who perpetrated one of the biggest blunders of the war by this method, and in so doing paved the way for the sinking of the cruiser *Hampshire* with Lord Kitchener, the Secretary of State for War, aboard. On 26 May 1916, a Norwegian named Lange, employed in the German Secret Service listening post at Neuminster, intercepted a message which, while on the face of it unimportant, none the less seemed extremely unusual. It was from a British destroyer to the Admiralty, saying that a channel west of Orkney had been swept clear of mines. Lange felt it strange that a destroyer should report direct to the Admiralty.

When the message was repeated four times in an hour he became convinced that there was something extraordinary about it.

Colonel Nicolai, in command of the listening station, rightly suspected that the passage was being swept to enable an important ship to use the route. Instructions were sent to the submarine minelayer U-75 to proceed at full speed to the west coast of Orkney to lay mines on the specified route. It was one of the mines laid by U-75 which sank the *Hampshire*.

THE ZIMMERMANN TELEGRAM

On 17 January 1917, the Reverend William Montgomery, then serving as a cryptanalyst in the diplomatic section of Room 40, intercepted a coded message from the German Foreign Secretary, Arthur Zimmermann, to the German Minister in Mexico. Even when only partially decoded it became obvious that the telegram would have world-shattering consequences:

BERLIN TO WASHINGTON STOP

MOST SECRET FOR YOUR EXCELLENCY'S PERSONAL INFORMATION AND TO BE HANDED TO THE IMPERIAL MINISTER IN [?] MEXICO WITH . . . BY A SAFE ROUTE STOP WE PROPOSE TO BEGIN ON FIRST OF FEBRUARY UNRESTRICTED SUBMARINE WARFARE STOP IN DOING THIS HOWEVER WE SHALL ENDEAVOUR TO KEEP AMERICA NEUTRAL . . . [?] IF WE SHALL NOT [SUCCEED IN DOING SO] WE PROPOSE TO [?MEXICO] AN ALLIANCE ON THE FOLLOWING BASIS STOP [JOINT] CONDUCT OF WAR [JOINT] CONCLUSION OF PEACE . . . YOUR EXCELLENCY SHOULD FOR THE PRESENT INFORM THE PRESIDENT SECRETLY [?THAT WE SUSPECT] WAR WITH THE USA [POSSIBLY] [JAPAN] AND AT THE SAME TIME TO NEGOTIATE BETWEEN US AND JAPAN . . . PLEASE TELL THE PRESIDENT THAT . . . OUR SUBMARINES . . . WILL COMPEL ENGLAND TO PEACE WITHIN A FEW MONTHS STOP ACKNOWLEDGE RECEIPT STOP

ZIMMERMANN STOP

Gaps in the deciphering still needed to be filled in, but clearly this was a threat of unrestricted submarine warfare. Equally it was an invitation to Mexico to attack the United States should the latter declare war on Germany and was an intimation that Japan, then a British ally, would be induced to change sides.

Zimmermann had sent his notorious cable by two channels to ensure its safe arrival: on what was known as the 'Swedish roundabout', which carried German telegrams via Stockholm first to South America, thence relaying them to Washington and Mexico City; secondly, by American diplomatic cables, a more direct route. But both lines passed through Britain, where they were intercepted by Room 40.

Within days the message was fully decrypted. The revised de-coding now read:

. . . WE INTEND TO BEGIN ON FIRST OF FEBRUARY UNRESTRICTED SUBMARINE WARFARE STOP WE SHALL ENDEAVOUR IN SPITE OF THIS TO KEEP THE UNITED STATES NEUTRAL STOP IN THE EVENT OF THIS NOT SUCCEEDING WE SHALL MAKE MEXICO A PROPOSAL OF ALLIANCE ON THE FOLLOWING BASIS STOP MAKE WAR TOGETHER STOP GENEROUS FINANCIAL SUPPORT AND AN UNDERSTANDING ON OUR PART THAT MEXICO IS TO RECONQUER THE LOST TERRITORY IN TEXAS, NEW MEXICO AND ARIZONA STOP THE SETTLEMENT IN DETAIL IS LEFT TO YOU STOP YOU WILL INFORM THE PRESIDENT [THAT IS PRESIDENT CARRANZA OF MEXICO] OF THE ABOVE MOST SECRETLY AS SOON AS THE OUTBREAK OF WAR WITH THE UNITED STATES IS CERTAIN AND ADD THE SUGGESTION THAT HE SHOULD ON HIS OWN INITIATIVE INVITE JAPAN TO IMMEDIATE ADHERENCE AND AT THE SAME TIME MEDIATE BETWEEN JAPAN AND OURSELVES STOP PLEASE CALL THE PRESIDENT'S ATTENTION TO THE FACT THAT THE RUTHLESS EMPLOYMENT OF OUR SUBMARINES OFFERS THE PROSPECT OF COMPELLING ENGLAND IN A FEW MONTHS TO MAKE PEACE . . .

The full message was forwarded to Washington and released to the press on 1 March, at a time when feeling was already running high against Germany because of the activities of her submarines. The telegram aroused a storm of protest throughout the USA, compounded by the fact that one copy had been sent to the German Ambassador in Washington over the private wire of the State Department, which the Germans had been given permission to use solely to facilitate the transmission of peace overtures. The telegram played a considerable part in inducing Congress to accept the idea of war with Germany, which was ultimately declared on 6 April 1917.

SIR ROGER CASEMENT

Richard Deacon, in his excellent book *The Silent War*, records one of the few truly unsavoury moments in the history of Room 40. The Department of Naval Intelligence had been determined to bring to book the Irish nationalist, Sir Roger Casement, since the early days of the war. Large sums of money were expended in obtaining intelligence on his movements in Germany and elsewhere; a yacht was even employed to spy around the west coast of Ireland, keeping watch for Casement's return from Germany. Eventually Room 40 intercepted a message from Berlin saying that Casement would be landed from a submarine off the coast of Ireland. As a result, in April 1916 he was arrested as he came ashore near Tralee. Casement was subsequently tried in London and sentenced to death.

Casement was highly respected both in Britain and overseas, not just as a diplomat but as a crusader against the ill-treatment of native workers in Africa and South America. To counteract the wave of sympathy for Casement, Admiral Hall privately circulated copies of a diary purporting to show that the Irishman had indulged in homosexual practices with boys in Latin America.

The diaries, which were forgeries, were wholly irrelevant to the charges brought against Casement and were not produced in court. Equally their informal distribution went well beyond the scope of Hall and his team. Yet they served their purpose. Casement was stripped of his knighthood and hanged. Some 50 years later, in an act of reconciliation, his remains were returned to Ireland, where they were reburied with full honours.

THE TABLES TURNED

The post-World War I German High Command was stung to discover the ease with which Room 40 had read its radio traffic and resolved never again to concede an enemy such an advantage. The army created the H.N.W. communications service and the Luftwaffe the Funkaufklärungsdienst, or N.-V.W. ('Intelligence and Signal System'). However the German cryptanalytic agency which had the greatest effect on the course of future events was the Kriegsmarine's 'B-Dienst', or 'Beobachtung-Dienst' ('Observation Service'). It had little contact with the other codebreaking agencies yet its success during World War II was out of all proportion to its minute size.

The penetration of British naval codes and ciphers began well before the outbreak of hostilities. When war eventually came it enabled German surface raiders to elude the British Home Fleet, spared German heavy ships from chance encounters with superior British forces, permitted surprise attacks on British warships, and helped sink six British submarines in the Skagerrak area between June and August 1940.

Arguably its greatest feat came in the invasion of Norway. Hitler approved the plan to invade Norway on 1 March 1940, but set no date for its implementation, fearful of the havoc that the Royal Navy might wreak on the invasion fleet. When B-Dienst reported that the Royal Navy planned to mine the entrance to the northern Norwegian port of Narvik, to block German ore shipments, the High Command decided to use this information to its advantage.

As soon as B-Dienst reported that the British mining fleet had sailed, Germany sent a decoy force to meet it. Sensing the possibility of battle, the Admiralty responded by ordering the Home Fleet and two cruiser squadrons north on an interception course. As soon as the British capital ships were too far away to intervene, the German transports crossed the Skagerrak free of Royal Navy interference, landing their occupation troops without a hitch.

THE U-BOAT WAR

The Battle of the Atlantic was without parallel. Its true beginning was in June 1940, when the German army reached the Atlantic coast of France. The capture of the Bay of Biscay ports gave the German submarine fleet a massive advantage, saving a round-trip of 1450 km (900 miles) to and from their favourite patrolling stations.

Both sides had a huge advantage unknown to the other. In July 1940 the German merchant raider *Atlantis* captured a copy of the 'BAMS code' used universally by British merchant shipping, together with a series of super-encipherment tables. Armed with this intelligence, the U-boat command had no difficulty in interpreting intercepted messages to the convoys and thereafter in deploying its submarines to maximum effect. By February 1943, B-Dienst had so effectively mastered the British crypto systems that it was even reading the British 'U-Boat

Even during the final stages of the war, the German U-boat fleet remained impressive.

Topham

173

Situation Report', which was regularly broadcast to the commanders of convoys at sea, telling them the known and presumed locations of U-boats!

The following month, March 1943, saw the climax of the Battle of the Atlantic and the near defeat of the convoy system. Within five days, B-Dienst reported the precise location of three convoys. Every U-boat available was sent to intercept and within three days 141 000 tons of Allied shipping was sent to the bottom, at the cost of only a single U-boat.

Britain was saved by the efficiency of her signals intelligence. In June 1941, Bletchley Park cracked the German Navy Enigma ciphers, enabling the Admiralty to monitor the incessant radio traffic to the U-boats. Convoys were rerouted around known 'wolf packs' and an estimated 300 merchant ships saved. Bletchley Park endured a Sigint blackout for nearly a year when the Germans altered their Enigma settings. However, the picture dramatically changed in spring 1943, when Bletchley Park regained its ascendancy and was once again able to direct the growing Allied might against the U-boats. German morale broke suddenly in May, when 31 U-boats were destroyed; on 24 May, Admiral Dönitz ordered the 'wolf packs' to disperse.

THE MODERN THREAT

SEABORNE INSERTION

Seaborne insertions became popular during World War II. Raiding forces and espionage parties were often carried to their targets by fishing boat, submarine, mini-submersible or canoe. In August 1942, the converted minelayer *Argonaut*, along with the *Nautilus*, delivered a raiding party of no fewer than 211 US Marines to Makin Island in the Gilbert Archipelago: they killed all 70 members of the Japanese garrison and destroyed a seaplane base. On 11 May 1943, *Argonaut* and *Nautilus* delivered a second unit to Attu atoll with equal success.

The Italian Navy made excellent use of its submarines to deliver miniature submarines and frogmen to the vicinity of enemy bases. Two boats of the 'Adua' class were converted to carry watertight containers for three assault craft, and two 'Flutto'-class boats had four such containers. Using such craft the Italian Navy not only sank some 63000 tons of Allied warships and 50000 tons of merchant shipping but also provided the Axis powers with invaluable intelligence on the potential movements of convoys in and out of Gibraltar.

However, despite these notable successes, the problems of landing covert parties on hostile shores were legion. Local commanders were rarely willing to release their best combat assets for espionage duties and few submarine commanders, who almost universally regarded themselves as hunters rather than transporters, relished risking their craft on missions of which they were told little.

Water infiltration remains popular. Much of NATO's northern and southern flank coast-lines (like those of her potential enemies) are long, rugged and exposed, creating an extremely difficult area to defend. Those attempting covert infiltration onto beaches today, however, must avoid not only the gaze of the enemy sentry but also very sophisticated radar and sonar arrays that cover the sea approaches to most countries. In effect this almost completely rules out the use of large surface vessels such as fishing boats. The canoe, however, remains a viable option. The sea-going Klepper or the latest generation of French and German canoes can be parachuted into the sea or launched from a submarine, and can be equally easily dismantled once ashore.

COVERT SWIMMERS

Every country of military significance employs marine special-purpose forces to execute reconnaissance and espionage missions, raids and acts of sabotage. These units are the elite and remain shrouded in secrecy, even to the point of certain countries refusing to concede their existence.

SPECIAL BOAT SERVICE

Britain has the Special Boat Service, a Royal Marines Commando elite within an elite. During World War II, a number of specialist units were raised to undertake beach reconnaissance and raiding duties along the European and Far Eastern coastlines. The value of these groups was so self-evident that they survived the inevitable post-war cutbacks and amalgamations to form the nucleus of the 'Small Raids Wing' attached to the Royal Marines Amphibious School.

During the next 20 years Special Boat Sections found themselves involved in reconnaissance and espionage missions against Chinese coastal emplacements during the Korean War, undertaking counter-insurgency operations in the Malayan Peninsula, supporting the Army in Borneo and working closely with 45 Commando in Aden. In 1977, in recognition of their consistently high standards, they were renamed the Special Boat Squadron. More recently they have been brought under the control of the Director Special Forces and renamed the Special Boat Service.

Although based at Poole in Dorset, the SBS operates world-wide. In recent years SB Sections have been deployed in Northern Ireland on border and coastal surveillance. During the Falklands campaign they were the first ashore on South Georgia, having initially flown from the United Kingdom and parachuted to a submarine in the freezing waters of the South Atlantic. They worked closely with 'B' and 'G' Squadrons of the SAS, providing intelligence for the beach landings, and may have been involved in espionage on the Argentine mainland itself, although this remains a matter of conjecture.

The SBS numbers some 150 members, sub-divided into a headquarters and three operational sections. An additional section is drawn from the ranks of the Royal Marines Reserve (RMR) and numbers some 50 members, who are selected, trained and exercised by their regular counterparts.

SPECIAL AIR SERVICE

Since its formation the Special Air Service (SAS), which currently has one regular and two Territorial regiments, has seen the advantages of using water as a means of espionage, intelligence gathering and infiltration, and has specialist teams formed into 'boat troops'. Traditionally the demarcation between SBS and SAS was the high-water line, but in the last decade circumstances, and to a degree unit rivalry, has caused this theory to be abandoned. This led to tragedy during the Falklands campaign when, unbeknown to each other, the SAS and SBS put patrols ashore in the same uninhabited area of the West Falklands. One man was killed and several injured when the patrols 'bumped'.

SPECIAL AIR SERVICE REGIMENT

Australia delegates the maritime reconnaissance and espionage role to the Special Air Service Regiment (SASR). The SASR was raised as a company at Campbell Barracks, Swanbourne, near Perth, Western Australia, in July 1957. It was quickly assimilated into the Royal Australian Regiment, the principal regular infantry element of the Army, but regained its independence on 4 September 1964. It was gradually expanded until, by 1966, it boasted three 'Sabre' squadrons, a headquarters, a base squadron, a training squadron and elements of 151 Signals Squadron.

Training Squadron has six specialist wings, of which Water Operations Wing is just one. No. 2 Squadron has two Water Operations Troops, made up of patrols of four to six men. Their role is parallel to that of the SBS, covering coastline surveillance, reconnaissance and beach survey. Sabotage and espionage against potential enemy positions are rehearsed and anti-smuggling patrols and surveys undertaken.

2ND REGIMENT ETRANGER PARACHUTISTE (REP)

France has a long connection with the history of diving and a strong tradition of covert swimming. The Fusiliers Marins, France's green-bereted Commandos, are trained in amphibious warfare and employ swimmers who are inserted into beach landing areas to survey the main landing zones. 2nd REP, the parachute regiment of the Foreign Legion, also employs covert swimmers. Its 3rd Company specialises in amphibious operations, and as such trains in the art of wet parachute drops, surface and underwater swimming, and the use of small boats.

An Italian two-man submarine of the type used during World War II. The craft is in transit mode, without the warhead fitted. Popperfoto

COMSUBIN

No country in the world has a prouder tradition of covert maritime warfare than Italy, whose special forces wrought havoc among the ships and installations of the British Mediterranean Fleet in the early part of World War II. Although modern fleets do not contain the huge capital ships of World War II, Italy is none the less well aware that the Mediterranean would play an important role in any future European conflict. Italian Navy Special Forces, known as COMSUBIN, ('Comando Subacquei Incursori') were formed in 1952 and now train for and specialise in all forms of covert maritime activity.

COMSUBIN is based at Varignano, a small centre near La Spezia on the north-west coast, and is under the direct control of the Navy Chief of Staff. It is organised into five units, two in support and three operational. The 'Incursori', the offensive arm of COMSUBIN, is small, consisting of less than 200 men of all ranks and is necessarily extremely secretive. Divided into logistics and operational cells, the 'Incursori' works in small teams of between two and 12. Its base at Varignano affords excellent underwater operational training areas. Friendly, but invariably unsuspecting, naval and merchant ships around the coast provide excellent material for the numerous simulated espionage and sabotage attacks made by each member of the 'Incursori' each year.

US NAVY SEALS

The US Navy SEALs were created on 1 January 1962 as an independent group capable of undertaking counter-insurgency operations, covert and overt, by SEa, Air and Land. Existing Underwater Demolition Teams (UDTs) were carrying out their duties of reconnaissance and beach clearance excellently, but theirs was felt to be too passive a role for development. Although SEALs are trained almost exclusively in offensive warfare they are none the less excellent at reconnaissance; they were used to monitor potential landing sites for Marine amphibious units in Grenada and the Gulf.

The 'Recon' Marines of the United States Marine Corps are trained to undertake deep reconnaissance before and during a landing when SEAL units are not available. 'Recon' Marines will move inland before a landing to seek out enemy defences and reinforcements and mark potential targets. They will move covertly so as not to draw the enemy's attention either to themselves or to the impending assault.

NAVAL SPETSNAZ

The role and organisation of the Russian Republic's special forces are still evolving. Prior to the disintegration of the Soviet Union, Naval Spetsnaz was the smallest and most secretive of its special forces. There were four operational Naval Spetsnaz brigades, one attached to each of the Northern, Baltic, Black Sea and Pacific Fleets. Each brigade comprised an anti-VIP Headquarters Company manned exclusively by regular servicemen, a midget-submarine group, three combat-swimmer battalions, a parachute battalion, a signals company and support units manned by conscripts.

Naval Spetsnaz have traditionally regarded much of their training, which was uncompromisingly harsh and physical, as 'active service', with many of its exercises carried out against the hulls of unsuspecting merchant ships. In time of war their tasks would have been as diverse as they would have been dangerous.

It has been suggested that manned Argus-class and unmanned 'Zvuk'-class submarines, designed primarily for scientific research, may have been used by Naval Spetsnaz to ascertain

WORLD-WIDE UNDERWATER SURVEILLANCE SYSTEM

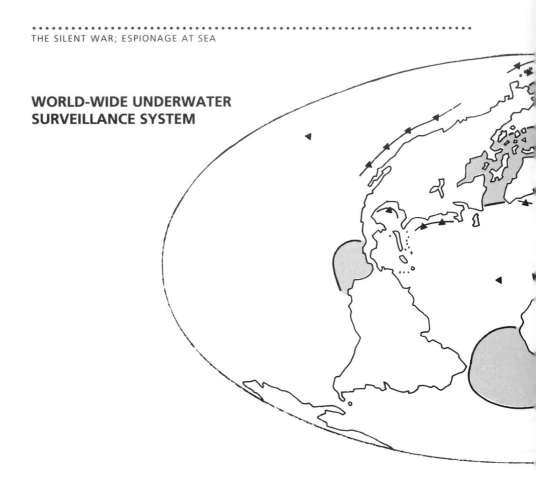

the position of underwater communications cables, with a view to destroying or tapping-in to them should the need have arisen.

Scandinavia was often visited by Naval Spetsnaz. Indeed, it seems highly likely that the vast number of territorial incursions complained of in the decade prior to the Soviet disintegration were carried out by Naval Spetsnaz forces operating from their base at Kronstadt, near St Petersburg (the former Leningrad).

SUBMARINE INSERTION

Espionage and reconnaissance patrols are frequently inserted from a patrol submarine. A transport aircraft carries the patrol from its base to a rendezvous with the vessel running at periscope depth. The submarine releases smoke to establish wind direction and an approximate drop zone. A decision is then made, dependent upon visibility, the sea state and the proximity of the enemy, on whether to surface.

The espionage team parachute into the sea carrying their personal equipment and breathing apparatus in waterproof containers. Extra equipment, such as inflatable boats and canoes, is dropped behind the men in containers. Once in the water the men don their masks and swimmer's fins before connecting themselves and their equipment to a rope, which is played out to its full length. The two outside divers activate transponder beacons, capable of making sufficient sound underwater to activate the submarine's sonar. The commander aims his vessel for the centre of the sonar signature and, running at reduced speed, allows the rope

Actual or probable US/Allied
sea bed sonar sites

Additional maritime ASW
patrol aircraft surveillance areas

to snag, causing the men and equipment attached to drift towards the rear of his boat. If the submarine is submerged, two swimmers dive down to open the stowage hatches and release a rope connected to a buoy, which floats to the surface. All equipment is then attached to the rope and guided into the stowage boxes. Once their equipment is secured British SAS and SBS infiltration teams tend to enter the boat via the five-man escape compartment. However, specialists from other countries prefer the claustrophobia of the torpedo tubes!

SHALLOW-WATER VEHICLES

Small inshore submersibles are being developed to allow the larger patrol submarines to remain in the comparative safety of deep water. A number, such as the 27 m (87 ft) Vickers 'Piranha' and the 3GST9, under evaluation for the US Navy SEALs, are designed to carry full teams of combat swimmers on offensive missions, and as such are too large for the greater subtleties of clandestine espionage work.

Other submersibles, such as Lieutenant-Commander Hugh Oswald's Subskimmer-80, are ideal. On the surface this remarkable craft resembles a powerful rigid-hull inflatable, powered by an 80 hp outboard motor. Close to the shore, the outboard's exhaust is sealed and a powerful suction pump is activated to suck the air out of the hull, enabling the boat to sink. 'Subskimmer' has a submerged speed of 8.5 km/h (4 knots). As it approaches its target, electric thrusters carry the craft on a power dive to greater depths, where it assumes the properties of a 'wet' swimmer delivery vehicle, capable of covering 9.66 km (6 miles) at 5 km/h (2½ knots).

It can be left on the bottom of a river or sea bed while the team infiltrates its espionage targets, and can later be recovered to return to the parent submarine or surface vessel.

THE SWEDISH EXPERIENCE

Soviet Naval Spetsnaz are known to have operated in covert missions from midget submarines in both Swedish and Norwegian waters, using larger conventional submarines for reconnaissance of the major areas of interest. Although the Soviet Union no longer exists, it would be facile to assume that Russia has not inherited a number of its espionage traits. It is wholly possible, therefore, that these incursions are continuing, albeit on a much-reduced scale.

It is probable that during the 1980s most incursions took place to establish places close to the Swedish mainland where Soviet nuclear ballistic-missile submarines might hide during a transition to war with NATO. Equally, the Soviets might well have wished to exploit the advanced Swedish road system through to southern Norway by landing a number of mechanised infantry divisions across the Baltic. To do this they would not only have had to reconnoitre landing sites but also establish in detail the potency of the Swedish coastal defences.

A major incursion took place at the Swedish base at Musko in October 1982. A number of Soviet submarines were involved, including three midget bottom-crawling craft of a type unknown to the Swedish authorities. During the same operation a midget submarine was reported to have entered Stockholm harbour. The craft used had twin tracks and single propellers and had been taken to the vicinity by a mother-ship, possibly an 'India'-class conventional submarine converted from underwater rescue duties. Incredibly, a photograph of the tracks left by one of these craft was published in *Pravda* in the mid-1970s, and said to be from a vehicle employed in the search for the lost city of Atlantis!

Soviet violations of Swedish territorial waters reached a peak in 1984, when no fewer than 20 incidents were reported. An improvement in Sweden's anti-submarine warfare (ASW)

The command position of a British Chariot two-man human torpedo.
Popperfoto

(Opposite) A Soviet miniature submarine suspended on its mother-ship, photographed by the Swedish Navy in 1981.
Topham

capabilities in the following year, coupled with the adverse publicity surrounding the submarine intrusions, caused the number of espionage sorties to diminish. However, it is certain that the incursions continued under an even greater mantle of secrecy.

In none of the numerous submarine searches have the Swedes succeeded in forcing the intruders to the surface, although they have mounted frequent heavy anti-submarine attacks. Indeed, in all but one case they have been unable to establish the identity of the intruders. The sea bed is considered to be too shallow, the target too small and the distortion created by the rugged coastline too great for conventional sonar to be effective.

In an incident which began on 24 February 1990 and lasted for several days, Swedish submarine hunters detonated underwater mines and fired anti-submarine grenades from a helicopter while chasing a suspected foreign submarine in the archipelago south-east of Stockholm. There was no evidence of any hit, and the search was eventually abandoned.

In October 1981, a Soviet 'Whiskey-II' class submarine ran aground off the Karlskrona naval base. The Soviets blamed navigational error and apologised, but the Swedes felt that the presence of the vessel during the testing of a new wire-guided torpedo in the vicinity was more than coincidence. World attention was attracted to the incident when the submarine was found to be carrying nuclear weapons; possibly depth charges, torpedoes or atomic demolition munitions. The submarine, which was extremely old and of a class no longer used for conventional patrolling in the Baltic, was also found to have been fitted with two attachment points, possibly for the coupling of midget submarines during transportation.

When the submarine was subsequently released it returned across the Baltic to the Soviet Union. Its commander was court-martialled, found guilty of negligence and sentenced to three years in a naval prison.

At the time the Soviet Baltic Fleet's independent intelligence service (RU) was headed by a Rear Admiral who reported to the chief of staff and thence to the Fleet commander. However,

(Opposite) A Soviet Whiskey-II class submarine of the type that ran aground near Karlskrona. Topham

(Below, left) The USS Liberty, *which was attacked by Israeli aircraft and torpedo boats, killing 34 American sailors. A torpedo hole can be seen on the waterline.* Popperfoto

the head of the RU was also responsible to the Chief of the 5th Directorate of the GRU, which in turn was controlled by the Department of Administrative Organs of the Central Committee of the Communist Party, and above that the Politburo and the Defence Council. The Baltic RU was therefore scarcely independent save in name, and must, one would have thought, have been deeply implicated in the 'Whiskey-II' affair. Thus it is extremely strange that the Admiral commanding the White Sea Fleet (and not the Baltic Fleet as might have been expected) was subsequently transferred to other duties.

SPY SHIPS

Although the Soviets operated some 40 spy ships, and the Russians continue to maintain a reduced number, the United States never had much luck with its signals intelligence (SIGINT) fleet. Within less than a year in 1967–68, they lost two vessels in distressing circumstances.

The USS *Liberty* was an old 10 000-ton freighter pressed into service as a SIGINT platform. When it appeared off the Sinai coast during the build-up to the Arab–Israeli Six-Day War in the summer of 1967 the Israelis objected. They realised that the ship's highly sophisticated monitors would be able to intercept battle orders on both sides, down to company level, and did not wish the United States to know the true extent of their victory.

Without warning, the USS *Liberty* was strafed by Israeli Mirage and Mystère jets, which effectively destroyed her electronic equipment. She was then attacked by three motor torpedo boats and ultimately surveyed for damage by a flight of reconnaissance helicopters. Casualties were high; in all 34 of the crew were killed and 75 wounded. United States military response was slow. An F-4 Phantom sortie was flown from the carrier USS *America*, but arrived too late to protect the ship from initial attack.

The Israelis issued a half-hearted apology, stating that *Liberty* had been mistaken for an Egyptian spy ship, but few in the intelligence-espionage world believed them. *Liberty* had been flying a large Stars and Stripes at the time of the incident. It was, in any case, unthinkable that an organisation as professional as Mossad would not have known of the existence and whereabouts of the United States ship.

The *Liberty* incident proved the vulnerability of spy ships to determined attack by a target more interested in preserving its secrets than adhering to the conventions of international law. In January 1968, the so-called *Pueblo* incident reinforced this unpalatable reality. *Pueblo*, a similar espionage vessel, was working off the coast of North Korea when it was attacked and boarded by a North Korean warship in January 1968. The crew, and a considerable quantity of secret papers and equipment which the captain did not have time to destroy, were captured.

The crisis provoked by this blatant act of piracy continued for a year. Eventually, in order to secure the release of the crew (on 23 January 1968), Washington was forced to confess to espionage activities under the terms of a complex deal arranged through the Mixed Armistice Commission at Panmunjom, and apologise.

Disillusioned by the two disasters, the US decommissioned its SIGINT fleet. However, the Soviet Union, confident that her ships would never become the victims of such blatant assault, had no such doubts and continued to rely heavily on its fleet of converted trawlers.

During the 1960s, the Soviets built up a spy-ship fleet of ex-trawlers with especially good sea-keeping qualities for their size. Generally referred to by their NATO designation of AGI (Auxiliary Vessel, General type, Intelligence), they became a familiar sight on the world's oceans, particularly in the proximity of a major Western naval exercise.

Traditionally the Soviets employed converted East German 'Okean'-class trawlers with a crew of 32. Increasing sophistication and larger crews, however, forced them to seek replacements. The newer 'Balzam'-class AGIs are of 4000 tons displacement, and have a crew of 180. The omnipresence of these ships in the proximity of NATO exercises undoubtedly provided the Soviet Navy with a wealth of information on Western tactics, strengths and deployment patterns. They would have helped establish the composition of battle and carrier groups and, most crucially, the operational relationship between the surface fleet and its mantle of protective submarines.

A number of AGIs follow well-established patrol lines, hunting for random intelligence in the process. Others spend months anchored to the same station monitoring the passage of target shipping in and out of key ports. British Polaris (and until recently United States Poseidon) nuclear submarines based on the west coast of Scotland have to pass along the Irish Sea where their presence is regularly monitored by at least one AGI.

A large part of the intelligence gained by AGIs must lose at least a degree of its value due to the delay caused by its having to be recorded and taken home for analysis. However, in the days of the Soviet Union, Tu-95RTs (NATO name 'Bear-D') aircraft frequently overflew the AGIs and it may be assumed that ship-to-aircraft links were established for the passage of the most

The Soviet research vessel 'Ayu Dag' made three illegal entrances into Oslo harbour over several years.　　　　Topham

A clear view of the USS Pueblo *showing a variety of LF, HF, and VHF antennae.*

Popperfoto

This 'Balzam' class AGI came within five miles of Pearl Harbor.

Topham

important intelligence. Today, most modern AGIs have rectangular housings on the bridge which are almost certainly employed to protect satellite-communications antennae.

SUBMARINE ESPIONAGE

Routine espionage is undertaken on occasions by virtually every fleet submarine. Most submarines have at least one periscope mast devoted to electronic sensors capable of detecting radio and radar transmissions. Although these are used primarily to warn the submarine of the impending approach of a hostile aircraft or ship, they can equally be used to monitor the movement of an enemy.

NAVAL AIR ESPIONAGE

Naval secrets are not safe simply because they are aired far from the land. All major fleets have air wings which constantly overfly their own and international waters in search of a potential enemy. Until recently the movements of the four Soviet fleets were monitored by NATO, fed into a central computer and analysed daily.

ELINT COLLECTING SHIP

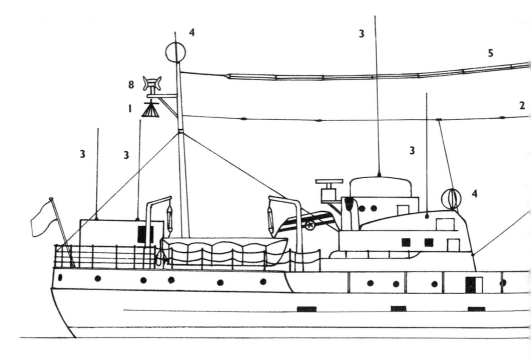

SUBMARINE SURVEILLANCE

Soviet submarines were electronically intercepted en route from their home bases to their patrol areas and monitored, possibly throughout the course of their entire mission.

When a submarine was positively identified, its unique acoustic signature was recorded. Thereafter, whenever that vessel passed within range of one of the many listening devices planted on the ocean bottom, it was identified and logged. Unfortunately this seemingly foolproof system of identification failed on at least one crucial occasion. During the early 1980s the Royal Navy maintained a record of the acoustic signatures of its NATO allies and Warsaw Pact rivals. It did not, however, keep a log of neutral submarines. When Britain went to war with Argentina over the Falklands, therefore, she was unable to utilise her most sophisticated intelligence-gathering systems to identify the enemy submarines threatening the exclusion zone. Fortunately for Great Britain, Argentina had only two submarines operational at the time, one of which, the *Santa Fe*, was forced aground on South Georgia early in the campaign.

Maritime patrol aircraft such as the British Nimrod, with their long endurance and ample accommodation, make ideal submarine-hunting platforms. A typical mission might last from eight to 14 hours and take the aircraft 1609 km (1000 miles) from base. Occasionally the aircraft will be armed with torpedoes or depth charges, and will certainly carry more than 100 sonobuoys and a variety of markers and pyrotechnic devices.

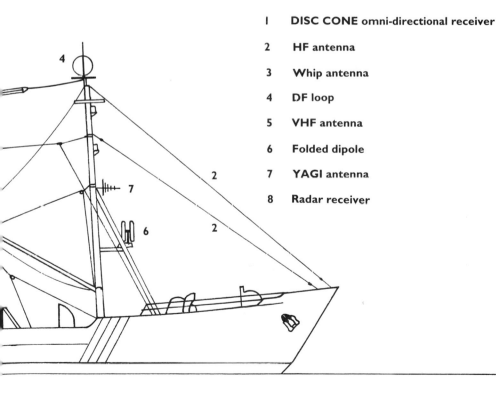

I	DISC CONE omni-directional receiver
2	HF antenna
3	Whip antenna
4	DF loop
5	VHF antenna
6	Folded dipole
7	YAGI antenna
8	Radar receiver

(Opposite, top) A Soviet sonobuoy found floating near Puget Sound. Interestingly, the electronic components are copies of American items. DOD/TRH

(Below, right) AQS-903 advanced acoustic processing system is now installed in RN Merlin ASW helicopters. GEC/Guy Taylor

SONOBUOYS

As sonobuoy performance is dependent upon the prevailing ambient conditions, a bathythermograph buoy will often be dropped first to monitor the ocean temperature and salinity at different depths. Once transmitted to the aircraft, this information will enable the crew to set the optimum operational mode for the sonobuoy.

Sonobuoys can be either directional or omnidirectional, active or passive. In all cases their hydrophone operating depth, surface-to-air transmission frequencies, buoy life and operating mode are pre-set in the aircraft prior to release; in the latest generation of sonobuoys, operating depth can be altered after the sonobuoy has entered the water in order to follow a target into a different temperature layer.

The United States currently buys some 289 000 sonobuoys annually and is in the process of introducing the SSQ-75 ERAPS (expendable reliable acoustic path sonobuoy), capable of operating at depths of between 300 and 4875 m (984 and 16 000 ft). The GEC Avionics AQS-902 Series Acoustic Processor, employed in Royal Navy Sea King Mk 5 helicopters, can handle up to eight NATO-specification sonobuoys simultaneously. The more advanced AQS-903 system being fitted to the EH-101 Merlin helicopter offers all-round cover, plain language analysis and display cues, and will interface with sonobuoy launch, navigation, tactical tracking and weapon release systems elsewhere to offer effective multi-targeting cover if required.

MAGNETIC ANOMALY DETECTION

Magnetic Anomaly Detection, or MAD, operates on the principle that a submarine's presence in the water can be detected by means of its deviation from the Earth's standard magnetic field. MAD is essentially a very short-range aid, the magnetic anomalies detected being minute. Although MAD is primarily carried on board search aircraft such as Nimrod, Atlantique and Orion, it can equally be housed on board the smallest naval helicopter, with the added advantages of low-level hover over target. The latest generation of MAD-equipped helicopters trail a detector 'bird' as far away from the aircraft as possible in order to reduce, to the absolute minimum, magnetic interference from the helicopter's own fuselage. MAD is used primarily in anti-submarine warfare and can work to depths of 90 m (295 ft); it is also suitable for surveillance, especially in choke points such as the Gibraltar Strait.

PHOTO-ESPIONAGE

Maritime patrol aircraft also carry out photo-reconnaissance missions over international waters. Although these missions cannot technically be classed as espionage, due to their international location, they can occasionally provoke retaliation. It is not at all unusual for 'spy' aircraft to be shadowed or to have flares fired into their probable flight path by a ship in the process of being photographed.

To avoid unnecessary danger a code of practice has evolved between the major participating nations. In May 1972, Supreme Commander of the Soviet Navy, Admiral S. Gorshkov and United States Secretary of State Warner signed the 'Incidents at Sea' Pact aimed at guarantee-

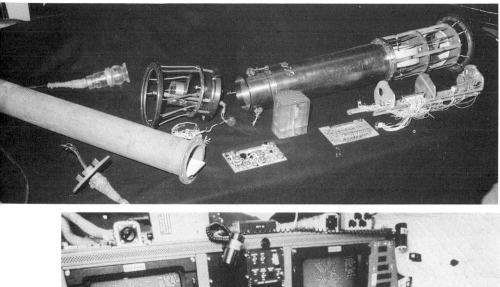

ing the safety of the warships and espionage aircraft of both nations when operating in international waters. Risky manoeuvres and direct overflights were banned and ultra-low flying in the vicinity of the other's aircraft without prior notice discouraged. For their part the European NATO members agreed to limit the number of passes made over a particular target during any single sortie.

Certain areas were considered too sensitive for random overflying. Thus Britain agreed not to fly its Nimrod reconnaissance aircraft in the far north of the Baltic, while NATO in general acceded to the Soviet wish that only Norwegian maritime aircraft should patrol the entrance to the Kola Peninsula. However, this concession did not prevent the USAF from overflying the area with its SR-71 'Blackbirds'.

Despite the plethora of highly complex equipments carried by naval espionage aircraft, the art of aerial photography remains quite primitive. Both the Nimrod and Atlantique are fitted with a removable opaque panel on the forward fuselage of the aircraft. Immediately before the photographs are taken the aircraft loses height and banks towards the target to enable the photographer to get as clear a run of pictures as possible. The window is then opened and the hand-held camera activated. Poor weather conditions, particularly heavy winds, make good photography very difficult and occasionally dangerous to the photographer. There have been a number of examples of photographers sustaining serious injuries when their arms have accidentally been caught in the slipstream.

However, the occasional excellent photograph makes the entire operation worthwhile. Warships have sometimes been caught with new radar or weapons sytems uncovered, and IRLS imagery has done much to help in the analysis of the nuclear propulsion systems of the latest generations of non-conventional craft.

In July 1976, a British Nimrod took the first needle-sharp picture of the flight deck of the Soviet carrier *Kiev* to be publicly released. The vertical take-off and landing (VTOL) Yak-38 'Forger' aircraft on board were not at all as expected, and led to an early re-evaluation (downwards) of the potential of the carrier-borne Soviet threat.

The Soviets began their own brand of naval airborne espionage in the 1960s when photographic reconnaissance versions of the Tu-16 bomber (NATO designation 'Badger-E') began to target United States and Royal Navy aircraft carriers. In 1968, nine Soviet Tu-16Rs in Egyptian colours began to pay close attention to the United States Seventh Fleet in the Mediterranean. In July 1972, the aircraft were moved to Libya, but continued to be manned by Soviet crews with the photographs going straight to Moscow.

Photo-reconnaissance Tupolev Tu-95MRs (NATO designation 'Bear-E') and converted Il-18 'Coot' civil airliners have more recently been seen patrolling potential flash points in the Gulf and Indian Oceans.

Soviet Tu-95 Bear bombers, with in-flight refuelling, are capable of extreme long-range maritime intelligence gathering flights.   Guy Taylor

MAJOR NAVAL ESPIONAGE AIRCRAFT

Beriev Be-12 Chaika

The Beriev Chaika (NATO designation 'Mail') is one of the few remaining operational amphibians. Production of the Be-12 began in 1963, with more than 200 models built. A weapons bay is located in the rear fuselage forward of the sonobuoy launchers. A MAD 'sting' is fitted aft of the tail as if to confirm the principal role of the aircraft as ASW. Other roles include maritime patrol and anti-ship, and at least one EW version has been reported.

Although the Be-12 has been gradually phased out of Russian service in favour of the Il-38 'May', an estimated 75 aircraft remain serviceable. The Be-12 is thought to have been the inspiration for the Chinese Harbin SH-5 flying boat, which also operates in a limited espionage-reconnaissance role.

Ilyushin Il-38 'May'

The Il-38 was derived from the Il-18 civil airliner, which first entered service with Aeroflot in April 1959. Subsequently 565 models were built at the GAZ-30 aircraft plant before production ceased in 1979. Two weapons bays were added to the converted Il-38, one ahead of the wing box and the other aft of the wing, and the entire wing structure moved forward.

The 'Wet Eye' surface search radar operates in J-band to maximise the angular resolution of the antenna and help reduce the effects of sea 'clutter' in the radar returns. A tail-mounted MAD is an obvious feature, as is a tiny chin fairing aft of the nose-mounted navigation/search/weather radar, which is thought to house an EO sensor. The Il-38 remains in service with the Russian Republic and has been exported to India.

Lockheed S-3B and ES-3A Viking

The Lockheed Viking is the world's only true carrier-based reconnaissance and espionage aircraft. The Viking is equipped to a high standard, with sonobuoy systems, FLIR, a MAD tail boom, radar, ECM and ESM equipment compressed into a relatively small airframe. A total of 40 of the 187 aircraft originally built have been converted to S-3B standard and retrofitted with an improved APS-137(V)1 radar, ARR-78 sonobuoy receiving system, UYS-1 Proteus acoustic processor and a GPS satnav system.

In 1988, work began on the conversion of 16 S-3A Vikings to ES-3A ELINT aircraft. The 61 sonobuoy tubes were removed and the area reskinned, and the weapons bay doors removed and replaced by cheek fairings. A long dorsal fin has been added with a radome covering an omnidirectional receiver antenna. Two smaller radomes and 35 assorted antennae have also been added to the fuselage. The on-board ELINT systems have been proven in the larger Lockheed EP-3 ELINT variant of the P-3 Orion.

British Aerospace Nimrod MR.2P and R.1P

The first production Nimrod MR.1 maritime patrol aircraft flew on 28 June 1968. A total of 46 production models were ordered by the RAF with deliveries beginning in 1969. Nimrod was effectively a Comet 4B civil airliner fitted with an unpressurised ventral section and powered by four 5520 kg (12 140 lb) Rolls-Royce Spey 250 turbofans.

Only five of the final batch of eight MR.1s were delivered; one became the prototype MR.2, while the remaining two became prototypes for the AEW Mk 3'. The service career of the MR.1

was relatively short, with conversion of 31 aircraft to the much-improved MR.2 standard beginning in 1975.

The RAF also operates three Nimrod R.1 aircraft. Little information has ever been released about their mission or capabilities, but it is highly likely that they carry highly sophisticated electronic eavesdropping systems.

Dassault-Breguet Atlantique

Construction of the twin-turboprop aircraft was carried out by the international consortium SECBAT (Société d'Etudes et de Construction du Breguet ATlantique). By the time that production ceased 87 aircraft had been built with 40 sold to France, 20 to Germany, 18 to Italy and 9 to the Netherlands. West Germany updated its fleet in the early 1980s, replacing the radar, ESM, tape recorder and sonobuoy ejection systems, modifying the acoustic processing system and installing an INS (International Navigation System). Since 1988 the French Aéronavale has received 30 completely new Atlantique 2 aircraft.

A Tu-16 Badger bomber, widely used for naval intelligence gathering.　　Guy Taylor

S I X

COMMERCIAL ESPIONAGE

THE OFFICE SECRETS

Business communications are not secure. The 1991 ASIS Technology Theft Survey of 165 companies indicated a marked increase of information theft by targeting commercial communications. This has now become one of the leading ways for foreign entities to target European and United States corporations both at home and abroad.

Most foreign governments, including those friendly to the source, can and do collect competitive business information from open source literature as well as from other human and electronic intelligence-gathering methods. This competitive intelligence is then passed on to local industrial interest on a regular basis.

While most agencies are reducing in size the French secret service is expanding to pry into friend and enemy alike. In 1992, President Mitterrand authorised a 10 per cent increase in the budget of the Direction Générale de la Sécurité Extérieure (DGSE), which is responsible for spying abroad. It must be assumed that France is preparing to increase its economic espionage, especially on its allies, including Britain and the United States.

The French learned the value of industrial espionage from a Soviet spy code-named Farewell. Until his arrest in 1982, Farewell worked in the industrial-espionage department of the KGB. Subsequently he told the French what information the KGB picked up abroad and how. He reported that in 1979 the KGB had collected 58 516 documents and 5824 industrial samples from the West, allowing them to start 162 new projects and accelerate 1262 others.

Not all subsequent French attempts at espionage were illegal. In 1991, two men were spotted rifling through rubbish outside a private house in a suburb of Houston, Texas. An off-duty police officer took the number of their van, which was traced to the French consulate. The house belonged to an executive of Texas Instruments. A French representative explained that the men were collecting grass cuttings to fill in a hole in the consulate garden!

The recent relaxation in military tension has led to a decrease in defence spending and an increase in redundancies in the world of armaments design and technology. Many once-secure specialists have combined with ex-security and military intelligence personnel to set up commercial surveillance organisations. It must be said that the vast majority of these firms are honest.

Typically they will concentrate on making pretext telephone calls to the target company in general to establish senior executives' private telephone lines, extensions and car telephone numbers; they will head-hunt key employees with amazing job offers as part of the process

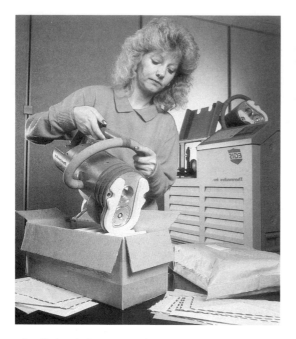

In the battle for commercial advantage the threat of sabotage is treated as seriously as that of espionage—here with the aid of an explosives 'sniffer'.
Zefa

of collating information about their current employers; they will sift through published literature such as glossy company files, public relations media, newspaper articles and technical journals for indirect information, and will even undertake rubbish searches.

A number of major organisations (including the UK Ministry of Defence on occasions) have neglected to clear their computer hardware properly when upgrading, and by this omission have inadvertently presented the purchasers with a wealth of commercial intelligence on their discarded hard disks.

ELECTRONIC EAVESDROPPING

In order to obtain the quality of commercial intelligence demanded by their clients, surveillance firms are increasingly able to rely on less covert methods of espionage, which in the majority of countries are still legal. A surprising number of business transactions take place via radio-based systems—cellular phones, cordless phones, delivery vehicle dispatch, buildings security, paging, inter-building and central office-to-vehicle data transmission. The only practical way for anyone to get communications on the move is via radio—yet few businessmen seem to realise the possibility of intelligence leakage through this obvious means.

Legislation on electronic surveillance differs widely around Europe. In Germany, one may manufacture, sell, buy, possess but not use electronic surveillance devices. Neither may one possess a radio receiver which can receive any of the controlled frequency bands. In Luxembourg, the laws relating to individual and corporate privacy are strict. In Britain they are virtually non-existent, save for the Interception of Telecommunications Act introduced to protect the national telephone networks against unauthorised bugging. The wide disparity of legislation within the European Economic Community makes the job of the professional eavesdropper far easier.

CORDLESS TELEPHONES

Cordless telephones offer little, if any, protection against eavesdropping. The original cordless phones had a range of between 100 and 200 metres/yards and used two radio frequencies, one at 49 MHz and the other at about 1900 MhZ, the approximate AM broadcast band. When cordless phones were legalised in the United Kingdom, the 49 MHz band was replaced by a handful of channels at 47 MHz. Operators wishing to intercept calls have merely to place their receiver within 200 yards or so of the target and scan between 46 and 49 MHZ until the signal is located. Having ascertained the frequency of the signal the operator can simply leave the scanner tuned and connected to a voice-activated tape recorder to monitor all calls on that line. More sophisticated recorders will even establish the date and time of each call.

Blatant eavesdropping on cordless phones is not illegal in Britain, and the Government has expressed no immediate intention of introducing legislation. In the United States the Supreme Court has ruled that eavesdropping does not violate the Fourth Amendment, as users have 'no justifiable expectation of privacy'. In the cold world of commercial reality therefore organisations which continue to transmit confidential information over cordless telephones have only themselves to blame if subsequently that information is compromised.

CELLULAR PHONES

Cellular phones are now used by a wide cross-section of the business population and are increasingly used not only for voice but also for data and facsimile calls on subjects ranging from sales and ordering to detailed discussions over takeover strategies. Cellular radio networks, although more secure than cordless telephones, are still far from safe.

The increasingly widespread use of cordless telephones has opened up a whole new field for eavesdroppers and counter-measures.   Zefa

Cellular telephoning, as its name implies, is based on a network of cells. Each cell has its own base transmitter operating on several independent duplex radio channels and connected to the central electronic telephone exchange network. In rural areas these may be 30 km (18½ miles) in diameter, whereas in cities the cell diameter might be as small as 2 km (1¼ miles). When a cellular phone user decides to make or receive a call the control channels allocate the phone a pair of actual frequencies (one for receiving, one for transmitting). As the cellphone owner is usually on the move the signal strength of the allotted channel tends to fluctuate. When it falls below a given strength the cellphone immediately scans around looking for another control channel with a stronger signal. If it finds one in a neighbouring cell any conversation taking place will have to be changed to a new pair of frequencies. This process, usually accompanied by a brief digital buzz, is known as 'hands off'. 'Hands off' will not inconvenience a bona fide listener to a call. It will, however, break the transmission for an unauthorised eavesdropper.

Thus a scanner set to the right frequency for a country and region (915–960 MHz in the United Kingdom, 820–840 MHz in the United States and 450 MHZ in much of the rest of Europe) will intercept a mass of part conversations. However, these will be anonymous and almost certainly too fragmented to be of commercial espionage value.

Interception with simple scanning equipment will occasionally be possible in rural areas,

(Left) A midget transmitter fitted into a cufflink box. (Right) A radio microphone and antenna.   Popperfoto

where cells are larger and 'hands off' correspondingly rarer. In November 1990, Richard Needham MP, a junior minister in the Northern Ireland Office, was driving in South Armagh and talking to his wife when his call was intercepted by an IRA cell. Detrimental comments about Prime Minister Margaret Thatcher, including the phrase 'I wish that cow would resign', were leaked to the Belfast press and published. Mrs Thatcher is said subsequently to have 'graciously' accepted Mr Needham's apology!

Eavesdropping in an urban environment is far harder. Operators capable of getting close enough may try to listen to the signals coming from the target cellphone itself (as opposed to the base station signal to the cellphone, which will always be 45 MHz higher). Although this signal will be much weaker the scanner will intercept signals only in the immediate vicinity, giving the operator a greater chance to identify his target. If the interceptor can follow the cellphone owner's car, when the 'hands off' takes place and the signal dies he will be in a far better position to relocate it.

A variety of more complex interception equipment exists for the purposes of detailed commercial espionage. Receiving equipment will listen on the control channels, interpret the information it hears and use either a pair of scanners linked to a computer or an adapted cellphone to move channel in sympathy with the target cellphone.

TELEPHONE TAPPING

Telephone tapping is the most widely publicised of all the eavesdropping techniques, and is the most difficult to defend against because telephone wiring gives the eavesdropper the advantage. He does not need access to the target building and he can attack anywhere before the telephone exchange.

In 1989, private detectives Michael Anderson, a former policeman, and Terry Rowe were convicted of intercepting the telephone of Comet director Peter Hooper. A few months later a convicted phone tapper, David Coghlan, appeared on television to describe in great detail a series of audio intelligence operations which he had undertaken over a period of eight years. These included the opening of British Telecom street cabinets to access the telephone system and drilling holes through window frames and external walls to place probe microphones in sensitive rooms. More recently the actress Koo Stark complained that private detectives have darted the wall of her home with a radio-probe microphone.

Once an operator has obtained details of routings from the telephone company he can identify a particular line, or group of lines, from among the many thousands in a joint or street junction box. He can then reroute the target line to another building or discreet area where he can attach his eavesdropping equipment.

Phone taps can be divided into three main groups; remote, hard-wire and inductive. Remote taps, which are often located by the top of a telegraph pole and use the line's own power to trickle-charge a Nicad battery, can remote a signal to a listening post several hundred metres away. Such devices normally operate only when the target telephone is being used, and, in addition, may be time-switched to coincide with the working day or remote-switched on and off during periods of particular interest.

Contrary to public belief, professionally fitted telephone taps are not readily detectable. There are no additional noises or clicks, nor is the clarity on the line degraded. Telephone tapping technology may be used just as easily to intercept a message sent by fax. A fax machine simply sends audio tones down a telephone line which are used by the receiving machine to construct the transmitted document. Stand-alone and PC-based fax and data intercept

The simple, but effective, microbug has been on the market for nearly thirty years.
Popperfoto

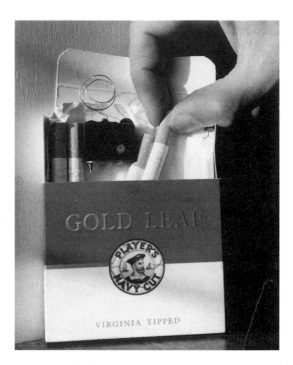

equipment exists which will covertly intercept and capture fax transmissions from any make or model of machine, regardless of its handshake or synchronisation signal.

A second form of telephone compromise involves the making of an electronic alteration to the microphone or ear-piece of a telephone handset. With the widespread use of plug-in phones, the simple substitution of a compromised set can be made in seconds. The rogue telephone will appear to operate normally. However, when not in use as a conventional telephone it will transmit all sounds from its location to an eavesdropping receiver.

Telephone wiring itself can also be compromised. Even optical fibres, which are increasingly being used to provide telecommunication links internally and externally, are liable to interception. A fibre optic may be intercepted by removing the outer covering and carefully bending around a cylinder of a particular radius. The minute leakage of data-carrying light (typically no more than 0.2 per cent) may be sufficient to reconstruct all the traffic passing along the fibre-optic cable.

RADIO BUGS

Miniature radio transmitters can be disguised as almost any piece of mundane office equipment and as such pose a tremendous threat to the security of the modern commercial organisation. Bugs have to be powered, either by batteries or by external power sources such as solar or mains. Battery technology has not kept up with advances in electronics, thus batteries (even lithium) are still quite large and this currently prevents the further shrinking of bugs to virtual pinpoint size. 'Parasitic' bugs therefore can have size advantage over battery-powered ones but can have their power supply interrupted.

Frequency, which can vary between 30 MHz and 25 GHZ in radio microphones, has a direct bearing on the size and range of a covert transmitter. Generally the lower the frequency the larger the device and the greater its range. Range is also affected by the output frequency, the antenna efficiency and the type of building construction; concrete and steel are far more conducive to long range than traditional bricks and mortar.

Modulation, the method of placing audio information on the radiating signal, is a vastly variable factor in modern bugging devices. Simple devices rely on amplified or frequency modulation (AM or FM), which is relatively easy for a sweeper to detect. More complex systems, however, resort to spread-spectrum, subcarrier, pulse-code and digital modulations, which are far harder to compromise.

Miniature audio transmitters are usually classified as 'quick plants', objects which can be left without notice or suspicion or exchanged for harmless objects by cleaners, visitors or maintenance staff. Typically they will take the form of pens, books, rulers, picture hangers, even lumps of chewing gum 'discarded' under the base of a desk or chair.

Installed devices, which tend to be larger and more powerful, are usually planted while a building is being built or refurbished. The transmitter is normally placed some distance from the microphone, is possibly mains-powered and is always difficult to detect.

In 1982, the United States shipped a number of new electronic typewriters to its embassy in Moscow, stored them in an unguarded warehouse, and then professed dismay when

This tiny transmitter bug costing £60 has a range of 229 m (750 ft) and will operate for 30 hours. Popperfoto

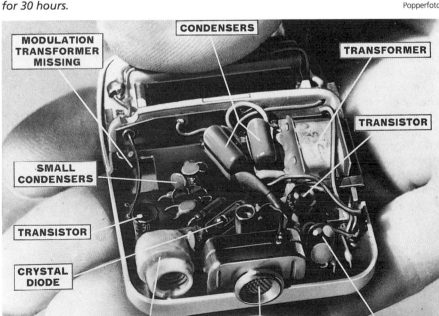

security officials reported that the machines had been expertly bugged. Data being typed onto the machines was being beamed outside the walls of the embassy to the waiting KGB listeners.

When the United States and the Soviet Union agreed to grant each other improved embassy facilities in 1968, the State Department found itself the victim of one of the most complete mass buggings in history. Soviet security zealously guarded the day-to-day construction of its new facility, employing one security adviser per two American construction workers on site. The blueprints were kept under lock and key and changed regularly. Rooms remained anonymous and were not marked for the purpose for which they were designated.

In Moscow things could not have been more different. Much of the building was prefabricated away from the actual site and beyond the supervision of the few security staff assigned. Blueprints were not kept secure and were clearly marked with the room's ultimate purpose—even the ambassador's office and code rooms were clearly shown. Not surprisingly early electronic security checks proved that the whole, partially finished embassy was in fact one gigantic KGB antenna. To compound the problem, thousands of chips and electronic components had been added to the concrete mixture, making it impossible to sweep for the genuine bugs. It was estimated by an embarrassed State Department that a new and smaller, more secure office would have to be built and the top three floors of the intended embassy completely rebuilt, at an additional cost of $40 million!

To add to the State Department's discomfort, it had to admit to hiring a Russian-speaking design engineer to supervise construction in Moscow. Perhaps not surprisingly the man, a Russian *émigré* but a United States citizen, subsequently opted to return to his motherland.

In 1980 the Soviet Embassy in Washington claimed that this bug had been planted in their new living quarters.
Popperfoto

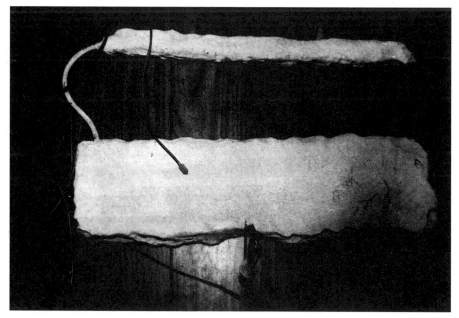

TRANSMITTER VARIATIONS

Infra-red microphones, which use similar technology to a television remote-control unit, cannot be seen by the human eye and make an excellent transmission medium for commercial espionage purposes. They suffer the potential drawback of requiring line-of-sight to operate but do have the advantage of being legal.

There are laser devices which operate in the near infra-red spectrum, close to visible light. They make ideal bugging devices, subject to the availability of a suitable reflective medium to radiate energy back to the source.

Perhaps the most difficult of all room bugs to detect are passive eavesdropping devices which receive and transmit radio energy. They operate in the extremely high microwave part of the spectrum, are small and require no batteries or maintenance.

TEMPEST

Untreated machines, such as visual display units, printers, disk-drives, modems, fax and telex machines, intercom and telephone systems, will emit to varying degrees an involuntary transmission, radiation or emission which, when analysed, can contain compromising intelligence. Unstable images of what the computer is displaying at any particular moment can be transmitted to an unauthorised screen nearby. Unless the pirate equipment is quite sophisticated, freeze and print-out facilities will not be available; and any letter or memo of more than 80 characters by 25 lines will be extremely difficult to read.

If, however, the operator has the facilities, and the estimated espionage retrieval value merits the financial outlay, additional equipment may be introduced. An image capture board can be linked to the pirate screen, as can Optical Character Recognition (OCR) equipment, which will translate a blurred image into characters which the computer has been programmed to recognise.

Known as 'Tempest' (Transcient ElectroMagnetic Pulse Emanation STandard), the entire phenomenon is complex and offers no guarantees of success. As such it is used commercially as an agency of last resort. Moreover, it has been successfully countered by Government agencies such as GCHQ and the NSA for some time. However, their precise techniques remain highly classified and have yet to be overtly released to the civil commercial market.

THE SAGA OF DAVID MELLOR

In July 1992, David Mellor became the victim of a relatively unsophisticated media bugging incident which ultimately compounded with other unrelated problems to cost him his ministerial career. His friend, an out-of-work actress, Antonia de Sancha, had recently taken a lease on a two-storey converted flat in a Georgian house in Finborough Road, West London. She had been advised by the owner, the entrepreneur and electronics specialist Nick Philp, that he was going away on business and would not require the property for some while. However, being aware of de Sancha's relationship with a top politician, Philp had bugged his own telephone. Her subsequent telephone conversations were taped by him and offered to the *News of the World*, which declined to purchase them.

The *People* newspaper showed more interest, but demanded concrete evidence before going to press. It decided to eavesdrop further, this time using its own investigators. Unknown to de Sancha an extension was fitted to Philp's telephone and run out through the window of a second-floor room and down the back of the house to a patio below.

The telephone socket in the second-floor room to which the extension lead was attached was hidden from de Sancha, whose tenancy agreement did not grant her access to the patio. A novelty silenced handset receiver, in the shape of a Jaguar car, was employed so as not to alert de Sancha when her telephone rang. Incoming calls were signalled when the car's headlights flashed. Conversations were recorded on a mini-cassette recorder linked to the telephone.

In all, the extension lead, the telephone and the recorder which gained the newspaper the evidence which it required prior to publication cost less than £100 to purchase on the open market. As a back-up, a listening device capable of picking up voices in the room and transmitting them to a receiver outside was placed behind a picture in the flat. The effect on David Mellor's career when the story was published is now history.

COMPUTER VIRUSES

Recent events have shown that computer viruses can cause catastrophic problems to commercial and defence networks. They have started a new kind of electronic warfare, the electronic insertion of a computer virus microcode into a victim's system. International terrorism has been quick to see the feasibility of using viruses to attack the technological heart of an enemy. In so doing it has become interwoven with the criminally less serious but commercially equally devastating world of the espionage hacker.

Viruses spread like wildfire. They comprise small software programs which duplicate themselves while hiding within another program. The speed with which they can travel from computer to computer is extraordinary. In their simplest form they make copies of themselves in any other program files they can find. They can mangle the files to a point where the system is no longer usable.

More complex viruses set out to ruin the entire structure of the target's hard-disk files, either by reformatting them or by completely wiping out the working storage, leaving much of the information unrecoverable. Given that information denial can be as lethal to a competitor as information compromise, viruses are beginning to enter the world of commercial espionage.

A recent study undertaken by the Ohio anti-virus specialists, Certus International, found some disturbing statistics concerning virus infection. Of the 2500 large sites with more than 400 personal computers which were investigated, half had experienced a computer virus infection. 3.3 per cent had suffered an infection before or during 1988, 11 per cent in 1989, 19 per cent during the first half of 1990, 16 per cent during the third quarter and 25 per cent during the final quarter of the same year. Most alarmingly, 26 per cent discovered a virus in January 1991 alone.

THE INTERNATIONAL HACKER

Traditionally computer security was regarded as the prerogative of companies with a large number of installations. However, the proliferation of personal computers and networked systems which hold sensitive company information has now taken security beyond the mantle of individual computer departments. To compound the problem, the recent growth in international scientific-based computer links has made non-attributable unauthorised access far easier.

In 1989, the then Soviet Union, Poland, Czechoslovakia, Hungary and Bulgaria applied to be connected to the European Academic Research Network (EARN). The link, which was approved in the following year, granted them access to Internet, a United States network serving defence, research and academic organisations world-wide. At a stroke the Soviets gained the ability to discuss scientific matters with Westerners working on similar projects without necessarily divulging their own identity. They gained easy access to the details of previously untapped institutions and individuals on the network; this was invaluable for later espionage targeting and opened the possibility of hacking into the network's closed data files. Although there is no suggestion that they have done so to date, it must be remembered that, in the so-called 'Hannover-Hacker' case in the 1980s, the Soviets used expert West German hackers to access United States restricted data bases, obtaining both software and defence-related intelligence in the process.

THE PRIVATE HACKER

Although there is no clear profile of the private computer hacker, the majority seem to share a number of common denominators. For the most part they are loners of above-average intelligence; they are interested in computers for their own sake, or in the technological challenge of breaking their security systems. Few are interested in financial gain, or regard what they are doing as illegal. Hardly any have contact with organised crime or industrial espionage networks. Most would not realise the full significance of valuable intelligence if they were to access it, and would have even less idea how to exploit their findings. Indeed it is true to say that the vast majority of stolen information gets no further than the hacker's wastepaper bin.

THE COMPUTER SPY

Unlike the 'pure' hacker, who is primarily interested in the challenge, the aim of the industrial spy is to gain as much information as he can from the confidential files of his target without getting compromised. The spy will study the target to see which part of his computer network is most vulnerable and which parts are therefore most likely to yield useful intelligence. Few large corporations employ only one computer system but prefer specialist networks for general database, payrolling, administration and personnel. A spy cannot hope to access every system and will therefore concentrate on the most vulnerable.

He will be able to discover details of his target's computer systems from a number of fragmented sources. A number of reference books and databases purport to cover most of the major computer installations, although their information is often out of date and incomplete. Specialist journals and even the commercial pages of certain newspapers often carry details of new contracts, occasionally supported by expansive articles prompted by the public-relations departments of the computer systems companies. The industrial spy, posing as a freelance technical journalist, will occasionally even be able to get further more detailed information from the potential victim itself, particularly if the target is keen to demonstrate its position at the forefront of new technology.

Increasingly companies are keeping the more intimate details of their financial status on personal computers located in the offices of the Financial Director, the Chief Executive or their immediate staff. Unless these machines have removable hard disks and are totally secure at all times they are among the most vulnerable.

Most computer compromise takes the form not of hacking but of simple theft by copying. A spy will gain access to a building using one of several guises: 'lost' visitor, engineer, new employee awaiting his security credentials (he may even be an established employee with a grudge). Once in the building he will locate the personal computer which he has carefully researched and, depending on the time and privacy available to him, copy all or part of the contents of its hard disk.

If the personal computer is connected to a mainframe or local-area network he may gain the added bonus of information from that source too. As soon as he is satisfied with his haul, he can simply place floppy disk or disks containing the stolen information in his pocket and head for the street. Few organisations exercise the right to search non-employees when leaving their premises.

Companies which practise personal computer as well as mainframe security can frustrate the espionage copier. The most secure commercial organisations that deal with classified information operate a 'locked door open cabinet, open door locked cabinet' policy designed to frustrate espionage by copying. When the occupier of a room leaves it temporarily he locks the door but leaves the cabinets open and computer running. When he has to leave the room for longer periods—for meetings, lunch or at the end of the day—he secures his cupboards, locks away his removable hard disk and leaves his office door open. Before leaving for home he will sign a declaration stating that he has physically checked his desk, computer and cupboards and that all are secure. Security staff will then check the room on a regular basis throughout the night.

HACKING TECHNIQUES

When simple copying proves impossible a commercial spy will resort to hacking. If he can gain access to the room in which the target computer is situated his initial attempts at compromise may be crude: he will check the immediate vicinity to see if the codeword has been recorded on a notice board or scrap of paper, he will try to overlook the legitimate user as he/she keys in the password or (if he is given the chance) attempt to guess the password using derivatives of the user's name, that of his/her spouse or boyfriend/girlfriend, or perhaps that of the boss.

If these rather crude methods do not work, and they frequently do, the commercial hacker must resort to rather more complex means. He may by-pass simple computer access control packages by using a fresh copy in the floppy drive and then rebooting. Alternatively, he may by-pass the access control by connecting his own desk-top computer to the target by one of the growing breed of special file transfer kits, which are normally used to move information at high speed between portable computers and desk tops.

Should all else fail he may resort to fake sign-on screens, which capture the passwords of legitimate users; password try-out programmes, which automatically offer guesses at a valid password from a dictionary of common variants; or password file decrypter programs. In the final analysis the greatest protection against both the hacker and copier lies in the constant physical supervision of ALL computers which hold any sensitive company information, wherever situated.

HUMINT AND COMMERCIAL ESPIONAGE

Humint, the exploitation of human resources for the gathering of intelligence, comes in many different forms. Overtly loyal employees boasting too openly about the exploits of their company after a Friday post-work pint-too-many provide one source of humint. Disloyal or sacked staff, or those 'headhunted' for a too-good-to-be-true position with an undisclosed

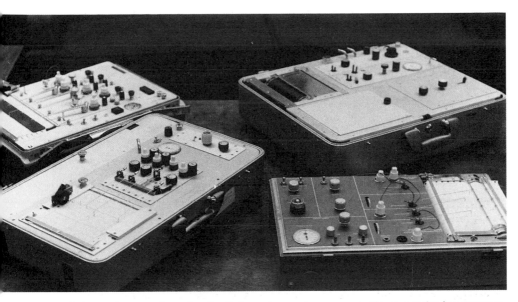

Polygraph screening of potential employees is now sometimes required to protect the highly valuable commercial intelligence. US Army/TRH

rival, are another. By its nature human intelligence from such sources tends to be patchy, subjective and difficult to verify, prone as it is to exaggeration and at times downright falsification.

THE PROFESSIONAL AGENT

More reliable humint can be obtained from professional agents such as private detectives. They follow rivals, watch their factories and offices, infiltrate staff into their premises, even scavenge their wastepaper for clues. Good professional agents are not easy to find. The larger, more established companies, who are eager to maintain an honourable name in a sullied world, tend to concentrate on major fraud investigations, asset hunting and the tracking down of counterfeiters, particularly in such fields as fake watches, perfume and pharmaceuticals. They will almost certainly not agree to any undertaking which might damage their reputation If disclosed. Where they do, they will invariably wish to employ sub-contractors.

The plethora of small detective agencies and security consultants who may have fewer scruples tend to specialise. Some concentrate on matrimonial compromise or process serving, others on personal injury, personnel vetting or insurance claims. Only a few will hold themselves out as physical security specialists, but, of these, very few have any real right to do so. Most physical security specialists will have an armed forces, often special forces, background or will be drawn from the retired list of the Government security services.

An SAS or MI5 background gives an operator a tremendous insight into the unusual. It does not, however, teach him or her how to make commercial enquiries or investigate fraud. Still less does it teach him about personal administration. Non-commissioned officers who have served perhaps half of their military lives with the SAS have learned to expect excellent research and training support facilities. When called upon to execute a mission they have become accustomed to others dealing with the preliminary and post-operational administration. Few seem capable of disciplining themselves to the mundane aspects of civilian commercial life; many who form small companies after leaving the Army suffer financial catastrophe within a few months.

This Minox miniature camera, made in Riga, Latvia, is 50 years old and is still highly valued by state and commercial spies.
IWM

COMMERCIAL INEPTITUDE

Not all security specialists work with the degree of consummate skill anticipated by their principals. In 1990, the *Sunday Times* Insight Team began to investigate the very real possibility of espionage in the unlikely world of private car parking. By 1985, National Car Parks (NCP) had become the largest car-parking operation in Europe, with a seemingly invincible control of the British market. It operated more than 650 car parks throughout the country, with a turnover of £151 million and profits of £37.5 million.

When Europarks, a rival company, started by the youthful Mancunian Stephen Tucker, began to take some of its prime contracts, George Layton, the chief executive and national chairman of NCP, started to wonder what the secret of Europarks' success was, and hired a group of former SAS soldiers to investigate. He contacted KAS, a firm set up by David Stirling, founder of the SAS, and an introduction was made to a director, Ian Crook, a former SAS colonel and Falklands veteran. It was agreed that KAS would use a freelance security consultant, David Patterson, to evaluate both NCP and Europarks in order to try to find out how Europarks were able to undercut their rival.

Mr Patterson, a former police officer in Zimbabwe, obtained a job interview with the directors of Europarks, from which he decided that their success was due entirely to their commercial efficiency. He was able to rule out the possibility of Europarks' infiltration of NCP management and urged that the operation should end. Not convinced, Crook ordered several employees, including an ex-SAS trooper, to get jobs as parking attendants with Europarks to gain more information. Europarks directors were followed home, where their dustbins were rifled for clues to their business and private lives.

By early 1989, Layton had become impatient with the pace of the investigation. KAS then recruited a 30-year-old female former army captain with SAS connections who, on the strength of a letter and CV which completely omitted her military service, got a job as personal assistant to Tucker, for whom she worked for four months. During this time she allegedly passed copies of management accounts to NCP and gave weekly briefings to them on Europarks' progress as well as providing a wealth of information about Tucker. She also allegedly provided details of contracts for which Europarks were bidding, with particular regard to how it was able so successfully to undercut its rivals.

The story broke shortly afterwards when a senior employee of KAS was dismissed and went to the Press. When the operation became public, Tucker filed a complaint with Scotland Yard, KAS went into liquidation and a police inquiry began. Tucker also issued a writ against NCP claiming substantial damages for industrial espionage. In an out-of-court settlement NCP paid Tucker an estimated £30 million for his controlling stake in Europarks and offered him a position as consultant on the NCP board.

FRATERNAL ESPIONAGE

Large political and industrial organisations are prone to espionage from within. In late 1992, left-wing leaders of Britain's biggest building union, UCATT, hired a private detective to monitor moderates whom they felt were being disloyal. UCATT's leaders suspected the moderates of conspiring to undermine the organisation by encouraging its members to desert to another union. The private investigator was sent to go through their rubbish in search of papers and documents to prove the accusation.

In late October, UCATT's solicitors used the rubbish collected to gain a Court order to search the homes of three men whom they accused of poaching members for the more moderate EETPU. Writs, which are being vigorously contested, were subsequently issued against the three individuals. In an interview with the *Sunday Times*, Noel Kelly, one of the defendants and a former UCATT convener on the Canary Wharf building site in London's

Docklands, described the union's action as, 'the kind of thing you would expect from the KGB or some right-wing reactionary government, not an organisation that is supposed to help its members'.

Miniaturisation has now been applied to visual surveillance. This car radio antenna houses a tiny lens which is connected to a remote recorder, shown here in the case.
Popperfoto

SPORTING ESPIONAGE

Sport is now big business. In many international events the difference between coming first and second can be measured not only in seconds but in a fortune in lost sponsorship. Skulduggery is commonplace during the America's Cup, a yachting event which costs millions to participate in, and which is held every four years at the home base of the previous winner. Fantastic steps are taken to preserve the design-integrity of each boat. Keels are kept covered when the yachts are not racing, areas of the dockyard are sealed off and armed guards are employed to deter intruders.

Matters reached a head during the January 1992 preliminaries when Amir Pishdad, a reservist in the US Navy SEALs, was discovered swimming beneath the hull of the New Zealand yacht. Pishdad was signalled to the surface. When he refused to comply Craig Kells and Eldon Archer, two New Zealand divers hired for just such a contingency, dived in after him, caught him, ripped off his face mask and removed his air pipe. This had the desired effect and Pishdad was hauled ashore to be secured in a headlock until the proper authorities could be summoned.

It was discovered that Pishdad had been carrying his airtank on his arm so that he could take a deep breath, leave the tank on the bottom and photograph the hull without leaving a tell-tale trail of surface bubbles. Pishdad denied that he had been hired by any of the seven rival boats (it later transpired that he was acting as a freelance) and was subsequently released without charge.

Pishdad's equipment was among the most primitive of the high-tech surveillance equipment then being utilised in the sporting-espionage war off the San Diego coast. Both New Zealand and Japan employed aerial reconnaissance helicopters in an attempt to photograph the keels of rival yachts in the crystal blue waters. Submersibles and two-man diving teams riding underwater sleds were spotted beneath the turning buoys. A huge powerboat named *Gazzini* even appeared to shadow the foreign yachts. Completely blacked out, its crew hidden from view, *Gazzini* was assumed to be 'tempesting' by using ultra-sensitive aerials to harvest electro-magnetic data from the computers aboard the rivals.

COUNTERING THE COMMERCIAL THREAT

Given the adage 'knowledge is strength' it is beholden on every corporation to keep its commercial strengths and weaknesses as secret as possible. Unfortunately, unless it is willing to remove its financial affairs to an 'off-shore' base, every limited company, public or private, has to produce readily accessible and increasingly comprehensive accounts. Whatever its geographical location, it has to justify its activities annually to its shareholders and offer enough information to its advertisers to make its products marketable.

RISK MANAGEMENT

Beyond the constraints of legal and commercial necessity, a company would be unwise to disclose anything that it did not have to. It needs to identify the information which most requires protection, establish its vulnerability and how best to guard it. This exercise is best carried out by a qualified team of managers and staff from departments dealing with proprietary information supported by experts in the fields of corporate security, human resources and corporate law.

The team should begin by identifying those components which give the company its competitive edge in the marketplace. These factors may include the quality of the product itself, the after-sales service, the price and manufacturing technology or distribution. Once it has identified them, the company should decide how best to protect its best assets. It must weigh the likelihood of espionage against the potential damage to the product if compromised and then decide whether or not it can afford the precautions necessary to ensure adequate protection.

HUMAN DEFENCES

A company which can convince its staff of the need for commercial awareness has won half the battle against espionage. Employees should understand that their professional well-being and progress depend on their company's success. They should be regularly reminded that profitability in large part depends on their vigilance in protecting the organisation's proprietary information.

Employees entrusted with answering the telephone should realise that this is a privilege, not a chore. They should be constantly aware of probing calls, or of unusual information being sought, and should be directed to terminate such conversations or pass them to the public relations officer. Secretaries should receive schooling in helpful evasiveness, with particular regard to the different interviewing methods available to an industrial spy.

Document classification and security is paramount. All proprietary documents should be classified according to the potential harm which might be caused by their loss or compromise. Where necessary they should be marked 'restricted' or 'limited access' and held in locked filing

Card access systems can be augmented by visual inspection using CCTV cameras.
Graphique Photography

Electronic access control systems eliminate the problem of master and sub-master keys which can be physically copied.
Graphique Photography

cabinets. Those with access to such cabinets should be vetted and have non-disclosure clauses added to their contracts of employment. Classified documents should be numbered and recorded in a central registry.

Photocopiers in the vicinity of the secure filing cabinets should themselves be secured and ideally disabled at night: options range from a secure power supply to a removable internal security component. Only specified personnel should be allowed to copy restricted documents, and where possible there should be a second member of staff present at the time, and all copies should be registered. Notes, drafts and memos should be treated with the same level of security as the source document. Once no longer required, a restricted document should be removed from the register, again by two independent members of staff, and shredded in the presence of both.

Visitors should be kept within a well-defined area as far away as possible from sensitive information. They should be escorted by their host at all times and should not be allowed to wander. In the past considerable intelligence has been gathered by company spies on their unescorted way to and from the lavatory. Plant tours should be discouraged unless absolutely necessary and should then be limited to known guests. In-house magazines, while remaining interesting, should divulge as little as possible about the company's aspirations or the private lives of its senior employees.

ELECTRONIC DEFENCES

Defences to protect a company from the risks of electronic espionage may be divided into two main areas: active technical surveillance and passive data and communication security. Active technical surveillance requires a lengthy (and expensive) visit by a properly equipped and trained technical-surveillance countermeasures (TSCM) team. Many of the smaller companies specialising in physical security will claim to offer this service, but realistically few have the requisite training or equipment. A TSCM team will concentrate on: the detection and prevention of information loss through eavesdropping; the security of communication circuits, telephone, data, facsimile, radio-phone and satellite communications; and finally the control of electronic (Tempest) emissions which might contain confidential information.

A trained team will be capable of detecting not only microphones with basic modulation such as frequency modulation (FM), amplitude modulation (AM) and subcarrier, but will also recognise pulse-code modulation (PCM), direct-sequence spread spectrum and slow to fast speed-hopping surveillance devices.

Following a technical counter-measures survey (TCMS), rooms should be secured. TCMS can only report the espionage state for the time being and suggest security improvements. It cannot foretell the future. A client company would be foolish to assume that, because bugging devices have been discovered, or even because an office has been found to be clean, that a subsequent attempt at espionage will not be made. A well-informed industrial spy will try to plant his devices after, rather than before, a TCMS.

Unlike active surveillance, which should be undertaken at least annually, passive security measures are relatively permanent and can be incorporated when an office is being designed. Where practical, a radio-secure area should be introduced. Proprietary screening material such as nickel-based formed fabric, which is both light and easy to apply, should be fitted to the walls, ceiling and floors and glass with an electrically conductive transparent coating fitted to the windows. Power, telephone, heating and air-conditioning vents should be filtered and screened to prevent them acting as a radio transmission path.

LAWFUL ESPIONAGE

THE SECURITY SERVICES IN DOMESTIC POLICING

THE FIGHT AGAINST TERRORISM

Covert policing in a democracy is never easy. It has to tread an almost impossibly fine line between a natural desire to succeed at any price and the constant need to keep within the law. Invariably opponents are less scrupulous and certainly less shackled. Having as their aim the destruction, or at the very least destabilisation, of that same society which the police are sworn to uphold, they have no regard for its mores.

Many counter-terrorist agencies, notably MI5 and MI6, regard themselves as intelligence gatherers and have no powers of arrest. Others, typically the Metropolitan Police Anti-Terrorist Branch, see themselves primarily responsible for law enforcement, with an overriding duty to bring the guilty to justice through the Courts. Ideally one would expect such agencies to work together by pooling their intelligence for the common good. The reality, however, could not be more different. Years of mistrust and professional jealousy have caused them to close internal ranks against their rivals regardless of the ultimate cost.

ANTI-TERRORIST ACTIVITIES

The ethos which caused MI6 and SOE to fight against rather than with each other in Occupied Europe lived on until recently in the fight against the Provisional IRA (PIRA). When the IRA first began its campaign in Northern Ireland in 1969, the British authorities believed that it could be dealt with quite quickly. They were wrong, yet until recently a strange mixture of stoicism, cynicism and complaceny permeated the domestic British attitude to the terrorists. With little initial sense of urgency, the relatively simple business of countering the bombers and assassins was allowed to falter and ultimately fail on the altar of entrenched attitudes.

Quite simply, too many agencies had become involved in what had rapidly become an intelligence quagmire. The principal bodies involved included: the Metropolitan Police Special Branch (MPSB), formed on 17 March 1883 to counter the growing incidence of Fenian bomb attacks in England; the smaller special branches attached to the 51 mainland police forces; MI5 to gather intelligence on the Loyalist threat in Britain and the IRA abroad; the Royal Ulster Constabulary (RUC) to combat terrorism in the Province; the Army, with its network of agents in Europe and Northern Ireland, Scotland Yard's Anti-Terrorist Branch; the Association of Chief Police Officers (ACPO), responsible for national coordination; and last but not least the Joint Intelligence Committee (JIC) responsible to the Prime Minister and Cabinet.

The core of the problem lay in the lack of dissemination of timely and reliable intelligence between the agencies. Traditionally the Special Branches of the RUC and the Republic of Ireland's Garda Siochana fed information to the mainland British forces via Scotland Yard. When it was discovered that this intelligence was being 'sanitized' before being passed on to the regions the RUC and Garda began to build up quite informal direct links with selected provincial police forces, by-passing the MPSB completely. This led to excellent transmission of intelligence between certain parties and the almost total starvation of others.

Whitehall realised that this situation could not be allowed to continue, and, in the wake of the assassination of Ian Gow, a Conservative MP and close friend of the Prime Minister, called for a large-scale security review, in July 1990. After years of debate, a report on mainland counter-terrorist organisations was completed in early 1992 by Ian Burns, an Under-Secretary at the Home Office. The report recommended the ending of Special Branch's sovereignty in mainland anti-terrorist intelligence-gathering in favour of MI5. It criticised the existing number of agencies involved and fuelled the cry for a single, national force capable of cutting through the then prevalent inertia. Such a force could be run on the lines of the FBI or the anti-terrorist forces in Germany and Italy, where 1970s terrorism had been crushed by central counter-terrorist overlords accountable to the Government but with otherwise almost dictatorial powers.

The ubiquitous East German 'VoPo'—a loyal government servant of a now discredited regime.
Mark Lloyd

The position of the MPSB was made more difficult in April 1992 when a report which was leaked to *The Irish Times* admitted that the Metropolitan Police had little 'hard' intelligence on the PIRA ASUs then operating in mainland Britain. Special Branch paranoia became even more acute later that month when it was reported that, as well as being asked to relinquish its leading role in IRA surveillance on the mainland, it might also be losing its diplomatic and VIP protection responsibilities.

As a part of the Metropolitan Police's 'proposals and options for change' it was proposed that the three Scotland Yard departments responsible for VIP protection—SO14, the plain-clothes officers who protect the Royal Family, SO16, the diplomatic protection branch, seen in uniform at embassies, and SO12, the political protection team—should merge into a single, uniformed entity. A previous attempt to combine the organisations had been dropped after the personal intervention of Prime Minister of the time Margaret Thatcher. However, the new Prime Minister, John Major, was regarded as less unyielding in his attitudes.

Light aircraft with sophisticated lightweight thermal imaging systems are being increasingly employed in the fight against terrorism.   Guy Taylor

THE ULSTER EXPERIENCE

Anti-terrorist activity evolved far more satisfactorily in Northern Ireland. During the 1970s the RUC and Army developed a vast network of agents and covert intelligence-gathering sources, using front companies such as video stores and laundries to gather together thousands of snippets of useful intelligence. In one instance a covert Army mobile laundry operating in Catholic West Belfast successfully identified a number of terrorists by submitting soiled clothing left for cleaning to forensic testing. Although this information could not be used to effect immediate arrests, it was invaluable to Military Intelligence in their attempt to establish the identities of the bomb-makers, couriers, and quartermasters behind the actual gunmen.

Occasionally these enterprises met with tragedy when the brave young soldiers manning them were compromised and killed. However, the intelligence gained, when added to that gleaned by troops manning covert observation posts, was considered well worth the risk.

Information gathered at vehicle control points (VCPs) and by random mobile foot patrols was fed into the intelligence computers at Lisburn until the security forces were able to establish family, street and even traffic patterns. Simple questions about an individual's movements could be verified within seconds and suspects found to be lying pulled in for more detailed questioning.

More recently the Army and RUC have increasingly come to depend on electrical intelligence and on agent penetration. Using powerful receivers and a network of ground-based listening stations, Royal Signals specialists regularly target known areas of IRA activity, sweeping the atmosphere for vital intelligence that might indicate the movement of known terrorists or reveal their planned bombings and assassinations.

A computer constantly scans telephone transmissions in search of key words: possibly the name of a terrorist, a known telephone number or a suspected safe house. Whatever key word or sequence of numbers the computer has been programmed to pick up, once spoken during a telephone call, the key activates the computer's recording facility and the conversation is relayed to the screen of the duty intelligence analyst.

Northern Ireland has an advantage over mainland policing in having a single Special Branch command. It also has a dedicated and near-autonomous military command network and a supportive political infrastructure directed by a single government minister. Equally, the authorities there have not forgotten that terrorism must be combated simultaneously on two planes. While gathering high-grade intelligence on potential terrorist activity from the various Elint sources available, they have not forgotten the importance of maintaining Humint and low-level intelligence gathering, utilising the computer back-up available for verification. It is perhaps sobering to note that when, in early 1993, Special Branch handed over responsibility for the prosecution of the mainland war against the IRA, it did not have a single computer network dedicated to the collection, collation and assessment of counter-terrorist intelligence.

MI5
A Second Police Force?

When the new anti-terrorist role for MI5 was confirmed in early 1993, a number of politicians and influential pressure groups expressed concern. They feared that the personnel intelligence-gathering facilities available to the security services in Northern Ireland would become available on the mainland and feared that this might lead to the targeting of a number of anti-establishment, though wholly lawful, organisations. They felt that the Security Service was expanding its intelligence-gathering activities beyond its traditional role and would lack accountability. They further argued that the end of the Cold War had left the 2000-strong agency massively over-manned, as a result of which it was desperately seeking a re-definition of its role. Suggestions that MI5 was also becoming involved in anti-narcotics operations and was investigating the possibilities of expanding into the fields of organised crime and fraud did nothing to alleviate such fears.

Stella Rimington, the newly appointed head of MI5, tried to defuse the fears. In an unusually open statement she declared that her service looked forward 'to strengthening (its) already close cooperation with the police service, and combining our skills even more effectively with theirs to help them bring terrorists to justice'.

(Above) The new London headquarters of MI5. Guy Taylor

(Opposite) A measure of MI6's openness is reflected in its choice of this new headquarters building near Vauxhall Bridge, London. Guy Taylor

Her speech met with little support from Ulster Unionist MP Ken Maginnis, who regarded the move as a step away from police primacy, nor from Social Democrat and Labour Party spokesman Seamus Mallon, who saw it as a move away from public accountability.

The police themselves, who of course have most to lose, have also been less than enthusiastic. The Metropolitan Police has started giving courses to MI5 personnel on the presentation of evidence in court in anticipation of their becoming more involved in criminal prosecutions, but it is difficult to see how they will be able to appear in the witness box while preserving their anonymity.

It is clear that in the eyes of MI5 the distinction between intelligence gathering and police operations is becoming blurred. Given that MI5 is thought to have stepped up bugging and tapping work in the commercial sector recently, a number of responsible police sources have now begun to query whether MI5 will be asked to take on the less-attractive aspects of police 'espionage', which is currently serving to ferment growing anti-police feeling in sectors of the population.

That MI5 can work successfully with the police was established in December 1991, when Post Office staff in the sorting office in Bangor, North Wales intercepted a number of incendiary devices contained in video cassette boxes. The four bombs had been intended for Welsh Office minister Sir Wyn Roberts, Conservative Party agent Elwyn Jones, the head of North Wales CID Detective Chief Superintendent Gwyn Williams and Detective Inspector Maldwyn Roberts, responsible for the special arson squad investigating the activities of the Welsh nationalist organisation, the Sons of Glyndwr.

Three suspects who had been seen experimenting with unknown devices were placed under covert surveillance by the police. Once sufficient grounds had been established to allow

them to do so, MI5 secretly entered their premises and photographed evidence which was subsequently used to bring the trio to trial.

Under New Management

The existence of MI5, an open secret since before World War II, was finally conceded in the Security Services Act, 1989. Two years later, in December 1991, the Government again broke with tradition when it announced the appointment of Mrs Stella Rimington in succession to Sir Patrick Walker as the agency's new head. Not only did Mrs Rimington become the first female head of an intelligence service in Europe, but was also the first Briton to have her appointment publicly proclaimed.

Mrs Rimington cut her teeth in MI5's F Branch, which is responsible for countering the activities of political subversives (including at one time, it is claimed, a number of Labour Party MPs and prominent trade unionists). She became head of F2, responsible for the analysis of the threat presented by political extremist groups: it was there that she came to the attention of Sir Patrick Walker. In the late 1980s she was promoted to the Directorship of Counter-Terrorism, dealing with Middle Eastern and Irish terrorism in Britain and the activities of the IRA abroad.

Mrs Rimington is ideally suited to the new, more open and accountable world of MI5. However, her lack of police experience may prove a disadvantage as she battles for supremacy in a politically hostile world. An unsuccessful attempt by MI5, reportedly sanctioned by her, to flood the City of London with undercover agents for a week-end in the hope of catching the IRA in the act of planting a car bomb, proved an embarrassing and expensive failure.

POLITICAL INTRIGUE

MI5 has never been popular with the political left. Although some of the horror stories relating to its covert activities against organisations with left-wing tendencies are certainly exaggerated, a number must be regarded as disconcertingly true. Under the leadership of Sir Michael Hanley, who succeeded Sir Martin Furnival Jones in 1972, MI5 became increasingly preoccupied with surveillance of groups such as the Socialist Workers Party (SWP) and the Workers Revolutionary Party (WRP), both of which had grown out of the student revolts of 1968.

In 1974, it is claimed that a group of MI5 officers actually hatched a plot to drive Prime Minister Harold Wilson from office. This group, which it must be emphasised was never large, planned to leak to the Press embarrassing confidential information on Wilson, his Cabinet and senior trade-union supporters. Allegations that Wilson was a suspected Soviet agent would, it was felt, almost certainly cause him to resign and leave him in no position to fight a general election thereafter.

The plot was aborted when senior MI5 officers refused to have anything to do with it. When the affair came to the attention of the head of the service some years later a number of those responsible were belatedly disciplined. Harold Wilson, who had at least an inkling of the plot, never forgave the service. After his resignation in 1976 (which had nothing to do with security service pressure) he made a variety of allegations against MI5, even seeking the assistance of the CIA to establish whether any of their operators had been implicated.

Stella Rimington is the first Director General of MI5 to be publicly acknowledged as such.
PA/Topham

Accountability

Recently MI5 has become the subject of considerable unwelcome debate on the topic of accountability. Although the Government has now put the security service on a statutory footing it has steadfastly refused to make it answerable to Parliament. A Security Service Tribunal has been appointed to investigate complaints against MI5, but its decisions have been specifically exempted from judicial appeal. Thus a victim of a hypothetical wrongful bugging may complain to the tribunal, but will be unable to take the matter further should the tribunal's finding prove unacceptable or evasive.

Strenuous attempts have been made by senior members of all political parties to increase MI5 accountability, particularly in the light of its new policing roles, but to date these have fallen on deaf ears. Indeed, when Stella Rimington was invited to appear before the Home Affairs Select Committee her attendance was vetoed by the then Home Secretary.

When addressing the House of Commons during the second reading of the Security Service Bill in December 1988, the Home Secretary made the following observation: 'An oversight body could not steer clear of secrets by confining itself to generalities. A body which had no access to secrets would have access to very little of interest or importance to the work of the security service. A body that worked and reported in ignorance would not be of much appeal to the House.

'If the body was inside the necessary ring of secrecy, it would have to report in monosyllables to those outside. People could not be expected to be content with that, whether they were members of the body or those who listened to the reports.'

Despite the reported support by the last three directors of MI5 for some kind of independent oversight, the Government shows no signs of yielding.

In December 1991, 90 innocent Arabs were interned as 'terrorists' at the start of the Gulf War. It subsequently transpired that none of them had links to terrorist groups. Information against them, which had been gathered by the Immigration Department, the Special Branch and MI5, was outdated and inaccurate. Although all three services were subsequently exonerated, the incident brought the question of government accountability to the fore.

A foreigner facing deportation as a 'national security risk' can appeal only to three Home Office-appointed advisers. He cannot be represented by a lawyer at the closed hearings, has no right of access to a court and is not allowed to know why he has been arrested.

Under certain extreme conditions the Home Secretary is empowered by the Prevention of Terrorism Act to sign an Exclusion Order denying British citizens access to the British mainland. The Home Secretary is not bound to divulge the evidence against the subject, which will normally have been provided by the Special Branch or MI5, and his decision is final.

In April 1993, there were 77 Exclusion Orders in operation, including one against John Matthews, cleared in open court of an attempted IRA bombing. In his defence, Home Secretary Michael Howard denied that exclusion was a response to the dropping of criminal charges. Instead he stated that he had evidence, which would have been inadmissible in court, that Matthews had been concerned in the 'commission, perpetration or instigation of acts of terrorism'. Under existing legislation neither Matthews nor his legal advisers have the right to question this accusation.

FOREIGN INVOLVEMENT

Unlike its sister agency, MI6 has yet to be put on a statutory basis. In 1973, its new head, Sir Maurice Oldfield, began to stamp his unique mark of authority on the agency. Operations were

Sir Maurice Oldfield was brought out of retirement to co-ordinate intelligence operations in Northern Ireland.
Topham

strictly controlled and scrupulous in their adherence to the wishes of the government of the day. The objectives of MI6 were also widened to take account of the increasing demand for commercial intelligence—on Britain's EEC partners, the Japanese and the Middle Eastern oil states in particular. A new government body, the Overseas Economic Intelligence Committee (OEIC), became a major customer for both MI6 and GCHQ. The OEIC would define areas where information was required and then analyse the information fed to it, distributing it in sanitised form to private commercial, as well as government, organisations.

During the 1970s, MI6 became heavily involved in Northern Ireland with often questionable results. In 1972, the organisation was deeply embarrassed by the infamous Littlejohn affair. The Littlejohn brothers, Kenneth and Keith, were known criminals operating in the Irish Republic. They were recruited by MI6 as informants in February 1972 and continued in that role until their arrest for bank robbery in the following October. Under cross-examination the brothers claimed that MI6 had provided them with arms and explosives to carry out bank raids and attacks on police stations in the Republic, knowing that these would be blamed on the IRA. They also claimed to have been given a list of known IRA men to assassinate.

MI6 emphatically denied any involvement, to the extent that Oldfield reportedly summoned his entire staff to a meeting to ensure that there was absolutely no truth in the story. None the less mud stuck, and the affair contributed to the decision in 1974 to reduce the MI6 presence in the Province.

Today MI6, with the CIA and new Russian intelligence service, is one of only three global intelligence networks. It no longer deals with IRA activities, having delegated these to MI5 world-wide. It is still interested in commercial espionage, although it would prefer to call it intelligence gathering, but is now also concerned with nuclear proliferation, (non-IRA) terrorism and drugs.

Particular attention is being paid to the Middle East, because of its instability and the extent of British interests; and to the former Soviet republics, because of their volatility. Other areas of prime interest include Hong Kong, China, South Africa, India and Pakistan.

Sir Colin McColl is not, as is often erroneously thought, designated the Director-General. His popular nomenclature, 'C', is in fact short for CSS, or Chief of the Secret Service. He has a staff of 2000 in Britain and an undisclosed, and probably fluctuating, number abroad. He has an open budget of £185 million, which he shares with MI5, and an undisclosed one which is probably far larger.

MI6 is far more liberal than in its recruiting policies than in the past. It accepted its first CND member in 1985 and now actively encourages the employment of non-public school personnel (Maurice Oldfield was its first grammar-school head). Many employees are actively recruited from the armed services, a policy also adopted by MI5. Salaries, based on a rigid civil service scale, are not high, deterring many worthy applicants not already enjoying the benefits of a police or military pension.

The recruitment of foreigners is said to be based on a 'hierarchy of loyalties'—whether it be political opposition to their own regime, professional failure in their ordinary job, an unstable social life or pure avarice.

BIG BROTHER IS LISTENING

LEGAL PHONE TAPS

The Government disguises the number of phone taps authorised each year. Although warrants may be as low as 500, several of these will cover entire organisations, or all the telephones to which a particular individual has access.

It is estimated that as many as 35 000 lines are tapped in Britain annually, the bulk of them for the security services and Special Branch. Since 1980, the number of specialist engineers employed by British Telecom to mount the taps has increased by 75 per cent.

A new high-security installation at Oswestry, Shropshire, which was opened in 1993, makes it possible for engineers to tap by computer without leaving the building. An individual line can be intercepted instantly and relayed to a listening centre anywhere in the country. The new system also allows 'treeing'; if target A makes a call to B, who then calls C, each call will be tapped instantly from Oswestry.

MI5, MI6 and Special Branch officers are known to have regular briefings at Martlesham, British Telecom's research establishment in Suffolk.

GCHQ

GCHQ, the Government Communications Headquarters on the outskirts of Cheltenham, is vast. Located as it is on the edge of the main A40 highway it is difficult to hide, yet it remains shrouded in secrecy. GCHQ is the British nerve centre of a global intelligence-gathering network, developed in partnership with the United States National Security Agency.

The electronic eavesdropping network incorporates the United States-built Menwith Hill and Morwenstow monitoring stations in Britain, a huge complex in the Troodos Mountains of Cyprus and a smaller centre in Hong Kong. GCHQ reputedly has some of the most sophisticated computer equipment in the world, capable of intercepting anything from huge international transfers to domestic chit-chat. It employs over 10 000 military and civilian personnel, the latter now banned from trade union membership as a security measure since 1984.

GCHQ works closely with the NSA, although certain information of a commercial nature is jealously guarded from United States eyes. Unlike domestic telephone tapping by MI5 and the police, which is governed by the Interception and Communications Act, 1985, GCHQ does not require warrants for its interceptions, nor is a rigid check kept on whose communications are targeted. GCHQ takes requests for commercial intelligence, although theoretically these must be limited to matters of national security. Notwithstanding this limitation, global interception cannot be selective at the point of interception. The GCHQ computers can be automatically triggered by commercial conversations alluding to dealings with particular countries or individuals under surveillance, however innocent such conversations may be.

Antennae such as these were once a common sight on embassy roofs. Susceptibility to eavesdropping has caused many delegations to change to satellite communications.

Guy Taylor

Companies can attempt to protect themselves from eavesdropping by installing expensive scramblers. However, the manufacturers of many of these work so closely with Cheltenham that GCHQ almost certainly has the capacity to descramble virtually every device on the market.

Considerable disquiet arose in June 1992 when the *Financial Times* published an interview with Robin Robinson, a former employee of the Joint Intelligence Committee between November 1988 and June 1989. Robinson stated that GCHQ had monitored Robert Maxwell's commercial dealings for years prior to the tycoon's death. His phone conversations and faxes had allegedly been intercepted by satellite for GCHQ from Israel and the Mediterranean. It is probable that communications from the yacht *Lady Ghislane*, from which Maxwell fell to his death in November 1991, were also tracked.

Robinson stated that details of Maxwell's activities, gathered from taped telephone conversations and faxes, were also passed to the Bank of England in 1989.

Both the Government and Bank of England denied receipt of such intelligence reports. It is highly possible that Maxwell was not specifically targeted but rather came to the attention of GCHQ because of his considerable commercial interests in the Communist world and Middle East. He was far too astute to have allowed himself the luxury of unguarded telephone conversations. Equally it is highly unlikely that anyone within GCHQ, who would have been monitoring his transmissions in search of entirely different information, would have gained an inkling of the full extent of Maxwell's transgressions.

ROYAL EAVESDROPPING

It is widely believed that the security services tap certain telephone lines in the Royal residences. It has been suggested that conversations between the Duchess of York and Steve Wyatt were intercepted by MI6 and their contents reported to the Queen.

Independent reports indicate that the now infamous conversation between the Princess of Wales and her friend James Gilbey, made when he was in his car and she was at Sandringham, was not recorded in the first instance by an amateur with a scanning receiver. It is far more likely that the conversation was in fact intercepted between the Princess of Wales' telephone and her local exchange.

In their detailed report, communications consultant John Nelson and audio analyst Martin Colloms state that the marked degree of 50 Hz hum on the tape is consistent with an attempt to record a telephone conversation by land-line. A narrow band spectrum analysis shows the 50 Hz hum to comprise two separate components, suggesting a remixing of the tape after the initial recording. Furthermore it is suggested that the particularly loud 'pips' on the tape, which would have been filtered out by a telephone exchange or cellular base station, are not genuine but were added later to the tape in an attempt to disguise the local tap.

In June 1992, as if to emphasise the growing concern over the question of interception and royal privacy, Prince Charles broke with tradition by employing an independent security firm rather than the police or MI5 to search Kensington Palace for bugging devices.

THE AGRICULTURAL ANGLE

In April 1992, it was announced that satellite-mounted spy cameras would be employed in the fight against potential agricultural fraudsters. Complex 'set-aside' provisions, by which farmers are paid not to grow crops, and the introduction of an oilseed rape subsidy based on acreage, require European Economic Community assessors to have measurements accurate to within 0.1 of a hectare—about a quarter of an acre—to enable them to make their assessments. Infrared colour photography will provide precise details of fields, and part fields, lying fallow and under oilseed rape cultivation.

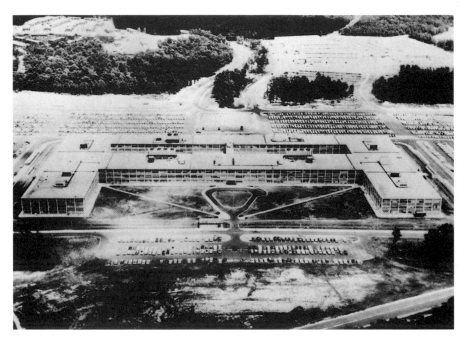

NSA headquarters at Fort Meade, Maryland, USA.   Popperfoto

FUTURE TRENDS

ESPIONAGE POST-PERESTROIKA

THE TAMING OF THE RUSSIAN BEAR

The collapse of the Soviet Union has brought with it a fundamental restructuring of the rules and aims of espionage in the region. In December 1992, Stella Rimington, head of MI5, paid a secret visit to Moscow to discuss 'prospects for cooperation and counter-terrorism'. At the same time Chancellor Helmut Kohl suggested that 'legal intelligence offices' be established in Moscow and Berlin to coordinate the fight against drug trafficking and international crime.

The growing rapprochement between the intelligence agencies of East and West was further boosted a few months later when the head of the CIA, Robert Gates, announced his intention to visit Sergei Stepashin, head of the Russian Republic's new Committee for Defence and Security.

However, in a moment of unusual candour, Yevgeny Primakov, head of the Russian FIS, the replacement for the 1st Main Directorate of the Soviet KGB, carefully defined the relatively restricted areas of potential cooperation between the world's major espionage agencies. Russia, he stated, had departed from Cold War confrontation in search of areas of mutual East–West interest; nuclear non-proliferation, drug trafficking and international terrorism. Significantly he made no mention of industrial espionage.

In reality Moscow has abandoned its political subversion and massive disinformation efforts, but has accelerated its campaign to steal the scientific and technical secrets of Japan and the West. The FIS has taken over the KGB's role of sending out 'acquisition tasks'—shopping lists of wanted plans and blueprints—to their agents all over the world. The Russian need to catch up with Japan and the West in the electronic revolution is paramount and they see espionage as the only way they can do it.

The GRU, less affected by the recent political turmoil, has never ceased this activity. Experts believe that about 150 ex-Soviet weapons systems depend on technology stolen from the West. KGB defector Oleg Gordievsky claims that the VPK, set up by Mikhail Gorbachev in the early 1980s to oversee Soviet weapons production, attempted to steal among other things the blueprints of the US B-1B strategic bomber. A recent announcement by the head of the GRU, Colonel General Yevgeni Timokhin, made it clear that such intelligence gathering would continue.

Russia's aspirations are being frustrated by three major factors: the near bankruptcy of its economy, the need to keep a close eye on its new neighbours, and the relative inexperience of many of its new agents. A number of key KGB agents either retired or defected to the West during the turmoils of Perestroika. Many of those who are left are disillusioned. Their salaries are low, particularly in comparison to their neighbours working for foreign subsidiaries, material perks no longer exist and the advantages of foreign travel are diminished in a country which now allows its citizens freedom to travel abroad. Although an unspoken fear, many of the older agents must also be mindful of the fate which befell their colleagues in the former East German Stasi when its records were made public by the new democratic government.

Russia has admitted that entrance standards for the FIS are lower than the KGB. Years of monitoring through Komsomol and DOSAFF are no longer possible and any aspirant graduate is being considered. When two young FIS agents, equipped with excellently forged British passports, were interviewed by the British Consulate in Helsinki, they were unable to volunteer the name of the British Prime Minister. They were returned to Moscow, chastened and embarrassed but otherwise unharmed.

There can be no doubt that the states of the former Soviet Union are busy spying on each other. In a telling interview in February 1992, General Shirkovsky, head of the Belarus KGB, complained that hundreds of foreign agents were infiltrating his country. Not only the CIA but his neighbours were widening their intelligence sources.

A RETURN TO THE GREAT GAME?

The Gulf War taught the United States a salutary lesson. Her sophisticated SIGINT and satellite intelligence was simply unable to foresee the Iraqi invasion of Kuwait. Thereafter her lack of good Humint denied her access to the somewhat erratic Iraqi military thought processes. This

KGB headquarters, Moscow.   Guy Taylor

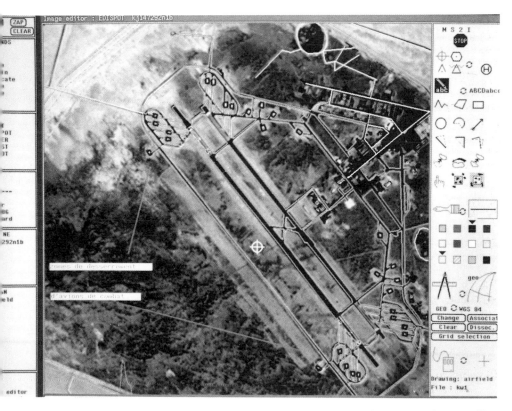

Military electronic systems are capable of accessing and enhancing civilian satellite imagery, as proved in the Gulf War.   MATRA/Guy Taylor

shortcoming might have been supplied by agents recruited from among the disillusioned elements of Saddam's military staff, had not such reliance been placed on technical means of intelligence gathering. Although satellites could detect mass movements of soldiers and armour, they could not identify units, or provide precise estimates of troop strengths, still less monitor the mood of the people.

The lessons of Iraq, coupled with the post-Cold War disintegration of the Soviet Union and the rise of Islamic fundamentalism in North Africa and the Middle East, have convinced the United States of the need for more agents on the ground.

In the 19th century, Britain was the great expert in the exploitation of human intelligence. Intelligence was the prerogative of young patriots from the great schools and major universities, overseen by retired generals and admirals in Whitehall. 'The Great Game', as it was dubbed, was played not for money but out of a sense of patriotism and loyalty to the Empire. At stake was the prevention of Tsarist expansion into Afghanistan and India; and stability in the Balkans, then as now a powder keg of ethnic unrest and political intrigue.

'The Great Game' foundered upon the political realignments of the inter-World War years and finally disintegrated with the emergence of the two post-war superpowers. However, the

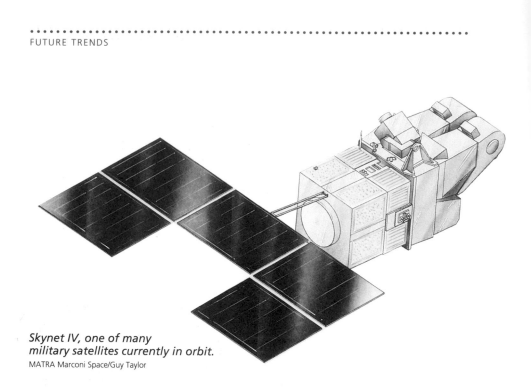

*Skynet IV, one of many
military satellites currently in orbit.*
MATRA Marconi Space/Guy Taylor

CIA headquarters, Langley, Virginia, USA.   Popperfoto

world of espionage has now turned full circle, and the day of the old-fashioned spy has perhaps returned.

Modern agencies are no longer recruiting exclusively from the social elite. MI6 in particular is now trawling universities and specialist army regiments, notably the SAS, for operatives. After training, recruits are being given 'cover posts' within the Foreign Office—such as commercial attachés and the ubiquitous passport control officers—and may expect to spend about 15 years in the field. The increased demand for new stations in the light of the emergence of so many new and potentially volatile states in Eastern Europe has led to an inevitable crash programme in language training. The CIA, with its far greater potential pool of native speakers, will probably continue to look to former Eastern bloc émigrés to fill such vacancies.

REDEFINING THE ROLE

The thawing of the Cold War has caused a number of national intelligence agencies to redefine their role in relationship to the commercial sector. In order to pursue their stated targets of unauthorised nuclear proliferation, organised crime and narcotics, the major Western agencies have had to recruit a new generation of criminologists and economists with few of the Old Order's paranoid obsession with excessive secrecy. The CIA has even taken to advertising in professional journals for men and women of the right calibre. Sympathetic journalists and writers have begun to receive unattributed briefings on various of the more open aspects of the secret services.

The movement of the secret services into the commercial sector is bringing with it its own problems. The aims and methods of political and commercial spies are rarely identical. Political allies are often commercial rivals. Intelligence agencies which at present afford excellent facilities to their political allies will quickly cease to do so if those facilities are seen to be used as bases for commercial espionage against themselves.

Commercial espionage will increasingly have to be carried out by proxy, using unattributable companies as agents. Mistakes will inevitably be made and the consequences may be severe. Closely guarded interception equipment, at present confined to official government use, will have to be released to these proxies, who may well then use the same equipment against wholly unrelated targets.

A PREVIEW OF NEW TECHNOLOGY

THE SPY SATELLITE

The spy satellite has been growing in strategic significance since the launch of the experimental Cosmos 198 in December 1967. Two Soviet satellites were subsequently launched within a few days of each other, each carrying a powerful radar for the location of ships in any weather and a radio-isotope thermal generator for the provision of power. These 'nuclear-powered' satellites were supposed to split into two on completion of their task, with the power element being boosted safely into high orbit. However, systems failures with Cosmos 954 in 1978 (when it crashed into northern Canada), and with Cosmos 1402 in January 1983, caused the Soviets to reappraise the entire use of nuclear power in space.

Two non-nuclear satellites were launched in April 1979, both capable of targeting NATO ships at sea. The most advanced Soviet satellite comprises a modification of the Salyut space station, with a capability at least equal to the United States' KH-11 (Key Hole). The programme is designed to be resupplied automatically by Progress spacecraft or by a manned shuttle, and has a known duration in excess of a year.

Traditionally the Soviets tended to launch directional satellites to cover particular crises. A satellite launched in May 1982 was perfectly positioned to spy on Anglo-Argentine naval engagements during the Falklands War. Although it seems highly unlikely that the Soviets actually passed any useful intelligence to the Argentines, they would have gained immensely from an analysis of Argentine shipping attacks and from the Royal Navy's defensive and offensive responses.

Despite her obvious financial problems, Russia is continuing the Soviet habit of launching a large number of satellites on a regular basis. Between 25 December 1992 and 26 January 1993, Russia launched a total of eight satellites; six in the Cosmos series, as well as Molniya-1 85 and Soyuz-TM 16.

Cosmos 2227 and Cosmos 2228, both launched on 25 December, were thought to carry ELINT payloads; Cosmos 2231, launched on 19 January, was a replacement photo-reconnaissance satellite (for Cosmos 2220); and Cosmos 2232, launched on 26 January, an early warning satellite, probably replacing Cosmos 2097.

The United States tends to launch fewer, but far more capable, satellites. The first KH-11 reconnaissance satellites were launched in December 1976. They operate in approximately 300–500 km (185–310 mile) orbits with inclinations of 97°. They weigh some 13 500 kg (29 750 lb) and measure about 12 m (40 ft) long and 3 m (10 ft) wide.

KH-11s carry relatively high-resolution cameras, allowing an average resolution of 30 cm (1 ft) depending on atmospheric 'wobble' or distortion. Other systems employ multi-spectral cameras, providing the ability to spy in good weather by day or night. Orbits are designed to ensure several passes per day over the Middle East and other strategic targets. Images are processed on board the satellites and stored as digital signals to be 'dumped' as the KH-11s pass over remote ground stations in Greenland and the Pacific.

Images are retransmitted to the National Photographic Interpretation Center in Washington via commercial communications satellites. From there they are passed to the White House, the CIA and other interested security agencies. Interpreted and analysed images are transmitted via satellite to field commanders, using small mobile terminals. The KH-12 reconnaissance satellite, which was rushed into limited service during the Gulf War, has the ability to transmit images direct to any suitably equipped command base around the world.

THE GULF EXPERIENCE

No fewer than 12 military satellite systems supported the Coalition forces during the Gulf War. Reconnaissance, ELINT, early-warning, communications, navigation and meteorological satellites were pressed into service to monitor Iraqi intentions.

Possibly three KH-11 and two KH-12 satellites were deployed, as was a Lacrosse reconnaissance satellite equipped with all-weather synthetic-aperture radar. Two Defense Satellite Communication System (DSCS) II and four DSCS III geostationary communications satellites provided the ground headquarters with immediate secure links to Washington, while the US naval forces were provided with ship-to-ship and ship-to-shore communications by US Navy FltSatCom and Syncom IV satellites.

Storm monitoring was provided by Atlas-launched, polar-orbiting Defense Meteorological Satellite Program (DMSP) satellites and early warning against the possibility of missile attack by three active and two back-up Defence Support Program (DSP) capsules. ELINT was comprehensively monitored by two shuttle-deployed Magnum spacecraft and one Titan 34D-launched Chalet satellite supported by up to five clusters each of three White Cloud ELINTs. The 14 Navstar Global Positioning System (GPS) satellites (out of a proposed total of 21) provided invaluable support for in-flight refuelling and ship navigation, although the dearth of receivers on the ground somewhat limited the system's effectiveness in the land war.

Images from the Spot IV civil observation satellite were used by the Coalition in the Gulf to augment military assets.　　　　　　　　　　　MATRA Marconi Space/Guy Taylor

JOINT STARS

The Grumman Systems Joint STARS, the most advanced ground surveillance system in the world, was rushed into service for the Gulf War. It provides real-time information on the

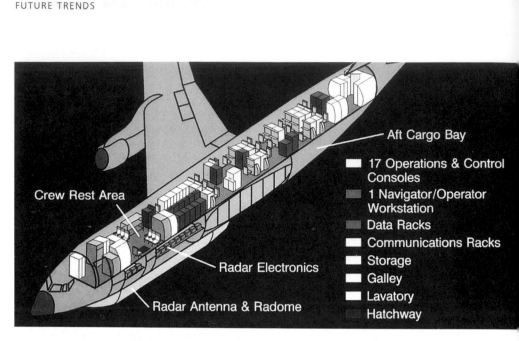

Aft Cargo Bay

■ 17 Operations & Control Consoles

■ 1 Navigator/Operator Workstation

■ Data Racks

■ Communications Racks

■ Storage

■ Galley

■ Lavatory

■ Hatchway

Crew Rest Area

Radar Electronics

Radar Antenna & Radome

The intelligence supplied by just two development aircraft was vital to the
Coalition success in the Gulf war. Grumman/Guy Taylor

detection, location, classification and tracking of moving and fixed objects and is capable of operating on-line, in real time, around-the-clock and in all weathers.

The Joint Surveillance Target Attack Radar System, to give it its full title, operates from an E-8 aircraft platform, effectively a militarised and modernised Boeing 707 civil airliner. A 7.32 m (24-ft) radar sensor is carried, housed in a canoe-shaped radome under the forward fuselage. A total of 18 operator consoles, high-speed data processors and secure voice and data links are positioned to the rear of the cockpit and crew rest area. Air-to-air refuelling permits flights lasting up to 20 hours, enabling the aircraft to support missions world-wide.

Joint STARS' wide-area surveillance/moving target indicator (WAS/MTI) radar will detect and provide the location of slow-moving targets, differentiating between tracked and wheeled vehicles. The synthetic aperture radar/fixed target indicator (SAR/FTI) produces a simulated photographic image or map of fixed targets or selected geographic areas. It is superimposed over SAR radar data maps showing the precise locations of fixed targets such as bridges, commercial installations and even stopped vehicles. Used in conjunction, WAS/MTI and SAR/FTI can provide detailed post-attack analyses by comparing stopped with previously moving targets.

The sector search (SS) radar offers a high-resolution, rapid revisit capability ideally suited to the automatic tracking of designated moving targets. Information is provided by Joint STARS aircraft to mobile ground station modules (GSMs) in real time, using secure data links. The GSMs process the radar data and provide a picture of the tactical situation directly to the command control and communications (C[3]) centres at corps and divisional headquarters, enabling the Army commanders to make an immediate intelligence appreciation. The data are transmitted simultaneously to the Air Force command via the Joint Tactical Information Distribution System (JTIDS).

Two E-8 Joint STARS aircraft were deployed to the Gulf. They flew 49 combat sorties and supported 100 per cent of mission taskings with a system availability rate of over 80 per cent. Operationally they logged 535 hours' flying-time, during which they located and identified POL storage sites, convoys, armoured concentrations and even SAM and artillery batteries. By day they operated with US Air Force F-16 fighters over the Kuwait Theatre of Operation (KTO), and by night with F-15Es, F-16s and F-111s seeking and destroying enemy convoys attempting to move under cover of darkness.

ASARS-2

ASARS-2 provided a further invaluable real-time reconnaissance link for the Coalition forces in the Gulf. The six airborne radar portions of the system are: the electronically scanned antenna, transmitter, receiver/exciter, control display unit, processor and power supply fit neatly into the available nose and fuselage space of the TR-1 aircraft. The system has a real-time, all-weather, day/night capability coupled with the unique ability to create constant-scale imagery in plan view.

ASARS-2 is designed to detect and accurately locate static and moving targets on either side of the TR-1's flight path. The radar gathers detailed information anywhere within the antenna field of view, feeding it via wideband data link to the ground station. Wide and spot, moving and stationary search modes are able to detect and locate targets, differentiating between static, slow and fast-moving vehicles.

ASARS-2 will remain a potent weapon in the United States espionage arsenal so long as the TR-1 remains flying, and no doubt for several years beyond that.

ATARS

Martin Marietta's Advanced Tactical Air Reconnaissance (ATARS), which is just entering service, provides yet another near real-time tactical imagery system. It can be pod-mounted or stored inside the fuselage of an F-16R or F/A-18D fighter. The reconnaissance package incorporates low- and medium-altitude electro-optical sensors and an infra-red line scanner, a digital tape recorder and a reconnaissance management system with a secure data link.

The management system controls the sensors and tape recorder using either manual inputs or a software system stored before the mission. The system provides live or recorded imagery which can be reviewed and edited in flight by the aircraft crew. The visible light and infra-red imagery can be stored using the digital tape recorder and transmitted to a ground or shipboard terminal for processing.

PHOENIX

In February 1985 the British Ministry of Defence belatedly placed an order for a replacement for the Canadair Midge Drone. Phoenix, which was developed too late to see service in the Gulf, provides Britain with her first fully equipped pilotless aircraft system for real-time remote targeting and battlefield surveillance. It comprises a small air vehicle with advanced avionics and an infra-red imaging system, an air/ground data link, a mobile ground station, logistics, launch and recovery vehicles.

Phoenix offers an active day/night, real-time capability. It is intended to operate at ranges of up to 50 km (31 miles) forward of the battlefield and has an endurance exceeding 4 hours.

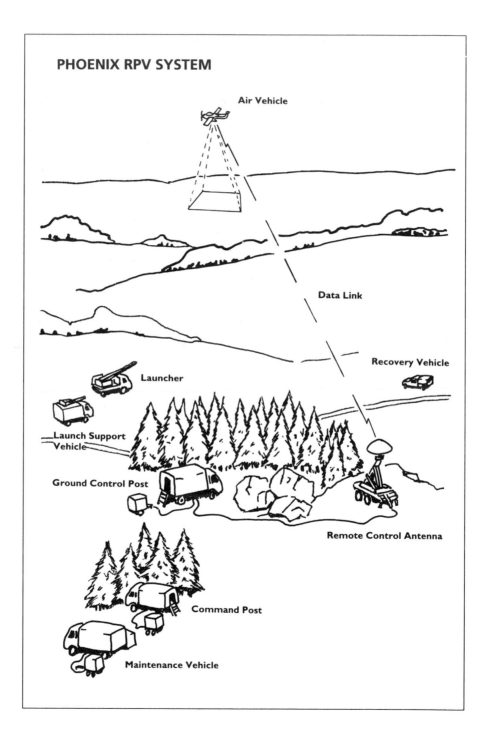

Its relatively small air vehicle is launched from a mobile hydraulic/pneumatic launcher to provide maximum operational flexibility and can be assembled, tested, loaded and launched in a matter of minutes. The landing site is pre-programmed during the mission planning stage, but can be altered at any time during the mission flight. A crushable shock absorber and parachute deploy prior to landing to reduce to a minimum the danger of sensor damage on impact.

The flight mission is controlled from the Ground Control Station (GCS), which relays instructions to the air vehicle via the Ground Data Terminal (GDT). Once the air vehicle has been launched, it climbs under autopilot control to a point where the initial data link is established and the flight plan is relayed as a series of way points from the GCS. The vehicle navigates using its Attitude and Heading Reference System, which is regularly updated by reference to the surveyed GDT position.

The operator monitors the position and track of the air vehicle from within the GCS, using a digital map display fed with the air vehicle position derived from data constantly updated by the GDT. Once an area of interest has been reached, or the air vehicle forward sensor has located an object of intelligence value, the operator can order an automatic or manual search. The real-time thermal imagery is relayed back to the GCS, where it is displayed on a work station manned by an imagery analyst.

To assist the Imagery Analyst in interpreting the thermal imagery in its relationship to the wider scenario, he can call on screen a digital map of the area displaying an overlay of the air vehicle's position, route and direction.

Phoenix was designed primarily to operate in northern Europe with the two Royal Artillery MRLS Depth Fire Regiments due to be deployed in support of the forward armoured divisions of 1 (British) Corps. In this it has been somewhat overtaken by political events. In the wake of German reunification, 1 (British) Corps has now been disbanded and over half of its troops returned to the United Kingdom. However, the secondary role of Phoenix, that of general surveillance, will remain crucial, particularly if the system should be called upon to deploy away from Western Europe in support of the Rapid Reaction Corps.

APPENDIX I

SOE ESTABLISHMENTS

The location of SOE training centres remained classified after World War II. Most were returned to their civilian owners. A few fell into disrepair while others, particularly those located on military property, remained in government occupation.

The following is a list of but a few of the more interesting SOE sites, a number of which are mentioned in the text. Where relevant an Ordnance Survey (OS) map number and grid reference have been given:

WANBOROUGH MANOR OS Sheet 186 Grid Ref SU 9349 (south-west of Guildford, off the Hog's Back)
One of the earliest special training schools established, used for preliminary training

ARISAIG OS Sheet 40 Grid Ref NM 6586, Scotland
No. 26 STS: West of Inverness/Lochailort. Field training base, 1st STS established at Inverailort House. Area later used by 1st Commando School.

MI R OS Sheet 165 near Aylesbury, Buckinghamshire
Originally based at 35 Portland Place before moving to The Firs, Whitchurch.

THE FRYTHE, Hertfordshire, OS Sheet 166 Grid Ref TL 225149 (near Welwyn Garden City)
Support weapons/equipment development centre.

ASTON HOUSE, Hertfordshire, OS Sheet 166 Grid Ref TL 2722 (Aston Village)
Training centre, specialist insruction including unarmed combat, run by Sykes and Fairbairn.

THE THATCHED BARN Barnet By-Pass (A1), Hertfordshire
Formerly a road-house. Used by SOE as a laboratory and production facility for special equipment, booby traps, etc.

DUNHAM MASSEY HOUSE Altrincham - Knutsford, Cheshire
First parachute training centre, later replaced by Tatton Park (Ringway).

2nd STAGE TRAINING CENTRES:
BROCKHALL—Daventry–Northampton
BELASIS—near Dorking, Surrey
CHORLEY WOOD—Hertfordshire
HATHROP CASTLE—Gloucestershire (home of 45 STS)

OTHER SPECIALIST CENTRES

HATFIELD (17 STS), Hertfordshire, Industrial sabotage, later wireless training; also some preliminary training.

BEDFORD, Bedfordshire, (40 STS) First wireless training (W/T) centre to be established.

BEAULIEU, Hampshire, Security and resistance to interrogation (R to I) school. 'Finishing school' and holding camp.

FAWLEY COURT Holding camp near Henley-on-Thames, Oxfordshire.

TEMPSFORD HOUSE, Bedfordshire, Holding camp near Tempsford airfield.

BICESTER, Oxfordshire, 53A Signals Station, established in the spring of 1942. Initially 3 workshops and 4 FANY coders increasing to 125 personnel within one year.

AYLESBURY, Buckinghamshire, 53B Signals Station, established in February 1943 with 83 FANY, increasing to 200 (including 60 coders) by October.

OTHER PREMISES (in London)

ST ERMIN'S HOTEL Caxton St, SW1. First offices.

62-64 BAKER ST. Next offices, mainly French section.

82 BAKER ST. St Michael House, back entrance in Mews.

83 BAKER ST. Norgeby House, 'Inter Service Research Bureau'

1 DORSET SQUARE RF Section.

CHILTERN COURT Scandinavian Section.

SANCTUARY BUILDINGS (Ministry of Pensions) interviews.

VICTORIA HOTEL Northumberland Avenue interviews.

Other buildings in: Berkeley Court, Portman Square, Oxford Square, Baker Street, Marylebone Street, Margaret Street (a European clothing factory) and Wimpole Street.

APPENDIX II

MAJOR KGB RESIDENTS FROM 1980 TO 1990

AUSTRALIA:
Lev Sergeevich Koshlyakov 1977–84
Yuri Pavlovich Tartsev 1985–89

CANADA:
Vladimir Ivanovich Mechulayev 1978–82
Aleksandr Alekseevich Metelkin 1982–84
Sergei Aleksandrovich Labur 1984–89

FRANCE:
Nikolai Nikolayevich Chetverikov 1977–83
Acting Residents only 1983–86
Anatoli Viktorovich Khramtsov 1986

ITALY:
Boris Aleksandrovich Solomatin 1976–82
Georgi Aleksandrovich Orlov 1982–86
Valentin Antonovich Akimov 1987

INDIA:
Gennadi Afanasyevich Vaulin 1977–81
Aleksandr Iosifovich Lysenko 1981–87
Feliks Ivanovich Tumakhovich 1988

NEW ZEALAND:
Nikolai Aleksandrovich Shatskikh 1977–82
Sergei Sergeevich Budnik 1982–87

REPUBLIC OF IRELAND:
Gennadi Aleksandrovich Salin 1980–83
Mikhail Sergeevich Smirnov 1983–85
Vladimir Vasilyevich Minderov 1985

UNITED KINGDOM:
Arkadi Vasilyevich Guk 1980–84
Leonid Yefremovich Nikitenko 1984–85
Oleg Antonovich Gordievsky 1985

UNITED STATES OF AMERICA:
Washington:
Dmitri Ivanovich Yakushkin 1975–82
Stanislav Andreevich Androsov 1982–86
Ivan Semyonovich Gromakov 1987
New York:
Vladimir Mikhailovich Kazakov 1979–85
Yuri Anatolyevich Antipov 1986–87
San Francisco:
Gennadi Ivanovich Vasilyev 1977–83
Lev Nikolayevich Zaitsev 1983–86

WEST GERMANY:
Yevgeni Izotovich Shishkin 1981–89

APPENDIX III

THE KGB RESIDENCY

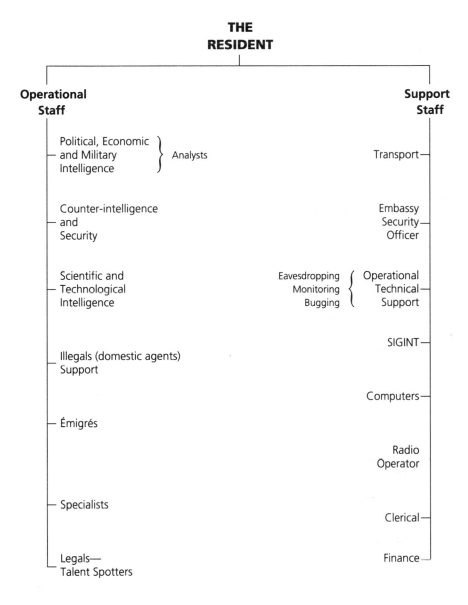

THE RESIDENT

Operational Staff

- Political, Economic and Military Intelligence } Analysts
- Counter-intelligence and Security
- Scientific and Technological Intelligence
- Illegals (domestic agents) Support
- Émigrés
- Specialists
- Legals— Talent Spotters

Support Staff

- Transport
- Embassy Security Officer
- Eavesdropping Monitoring Bugging } Operational Technical Support
- SIGINT
- Computers
- Radio Operator
- Clerical
- Finance

APPENDIX IV

THE ESPIONAGE CYCLE

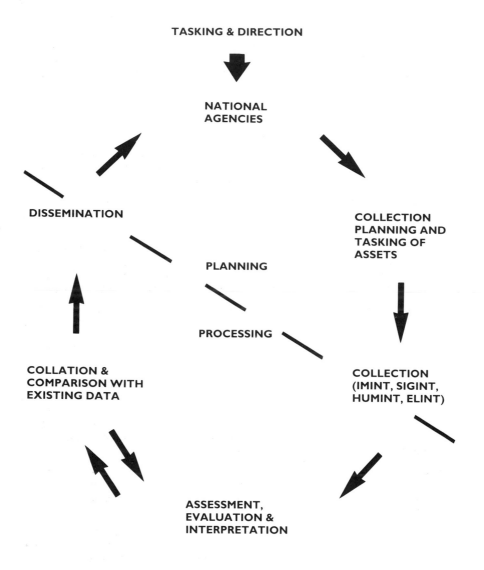

TASKING & DIRECTION

**NATIONAL
AGENCIES**

DISSEMINATION

**COLLECTION
PLANNING AND
TASKING OF
ASSETS**

PLANNING

PROCESSING

**COLLATION &
COMPARISON WITH
EXISTING DATA**

**COLLECTION
(IMINT, SIGINT,
HUMINT, ELINT)**

**ASSESSMENT,
EVALUATION &
INTERPRETATION**

APPENDIX V

PRINCIPAL ESPIONAGE AGENCIES

AL MUKHABARAT Iraq: literally translates as 'the Listening Post'. Formed when the Ba'ath Party gained control in 1968 to combine military and civilian intelligence services. Linked with the KGB during the 1970s. Responsible for a number of assassination and terrorist attempts world-wide.

ASIO Australia: Australian Security and Intelligence Organisation. Formed originally to counter the threat of a Japanese invasion, it grew into a credible counter- intelligence organisation in the 1950s. Early close links with MI5 and MI6 have recently weakened due to government rifts. Controlled by a Director-General and monitored by the Inspector General of Intelligence and Security and the Joint Parliamentary ASIO Committee.

BfW West Germany: Bundesamt für Verfassungsschutz or Office for the Protection of the Constitution. Formed in 1950 with strong British support. Until reunification heavily infiltrated by East German agents. Debased by a long history of internal scandals.

BND West Germany: Bundesnachrichtendienst or Federal Intelligence Agency. Formed in 1956 with CIA backing. Early attempts to infiltrate large numbers of agents into East Germany and the Soviet Union met with disaster. Like the BfV, debased by infiltration and scandals.

BOSS South Africa: Bureau of State Security. A reputation for utter ruthlessness, it traditionally operated with scant regard for international law. Reorganised after the 'Muldergate Scandal' in 1979 and now succeeded by the more moderate NIS.

CELD China: Central External Liaison Department. Concerned with the analysis of foreign intelligence, it links closely with the Party and State Council—which itself has connections with the Ministry of External trade and Military Intelligence Department of the General Staff. It provides a global, though politically constrained—and therefore not always efficient—intelligence service.

CESID Spain: Centro Superior para la Informacion de la Defensa. Formed after the death of Franco, it employs a large number of former Army officers and as such is still not completely trusted by the political Left. It scored a major success in 1982 when it frustrated a right-wing coup by senior elements within the army. In 1984 its eight departments were merged under a single director responsible solely to the Prime Minister.

CIA USA: Central Intelligence Agency. Founded in 1947 as the C.I. Group to counter the Soviet NKVD, it suffered in its early years from a multitude of inexperienced directors. Improved and expanded in the 1950s it has a current staff of nearly 20 000 and a massive headquarters in Langley, Virginia. Despite a number of embarrassing gaffs the CIA is generally respected as an intelligence gathering agency, although there have recently been suggestions that it lacks Humint input and has become over-reliant on technology.

CSIS Canada: Canadian Security Intelligence Service. Formed in May 1983 to deal with internal security and counter-espionage, it has sweeping powers to tap telephones, use listening devices and intercept mail. Many of its original employees were drawn from the RCMP, although it now recruits largely from the military and universities.

DGI Cuba: Direccion General de Inteligencia. Formed by Fidel Castro and until recently financed by the Soviet Union, the DGI was traditionally a puppet for the KGB, training terrorists and involving itself in espionage activities when required. In the past it has nurtured close connections with groups such as the Red Brigade, the PLO and the IRA. Its influence has waned considerably in the last few years, to the extent that it has now been forced to concentrate on the countering of internal subversion.

DGSE France: Direction Général de Sécurité Extérieure. Formed by President Mitterrand from the

SDECE it is one of the most successful, and ruthless, intelligence agencies in the world. Exceptionally well informed on the Arab world, it has recently concentrated its resources in support of French trade deals, occasionally at the expense of her political and military allies.

DS Bulgaria: Darjavna Sugurnost. The former Communist state security service, it was almost wholly dominated by the KGB on whose behalf it carried out a number of assassination attempts. Ruthless in its attitude towards defectors and *émigrés*, it was responsible for the umbrella-gun murder of Georgi Markov in 1978.

DST France: Direction de la Surveillance du Territoire. Regarded as one of the finest counter-espionage agencies in the world during the days of the Cold War, it is now occasionally accused of putting the interests of France before the international good.

ESPIONAGE ABTEILUNG Switzerland: Formed during World War II to help ensure Swiss neutrality, it is now responsible for counter-espionage.

FBI USA: Federal Bureau of Investigation. Responsible for counter-espionage, internal subversion, crimes against the government and those in which state jurisdiction is unclear. Although it took a number of years to become really efficient it did enjoy a number of early successes, particularly in the battle against organised crime. It is wholly independent of the CIA, which cannot access its files, and which may only obtain intelligence from it upon request.

GCHQ United Kingdom: Government Communications Headquarters. Established in 1952, it intercepts communications—diplomatic, military and commercial—from all over the world. It employs approximately 12 000 personnel, has several stations in other parts of the world and works in close cooperation with Australia, Canada and the United States.

GRU Soviet Union: Glavnoye Razvedyvatelnoye Upravleniye. Traditionally, Soviet Military Intelligence worked with the Communist Party and KGB to ensure stability within the Soviet Union. It remains responsible for all facets of military intelligence and intelligence gathering, for which it has covert agents posted in every major Russian consulate and embassy in the world.

KGB Soviet Union: Komitet Gosudarstvennoy Bezopasnosti. The Committee for State Security grew from the NKVD into one of the most powerful intelligence services in the world. It had its own army of nearly 350 000 personnel, including special forces and a hostage rescue unit, armoured and artillery regiments, and was exclusively responsible for the preservation of the old Soviet borders.

KISS South Korea: Korean Intelligence and Security Service. Tough and ruthless, KISS has its antecedents in the South Korean Central Intelligence Agency formed with United States assistance after the Korean War. It has enjoyed a number of successes in the on-going battle against North Korea, and undoubtedly continues to offer considerable assistance to the CIA.

MfS East Germany: Ministerium für Staatssicherheit. Established on 9 February 1950, the East German Ministry for State Security was the largest and most powerful intelligence agency in the Soviet bloc after the KGB. At one stage it had an estimated 20 000 agents, including sleepers, in West Germany alone. It had a dedicated uniformed branch, the Felix Dzerzhinsky Guard Regiment, estimated at 6000 officers and men, which performed security as well as ceremonial duties. When East Germany collapsed its population was shocked to discover the sheer quantity of files held by the MfS on virtually every citizen.

MI5 United Kingdom: Traditionally responsible for counter-intelligence, MI5 has recently assumed responsibility for Irish terrorism, organised crime and narcotics. It has also been put on a statutary basis and has opened its doors (albeit slightly) to the Press.

MI6 United Kingdom: Originally Military Intelligence, Department 6, it is today more often known by its alternative title, the Secret Intelligence Service. It works closely with GCHQ and the Foreign and Commonwealth Office and is responsible for intelligence gathering world-wide.

MOSSAD Israel: Mossad Le Aliyah Beth. The Institution for Intelligence and Special Services, Mossad is arguably the finest intelligence service in the world. Single-minded and utterly ruthless, it recorded some considerable successes prior to the Six-Day War and (to a lesser extent) the Yom Kippur War in 1973. It has, however, suffered a number of setbacks. Three agents were killed by the PLO in Cyprus in 1985.

MUKHABARAT Libya: Formed by Colonel Gaddafi it has been heavily influenced by the KGB and MfS and in the past has worked closely with the Syrian secret services. Blatant in its support of revolutionary movements such as the PLO, Red Brigade and IRA, it has supplied such organisations with arms, equipment and expertise whenever asked.

NCNA China: New China News Agency. Staffed by politically reliable personnel, the foreign-based employees of the NCNA have long been used by China as a recruiting agency and to gain low-grade intelligence abroad.

NIS South Africa: National Intelligence Service. Created in 1979 as a replacement for the discredited BOSS, and briefed to concentrate on the collection of intelligence, it no longer involves itself in the almost indiscriminate smear campaigns which so discredited its predecessor. It has gained a number of successes in the field of counter-espionage.

RCMP Canada: Royal Canadian Mounted Police. Until 1979 the RCMP was responsible for intelligence and counter-espionage in Canada. It was concerned mainly with internal security but occasionally became involved in highly successful intelligence-gathering activities, particularly during and immediately after World War II. During the late 1960s the RCMP encountered problems with the Quebec Liberation Front (FLQ) which was ultimately destined to destroy it as an intelligence-gathering agency. In 1977, a Commission of Inquiry upheld allegations of illegal wire-tapping and breaking and entering against members of the RCMP operating against the FLQ. A separate security service was established as a direct result. In May 1983, the CSIS took over responsibility for all intelligence and counter-espionage activity.

SAVAK Iran: Formed by the Shah to counter the threat of Arab fundamentalism, SAVAK was formed with the help of the CIA, MI6 and Mossad. It quickly developed a reputation for ruthlessness, torture and repression. After the fall of the Shah, Muslim hardliners took control, executing the former leader, General Nematollah Nassiri, without trial. SAVAK retains close contacts with Mossad, not least because of their common enmity towards Iraq.

SB Poland: Sluzba Bezpieczenstwa. The SB was formed under the wholesale control of the KGB, which manipulated its every activity. None the less during the Cold War it engineered a number of coups in its own right, particularly at the expense of the United States. For over a decade a number of its agents accepted United States cash by pretending to be members of an infiltrated CIA underground espionage organisation. The SB did not survive the fall of the Communist regime.

SHIN BETH Israel: The Security and Counter-Espionage Service, although primarily a counter-espionage department, also has an interest in the collection and collation of military intelligence. It has a purely counter-espionage section known as Sharuth Bitakhon Klali, more usually known as Shabak.

SIS New Zealand: Security Intelligence Service. Set up in 1947, SIS has an exclusively counter-espionage responsibility. It recruits largely from the army and police and until recently was highly secretive. After the *Rainbow Warrior* incident in July 1985, however, it became more public. External intelligence is dealt with by the Government Communication Security Board (SIGINT).

SIS United Kingdom: Secret Intelligence Service. See MI6.

STASI Ministerium für Staatssicherheit.

ACRONYMS

Abwehr — World War II German Military Intelligence
ACPO — Association of Chief Police Officers
AEW — Airborne Early Warning
AFSATCOM — Air Force Communications Satellites
AGI — Auxiliary Vessel, General type, Intelligence (Soviet spy ship)
AM — Amplitude Modification
APIC — Army Photographic Interpretation Centre
ASU — Active Service Unit
CAP — Combat Air Patrol
Cheka — Extraordinary Commission for Combating Counter-Revolutions (formed by Feliz Dzerzhinsky after Russian Revolution)
CEO — Chief Executive Officer (within SOE) Cheng pao k'o Political Security Section (People's Republic of China)
CIA — Central Intelligence Agency (United States foreign intelligence service)
COMINT — Communications Intelligence
COMSUBIN — Comando Subacquei Incursori (Italian Navy Commandos)
DAIO — Divisional Artillery Intelligence Officer
Dept STS 33 — Department responsible for SOE parachute training
Depts IX/XVII — Departments responsible for training SOE in sabotage techniques
DF — Direction Finding
DGER — Direction Générale des Etudes et Recherches (successor to DGSS formed by de Gaulle after liberation of Paris)
DGSE — Direction Générale de la Sécurité Extérieure (French exterior intelligence agency)
DGSS — Direction Générale des Services Spéciaux (World War II Gaullist intelligence service)
DIA — Defense Intelligence Agency
DMSP — Defense Meteorological Satellite Program
DOSAAF — Soviet Union's All-Union Voluntary Society for assistance to the Army, Air Force and Navy
DLB — Dead Letter Box
DMI — Director of Military Intelligence
DNI — Director of Naval Intelligence
DSP — Defence Support Programme
ECM — Electronic Counter-Measures
E.Dienst — Entzifferungsdienst (German Naval Decoding Service)
ELINT — Electronic Intelligence
ENIGMA — Code-name for German encoding machine defeated by the British during World War II
EW — Electronic Warfare
FANY — First Aid Nursing Yeomanry
FBI — Federal Bureau of Investigation
FICON — Fighter Conveyor (converted RB-36 bombers)
FLIR — Forward-Looking Infra-red
FM — Frequency Modulation
FMS — Forward Motion Compensation
F-Section — Section of SOE responsible for France
GC&CS — Government Code and Cipher School (predecessor to GCHQ)
GCHQ — Government Communications Headquarters (Cheltenham)

GCS	Ground Control Station
GDT	Ground Data Terminal
Gestapo	Geheime Staatspolizei (World War II German Secret state Police)
GPS	Global Positioning System—satellite navigation
GPU	The State Political Administration (successor to Cheka brought under control of NKVD)
GRU	Glavnoye Razvedyvatelnoye Upravleniye (Soviet Military Intelligence)
HUD	Head-Up Display
HUMINT	Human Intelligence (intelligence obtained from a human source, usually an agent)
IFF	Identification Friend or Foe
IMINT	Imagery Intelligence (pictures of film obtained from an RPV, aircraft or satellite)
INO	Foreign Department of 1st Directorate of KGB
INS	International Navigation System
IO	Intelligence Officer
IR	Infra-red
IRLS	Infra-red Line Scan
JARIC	Joint Air Reconnaissance Intelligence Centre (RAF Brampton)
JIC	Joint Intelligence Committee
JTIDS	Joint Tactical Information Distribution System
KGB	Komitet Gosudarstvennoy Bezopasnosti (former Soviet Intelligence Service)
KISS	(South) Korean Intelligence and Security Service
LOROP	Long-Range Oblique Photography
MAD	Mutually Assured Destruction
MAD	Magnetic Anomaly Detection
MI	Military Intelligence
MI5	Department of British Security Services responsible for counter-espionage within the UK
MI6	Department of British Security Services responsible for security and espionage services outside the UK (also known as SIS)
MI9	World War II department responsible for escape and evasion
MI19	World War II department responsible for refugees and enemy prisoners
MOSSAD	Mossad Le Aliyah Beth (Institution for Intelligence and Special Services—Israeli intelligence agency)
MPSB	Metropolitan Police Special Branch
NACA	National Advisory Committee for Aeronautics (predecessor of NASA)
NASA	National Aeronautics and Space Administration
NATO	North Atlantic Treaty Organisation
NID	Naval Intelligence Division
Ninja	Ninijitsu—the art of making oneself invisible
NIS	Netting-In Signal (used to tune in a clandestine radio)
NKVD	Narodny Kommissariat Vnutrennich Dyel (People's Commissariat for Internal Affairs—predecessor of KGB)
N-PIC	National Photographic Interpretation Center (Washington)
NSA	National Security Agency (US Signals Intelligence)
OEIC	Overseas Economic Intelligence Committee
OGPU	Unified State Political Administration (successor to GPU)
OLs	Operating Locations (for U-2 flights)
ONI	Office of Naval Intelligence (formed by the US Bureau of Navigation in 1882)

OSS	Office of Strategic Services (first US espionage agency which combined intelligence gathering with paramilitary activities)
PIRA	Provisional IRA (Irish Republican Army)
PSYOPS	Psychological Operations
RAM	Radar-Absorbent Material
RAF	Royal Air Force
REC	Radio Electronic Combat (Soviet term for electronic warfare)
REP	Regiment Etranger Parachutiste (French Foreign Legion)
RFC	Royal Flying Corps—predecessor of RAF
RN	Royal Navy
RPV	Remotely Piloted Vehicle (unmanned aircraft)
Reseau	Resistance group operating in occupied Europe
RUC	Royal Ulster Constabulary
SAM	Surface-to-Air Missile
SAR/FTI	Synthetic Aperture Radar/Fixed Target Indicator
SARA	Système Aéro-Transportable de Reconnaissance Aérienne
SAS	Special Air Service
SASR	Special Air Service Regiment (Australian Army)
SATCOM	Satellite Communications
SATNAV	Satellite Navigation
SBS	Special Boat Service (formerly Squadron)
SD	Sicherheitsdienst (World War II German security service)
SDECE	Service de Documentation Extérieure et de Contre-Espionage (French foreign intelligence service)—predecessor of DGSE
SEALs	Sea Air and Land (US Naval Special Forces)
SEMA	Special Electronic Mission Aircraft
SIGINT	Signals Intelligence
SIME	Security Intelligence Middle East
SIS	Secret Intelligence Service (see MI6)
Skeds	Schedules—the life blood of SOE radio operators
SKM	Signalbuch der Kaiserlichen Marine (principal German Naval Code of World War I)
Skunk Works	Advanced Development Projects, Lockheed, California
SLAR	Sideways-Looking Airborne Radar
SOE	Special Operations Executive
SOTAS	Stand-Off Target Acquisition System
SSM	Surface-to-Surface Missile
TACAMO	Take Charge and Move Out (USN communications aircraft)
TC	Troop Commander
TCMS	Technical CounterMeasures Survey
TELINT	Telemetry Intelligence
TEMPEST	Transcient ElectroMagnetic Pulse Emanation Standard
TEREC	Tactical Electronic Reconnaissance
TSCM	Technical Surveillance CounterMeasures
UDT	Underwater Demolition Team
UHF	Ultra High Frequency
ULTRA	Code-name for exploitation of intelligence gathered by GC&CS
USAF	United States Air Force
USN	United States Navy

VB	Verkehrsbuch (World War I Imperial German Naval Code for communications with Naval Attachés, overseas warships and Flag Officers
VCP	Vehicle Control Point
VHF	Very High Frequency
VLF	Very Low frequency
V-Manner	World War II German double agent 'turned' by the Abwehr or Gestapo
VTA	Voeyenno Transportnaya Aviatisya—former Soviet Military Transport Aviation
VTOL	Vertical Take-Off and Landing
WAAF	Women's Auxiliary Air Force
WAS/MTI	Wide-Area Surveillance/Moving Target Indicator
XX Committee	Double Cross Committee (World War II organisation formed by British counter-intelligence to handle 'turned' agents)
Y Service	World War I Naval Radio Interception Service

BIBLIOGRAPHY

- Adams, James: *Secret Armies, The Full Story of the SAS, Delta Force and Spetsnaz* (Hutchinson).
- Adams, James, & Morgan, Robin: *Ambush; The War Between the SAS and the IRA* (Pan).
- Andrew, Christopher, & Gordievsky, Oleg: *KGB, The Inside Story* (Hodder & Stoughton).
- Andrew, Christopher, & Gordievsky, Oleg: *Instructions from the Centre: Top Secret Files on KGB Foreign Operations 1975–1985* (Hodder & Stoughton).
- Andrew, Christopher, & Gordievsky, Oleg: *More Instructions from the Centre* (Frank Cass).
- Barron, John: *Breaking the Ring* (Avon Books).
- Beesly, Patrick: *Room 40, British Naval Intelligence 1914–18* (Hamish Hamilton).
- Bishop, Chris, & Drury, Ian: *Combat Guns* (Temple Press/Aerospace).
- Boar, Roger, & Blundell, Nigel: *The World's Greatest Spies and Spymasters* (Octopus Books).
- Braddon, Russell: *Nancy Wake* (Pan).
- Burgess, Maj William H.: *Inside Spetsnaz* (Praesidio).
- Clutterbuck, Richard: *Terrorism and Guerrilla Warfare* (Routledge).
- Cornwall, Hugo: *The Industrial Espionage Handbook* (Ebury Press).
- Crankshaw, Edward: *Gestapo, Instrument of Tyranny* (Greenhill Books).
- Churchill, Winston S.: *The Second World War* (Cassell).
- Deacon, Richard: *A History of the British Secret Service* (Granada).
- Deacon, Richard: *Spy!* (BBC Publications).
- Deacon, Richard: *Spyclopaedia: The Comprehensive Handbook of Espionage* (Futura).
- Deacon, Richard: *The French Secret Service* (Grafton Books).
- Deacon, Richard: *The Israeli Secret Service* (Hamish Hamilton).
- Deacon, Richard: *The Silent War* (History of Western Naval Intelligence) (David & Charles).
- Deacon, Richard: *The Truth Twisters* (Macdonald).
- Dobson, Christopher, & Payne, Ronald: *The Dictionary of Espionage* (Harrap).
- Eaton, Capt H.B.: *APIS, Soldiers with Stereo* (Intelligence Corps Museum).
- Elton, G.R.: *England Under the Tudors* (Methuen).
- Farson, Stuart, & Stafford, David: *Security and Intelligence in a Changing World* (Cassell).
- Foot, M.R.D.: *MI9, Escape and Evasion 1939–1945* (Bodley Head).
- Foot, M.R.D.: *SOE, The Special Operations Executive 1940–46* (Mandarin).
- Grant, R.G.: *MI5, MI6 Britain's Security and Secret Intelligence Services* (Gallery Books).
- Gunston, Bill: *Spyplanes and Electronic Warfare Aircraft* (Salamander).
- Gunston, Bill: *USAF The Modern US Air Force* (Salamander).
- Hayden, Lt Col H., USMC: *Shadow War: Special Operations and Low Intensity Warfare* (Pacific Aero Press).
- Healey, Tim: *Secret Armies* (Purnell).
- Hinsley, F.H.: *British Intelligence in the Second World War* (HMSO).
- Howarth, Patrick: *Undercover; The Men and Women of the SOE* (Arrow).
- Jones, Liane: *A Quiet Courage* (Corgi).
- Jones, R.V.: *Most Secret War* (Hamish Hamilton)
- Kahn, David: *Seizing the Enigma, Race to Break the German U-Boat Codes* (Souvenir Press).
- Kahn, David: *The Codebreakers* (Weidenfeld & Nicolson).
- Kemp, Anthony: *The Secret Hunters* (Michael O'Mara Books).
- Kingston, Gen Robert C., US Army (Retd): *Inside Spetsnaz* (Presidio).
- Knightly, Phillip: *Philby, KGB Masterspy* (Pan).
- Loran, Pierre: *Secret Warfare, The Arms and Techniques of the Resistance* (Orbis).
- Macdonald, Peter: *The Special Forces* (Viscount).
- Montgomery Hyde, H.: *George Blake, Superspy* (London, Constable).
- Moore, Capt J.E., RN, & Compton-Hall, Cdr, RN: *Submarine Warfare Today and Tomorrow* (Michael Joseph).

Munro, Neil: *Electronic Combat and Modern Warfare* (Macmillan).

Norman, Bruce: *Secret Warfare, The Battle of Codes and Cyphers* (David & Charles).

Paine, Lauran: *The Abwehr, German Military Intelligence in World War II* (Hale).

Palmer, A.W.: *A Dictionary of Modern History 1789-1945* (Penguin).

Parritt, Brig B.A.H., CBE: *The Intelligencers; The History of British Military Intelligence to 1914* (Intelligence Corps Association).

Penkovsky, Oleg: *The Penkovsky Papers* (Collins).

Ranelagh, John: *The Agency, The Rise and Decline of the CIA* (Weidenfeld & Nicolson).

Richardson, Doug: *Modern Spyplanes* (Salamander).

Seith, Ronald: *Encyclopedia of Espionage* (New English Library).

Stevenson, William: *A Man Called Intrepid, the Secret War 1939–1945* (Sphere).

Suvorov, Viktor: *Soviet Military Intelligence* (Grafton).

Sweet-Escott, Bickham: *Baker Street Irregulars* (Methuen).

Tolstoy, Nikolai: *Stalin's Secret War* (Pan).

Van der Aart, Dick: *Aerial Espionage* (Airlife).

Welham, Michael: *Combat Frogmen* (Patrick Stephens Ltd).

West, Nigel: *MI5 : British Security Operations 1909–45* (London).

West, Nigel: *MI5 1945–72: A Matter of Trust* (Weidenfeld & Nicolson Ltd).

West, Nigel: *Seven Spies Who Changed the World* (Mandarin).

West, Nigel: *The Friends; Britain's Post-War Secret Intelligence Operations* (Weidenfeld & Nicolson).

West, Nigel: *The Story of SOE* (Hodder & Stoughton).

White, Terry: *Swords of Lightning* (Brasseys).

Wright, Peter: *Spycatcher* (Heinemann).

Wynne, Greville: *The Man From Odessa* (Hale).

TELEVISION PRESENTATIONS
Inside Story: BBC
Mordechei Vanunu: BBC Open Space

MANUALS
GEC Avionics: *Battlefield Surveillance Systems for the British Army*
Grumman: *Eyes of the Storm—Joint STARS*
HMSO: *Report of the Security Commission, May 1973 Cmnd 5362*
Hughes Electronics: *ASARS-2*

NON-ATTRIBUTED
Revealed: Secrets of the KGB's 'Unruly Mail' (Sunday Times 22 Sep 91)
Spies, Scouts and Raiders – The US Civil War (Time Life Books)
Spying on Saddam (Flight International Aug 90)
Storm Support From Space (Flight International Apr 91)
The World At Arms (Readers Digest)
ARTICLES
Adams, James/Clarke, Liam/Prescott, Michael: *Bombers v Bunglers* (*Sunday Times*, 19 May 92).
Beever, Antony: *Xan Fielding, An Obituary* (*Independent*, 20 Aug 91).
Bower, Tom: *Red Web* (*Sunday Times*, 6 Aug 89).
Branson, Louise, & Sekoloff, Connie: *Yard Has Key Evidence in Umbrella Murder* (*Sunday Times*, 9 Jun 91).
Clark, Philip: *Worldwide Spacecraft Launches* (*Janes International Review*, May 93).

Flanagan, William/McMenamin, Brigid: *The Playground Bullies Are Learning How To Type* (*Forbes*, Dec 92).

Furbisher, John: *Union Spied on its Disloyal Members* (*Sunday Times*, 17 Jan 93).

Galeotti, Mark: *KGB; RIP* (*Janes International Review*, Jan 92).

Hansen, Michael: *Counter Espionage Techniques That Work* (*Security Management*, Sep 92).

Heffernan, Richard J: *Who's On The Line* (*Security Management*).

Ivanov, Yevgeny: *Sex, Spies and a Girl Called Christine* (*Sunday Times*).

Karch, Col Lawrence, USMC: *Very Low Cost UAVs: Why We Need Them* (*Marine Corps Gazette*, Mar 91).

Lovece, Joseph A.: *UAV Programmes Experience Growth Pains* (*Armed Forces Journal*, Jul 91).

Millar, Peter: *Someone To Watch Over Me* (*Sunday Times*, 18 Apr 93).

Munson, Kenneth: *RPVs – Who Are The Real Pilots* (*JDW*, 8/85).

Noack, Ernst: *Drones and RPVs Today and Tomorrow* (*Miltech*, 10/83).

Perkins, Maj Gen Ken: *An Interview* (*Independent*, 21 Sep 91).

Phillips, Jim: *Espionage In The Countryside* (*Intelligence Quarterly*).

Plugge, Matthias: *Soviet Special Forces Used to Maintain Law and Order* (*IDR*, 3/91).

Plunkett, Sandy: *Sabotage On Screen* (*Business Review Weekly*, Feb 93).

Pretty, Ronald T.: *Israeli Mini-RPV Experience* (*JDW*, 7/84).

Rufford, Nick/Leppard, David/Burrell, Ian: *Revealed; The Bugs That Trapped Mellor* (*Sunday Times*, Jul 92).

Soyster, Lt Gen H.E.: *The Changing Face of the American Spy* (*Intelligence Quarterly*).

Speers, Michael F.: *A Biased State* (*Intelligence Quarterly*).

Streetly, Martin: *Airborne Battlefield Surveillance* (*JDW*, 10/84).

Tanzer, Marc: *Foiling the New Corporate Spy* (*Security Management*, Sep 92).

Terenichev, Col A.: *Pilotless Means of Attack* (*Aviatsiya Kosmonoutika*, 1986).

Terraine, John A.: *Battle to Break the U-Boat Blockade* (*Independent*, 21 Jun 93).

Turnill, Reginald: *Military Satellites* (*JDW*, 9/84).

Vaviadis, Nicholas: *Cellular Radio; Vulnerable to Attack* (*Telecommunications*, Feb 89).

Vaviadis, Nicholas: *Electronic Threats and Espionage in the 90s* (*International Security Review*).

Vaviadis, Nicholas: *The 'Buggist' and How To defeat Him* (*Security Times*, Jul 89).

Vigo, Dr Milan: *Shallow Water ASW; Sweden's Problems* (*JDW*, 18 Jan 86).

West, Nigel: *Soviet Defectors; The British Record* (*Intelligence Quarterly*, Aug 89).

INDEX